LEARNING AND TEACHING IN THE VIRTUAL WORLD OF SECOND LIFE

LEARNING AND TEACHING IN THE VIRTUAL WORLD
OF SECOND LIFE

Eds. Judith Molka-Danielsen and Mats Deutschmann

ℯ tapir academic press

© *Tapir Academic Press, Trondheim 2009*

ISBN 978-82-519-2353-8

Layout: *The Authors*
Printed by: *AIT AS e-dit*
Cover Design: *Design Container AS*

*Our gratitude is given to Molde University College for the financial contribution of
NOK 20 000 in assistance of the publication of this book.*

J. Molka-Danielsen@hiMolde.no

Mats. Deutschmann@miun.se

Visit the book`s website at: www.tapirforlag.no

*Tapir Academic Press
NO–7005 Trondheim, Norway
Tel.:   + 47 73 59 32 10
Email: post@tapirforlag.no
www.tapirforlag.no*

Publishing ed.: lasse.postmyr@tapir.no

Table of Contents

Part I: Pedagogic Design

Part II: Learning Projects

Preface

Graham Davies
Professor Emeritus of Computer Assisted Language Learning
Member of the EUROCALL Executive Committee

Virtual worlds have been in existence for much longer than most people think. I first became acquainted with what could be loosely termed a virtual world in 1979, while I was attending a one-week course in programming in the humanities. During one of the coffee breaks the conversation turned to a computer simulation known as Colossal Cave Adventure – or simply Adventure for short. A version of Adventure was available on the mainframe computer which we were using for our course, and a number of the course participants had discovered it. The simulation was designed by Will Crowther in 1975–76 and based on a real cave network in Kentucky that he had explored as an amateur speleologist. When I returned to my college after the course I asked staff in the computer studies department if they had heard of Adventure, and I was told that there was a version on the college's Prime minicomputer. I was immediately hooked, spending hours exploring the colossal cave and swapping experiences with a colleague who was similarly addicted.

At that time most computers produced only text output, and the normal way of inputting text was via the keyboard. In keeping with these limitations, Adventure was a text-only simulation in which the user communicated with the computer by typing commands at the keyboard and had to imagine how the cave network looked. The user could give commands to follow a certain route and to pick up objects that might be useful at a later stage of the simulation, for example a weapon for slaying potentially hostile beasts. There was even a primitive teleport command. Adventure spawned many imitations, including variants that ran on the early home microcomputers. The 1980s saw the arrival of a number of Adventure-like simulations that were specially designed for language learners: for example, Osman Durrani's Schloss Schattenburg (Camsoft), Roger Woodward's Manoir des Oiseaux (Camsoft), and Barry Jones's imaginative Granville (Cambridge University Press), which was a virtual representation of a real French town.

The next landmark in the history of virtual worlds was Multi-User Dungeon (MUD), the brainchild of Roy Trubshaw, who developed the first version of the program in 1978 while he was an undergraduate student at the University of Essex. MUD was the first major simulation to be available over a wide area network when it was adopted by CompuServe in the mid-1980s and renamed British Legends. Like Colossal Cave Adventure, it was text-only, with the difference that it was available to a much wider audience. British Legends still exists in an online form and continues to be popular with retro-computing enthusiasts.

The name Multi-User Dungeon was probably a disadvantage because it was too closely associated with the Dungeons and Dragons board game and lacked appeal to educators, but then the generic term Multi-User Domain emerged as a more acceptable term to describe programs of this type. This led on to the next major landmark in the development of virtual worlds, the MOO (Multi-User Domain Object-Oriented). At first sight this appears to be an impenetrable term. The important thing that makes a MOO different from a MUD is that it not only allows text chat between its participants but it also allows them to build their own "objects", for example a room into which they can retreat and entertain their friends. The objects are not visual objects, however, but written descriptions of them. In this respect MOOs, like their text-based predecessors, rely on the imagination of their participants. Participants can also create a description of themselves, forming the basis of their online personality – a described avatar, as it were. MOOs have been used in education since the early 1990s, and a number of MOOs have been designed specifically for learning foreign languages and for intercultural exchanges: schMOOze University, Dreistadt, MOOlin Rouge, MOO Français and Mundo Hispano. See Donaldson & Kötter (1999) and (Shield 2003).

The next important breakthrough was the development of a graphical user interface for communication and the development of a visual virtual world. A primitive graphical interface was incorporated into Quantum Link online service. One of the products developed for Quantum Link was Lucasfilm's Habitat, an online role-playing game (1986), which in many respects was a forerunner to the virtual worlds that we know today, but it was only two-dimensional. Each game player used a home computer to connect to the mainframe host that received messages and relayed messages input by the player, while the client software stored on the player's computer generated a real-time animated display of the Habitat environment. Players in this virtual world were represented by visual avatars who could interact with one another using text chat.

Traveler (1996) was another important development, adding the possibility of audio communication between avatars who were represented as disembodied heads in a three-dimensional abstract landscape. In this respect Traveler comes close to the virtual worlds that we know today. Its lip-synchronisation technology creates an impression of someone actually talking and therefore it is particularly suitable for teaching foreign languages. A drawback, however, is that it does not include text chat.

Now there is wide choice of virtual three-dimensional virtual worlds, many of which are catalogued in the online Virtual Worlds Review. A number of them have been used for educational purposes, especially Traveler and Active Worlds (Svensson 2003).

Second Life was launched in 2003 and is now the fastest-growing virtual world in the Web. When I first ventured into Second Life in early 2007 I was not particularly impressed. I had already had some experience of using virtual worlds such as Anarchy Online and Active Worlds, and my first impression of SL that it was just another online game. I struggled to control my avatar, who proved to be an inept creature, blundering into numerous objects and other avatars, falling off buildings and precipices, and occasionally engaging in text chat with other visitors to this virtual world, most of whom did not seem to have much to say. I could not see that SL offered anything new and exciting, especially for education. Nevertheless, spurred on by recommendations in messages posted to the online discussion list of the European Association of Computer Assisted Language Learning (EUROCALL), I thought that Second Life was probably worth a "second look". I registered for the first SLanguages conference, which took place on one of the EduNation islands on 23 June 2007. At that time voice chat in SL had not been implemented, so the speakers and participants had to run SL in tandem with the Ventrilo audioconferencing software, combined with standard SL text chat. Speakers' and participants' voices came through very clearly on my computer, and the speakers were able to put up PowerPoint slides on a large display at the EduNation conference venue, the Glass Pyramid. In the discussion sessions, participants could use text chat with the presenters or they could illuminate a light bulb on their head to indicate that they wished to speak, and then the chair would call upon them in turn. This approach to conferencing was new at the time, but it worked surprisingly well. In the meantime it has become commonplace now that SL has introduced its own voice chat facility.

I was encouraged to explore SL further. I began to look around for online language courses in SL. It was easy to find them. It took me very little time to discover Avatar Languages, English Village, Language Lab and Languages United. As a former teacher of German, I began to discover German-speaking SL sims such as Munich and Apfelland, where many of the signs and instructions are written in German and where one is likely to meet German-speaking avatars – ideal environments for exploratory and task-based approaches to language learning.

I was now convinced that it was time for EUROCALL to set up a base in SL, and I persuaded the EUROCALL Executive Committee to make funding available for a headquarters building on EduNation III Island, one of a group of islands maintained by The Consultants-E, Barcelona, and dedicated to education in SL. I was given the task of furnishing and equipping the EUROCALL HQ. It was a challenging task, but it taught me a lot about Second Life. The HQ is now fully furnished and equipped with slide presentation screens and a media player. It has proved to be very useful for small meetings and for delivering online training for newcomers to SL. There is also a EUROCALL SL Group that you can join. EUROCALL's sister organisation in the USA, CALICO, maintains a CALICO SL Group too and has recently (2008) set up a Virtual Worlds Special Interest Group.

The publication of this book is timely. It gathers together experts from around the world who approach education in SL in a variety of different ways. Their contributions range from practical advice to ongoing research, covering task-based learning, assessing learners' language skills, role-play in a business studies context, collaborative creative projects, and the use of SL as an alternative stage for the performing arts. The important message that comes across in the chapters of this book is that virtual world technology offers new opportunities for enhancing learning and teaching. Although SL is relatively new, it is clear that from the contributions to this book there is already a wealth of knowledge about its potential in promoting education, and there are many existing examples of good practice for others to build upon.

References

Active Worlds: http://www.activeworlds.com

Anarchy Online (English): http://www.anarchy-online.com

Avatar Languages: http://www.avatarlanguages.com

British Legends: http://www.british-legends.com

CALICO Virtual Worlds Special Interest Group: http://colanmc.siu.edu/virtualworlds/

The Consultants-E: http://www.theconsultants-e.com

Donaldson R.P. & Kötter M. (1999) "Language learning in cyberspace: teleporting the classroom into the target culture", CALICO Journal 16, 4: 531–558.

Dreistadt (German): http://cmc.uib.no/dreistadt/

English Village: http://englishvillage.asia/

EUROCALL (European Association of Computer Assisted Language Learning): http://www.eurocall-languages.org

Felix U. (ed.) (2003) Language learning online: towards best practice, Lisse: Swets & Zeitlinger.

LanguageLab: http://www.languagelab.com/en/

Languages United: http://www.languagesunited.co.uk/learning-on-line.html

MOO Français (French): http://www.umsl.edu/~moosproj/moofrancais.html

MOOlin Rouge (French): http://cmc.uib.no:9000/

Mundo Hispano (Spanish): http://www.umsl.edu/~moosproj/mundo.html

Shield L. (2003) "MOO as a language learning tool". In Felix U. (ed.) Language learning online: towards best practice: Lisse: Swets & Zeitlinger.

schMOOze University: http://schmooze.hunter.cuny.edu

Svensson P. (2003) "Virtual worlds as arenas for language learning". In Felix U. (ed.) Language learning online: towards best practice: Lisse: Swets & Zeitlinger.

There: http://www.there.com

Traveler: http://www.digitalspace.com/traveler/

Virtual Worlds Review: http://www.virtualworldsreview.com

Overview of the Book

Virtual worlds are increasingly incorporated into modern universities and teaching pedagogy. Over 190 higher education institutions worldwide have done teaching in the virtual world of Second Life® (SL). This book is based on the first Scandinavian project to experiment with the design and testing of teaching platforms for lifelong learning in SL. In 2007 it created a virtual island or "sim" in SL called "Kamimo Education Island". The project funded by "Norgesuniversitetet" (a state run organisation a.k.a. "Norway Opening Universities" in 2007 and 2008), generated a number of courses taught in Second Life, and instructed educators in the use of SL. This book disseminates the experiences and lessons learned in that project and from other educational projects in SL. Kamimo Education Island can be found in Second Life at:

http://slurl.com/secondlife/Kamimo_Island/127/148/25

This book identifies the gaps in traditional forms of education. It provides a roadmap on issues of: instructional design, learner modelling, building simulations, exploring alternatives to design and integrating tools in education with other learning systems.

The target audience for this publication is educators and learners in higher education looking for inspiration to support teaching/learning activities in virtual 3D environments such as Second Life (SL).

Outline of the book is broken into two parts. Part 1 is on Pedagogic Design and Part 2 Learning Projects relates lessons learned through research and educational projects that are recent or ongoing in Second Life.

Part I: Pedagogic Design

Chapter 1: The New Learning and Teaching Environment
Motivation and tone for this book are set in the opening chapter by Dr. Judith Molka-Danielsen from Molde University College in Norway (hereafter abbreviated HiMolde). This chapter provides a clear picture of why SL may be chosen as an environment for learning and teaching through giving a theoretical foundation and then a set of examples of its use. It introduces definitions and a set of terminology that may be new to many educators and are presently used with virtual worlds both in work, education and entertainment. This chapter clearly highlights the major enhancements and opportunities that virtual worlds such as SL can offer to learning and teaching.

Chapter 2: Instructional Design, Learner Modeling, and Teacher Practice
One great challenge for educators is to design tasks and promote teacher-learner interaction that encourage learner engagement, participation, autonomy and creativity within the practical constraints of SL and the administrative demands of the institutions we operate in. This chapter by Dr. Mats Deutschmann from Mid Sweden University in Sweden and Dott.ssa Luisa Panichi from the University of Pisa in Italy more deeply addresses issues: identifying tasks

that SL is suited for; creating tasks where the learners become a source of content; creating the social and technical prerequisites for a social learning situation to occur; and teacher role/best practice issues such as facilitator.

Chapter 3: Assessing Student Performance

Here David Richardson from University of Kalmar in Sweden contributes as an active teacher of flexible courses in English and is assisted by Dr. Judith Molka-Danielsen (with HiMolde). They introduce experiential and theoretically based approaches to assessment in teaching that address the affective advantages and disadvantages of the environment. For example, levels of learner comfort in various situations and the impact the environment may have on the learners' willingness to participate. Practical and pedagogic concerns about learner assessment within SL (i.e. oral assessment in language learning or the assessment of artefacts by digital design students) and of student work carried out in SL but not assessed within the environment itself (for example, student reports/essays about their SL experience).

Chapter 4: Sim Creation and Management for Learning Environments

This chapter presented by Dr. Judith Molka-Danielsen (with HiMolde) and Linn-Cecilie Linnemann who is manager and consultant for the marketing firm Design Container in Oslo, Norway. This chapter addresses practical issues related to the creation and management of a virtual sim. The first phase of sim creation is to obtain virtual space or parcel. This begins with either a purchase or rental of server sims from the Linden Lab grid. After purchase the owner will need to modify the terrain of the sim, to their personal needs. The choice is to do-it-yourself or it can be outsourced to those that specialize in SL design and building. Adding tools for the support of education is part of this design process. Sim creation is followed by the need to manage the new virtual learning environment (VLE). Management means allowing the right users to share the developed resources, to provide security and privacy where it is needed, and to allow openness where desired. Finally, once a working platform of services, groups and rights are created, the users will need to be educated about how to access and use the VLE.

Part II: Learning Projects

The remaining chapters are classified as Case studies on education projects in SL. The authors give guidance to a range of issues including their experiences related to creation and administration of their active environments, specific pedagogic design issues and illustrate how SL came to be used in a variety of teaching and subject domains (language, art, history, etc).

Chapter 5: Creating Effective Learning in Construction of a Teaching "Artifact"

The authors Dr. Clare Atkins and Mark Caukill present a case study that bridges the gap between "serious fun" and "serious learning". They describe the lessons learned in a Bachelor of Information Technology student project at Nelson Marlborough Institute of Technology in New Zealand. The student's final year project was to explore SL educational capabilities and assess if it was up to a level where teaching can take place effectively. It was also to encompass the building of an educational activity to test how feasible it would be to construct a teaching 'artifact' and whether it might aid in teaching and learning. The artifact was a build to demonstrate an Internet Protocol v4 (IPv4) sub-netting tutorial.

Chapter 6: Action Learning in Second Life
Lindy McKeown, advisor to the New Media Consortium (NMC) and PhD student with University of Southern Queensland in Australia, gives a brief explanation of how Action Learning works and why it is such a widely used learning strategy. Her chapter will explore how to use a virtual world as a location for Action Learners.

Chapter 7: Enhancing Virtual Environments
Dr. Bryan Carter from the University of Central Missouri in USA describes ways to design learning environments with a philosophy of creating enduring engagement among participants. He explains that since it's inception in 2003, Second Life has offered educators an opportunity to engage students on a level never before possible in a traditional classroom setting. Through the creation of historical or futuristic environments, interactive assignments and multiple ways to communicate and collaborate, SL is the pedagogical compliment for which many educators have been waiting. Examples are builds such as Virtual Harlem and Virtual Montmartre where the Jazz Age is highlighted and experienced. SL encourages engagement, communication and interaction with both the environment and other residents on the same level if not more so than that which occurs in the real world. How, then, might an environment designed in such a way, be enhanced to increase that which is already at such a high level? The current state of technology suggests several very real possibilities; one of which is already deployed on Virtual Harlem. Artificial Intelligent Agents is one compliment to Second Life that may offer educators an additional way to engage students both in-world and out.

Chapter 8: Pilot Role Play Study in a Purchase Management Class
Dr. Bjørn Jæger and Dr. Berit Helgheim from Molde University College in Norway give general background of role play in education in particular its potential application to Business studies and Purchase Management in practice. They give a detailed account of the role play model as in applied in a Purchase Management class using the case example of the buying and selling of an Enterprise Resource Management system.

Chapter 9: Learning by Creating Historical Buildings
The tight research team from the University of Pisa in Italy of students: Marco Bani, Francesco Genovesi, Elisa Ciregia, and Flavia Piscioneri; with professors Beatrice Rapisarda, Enrica Salvatori, and Maria Simi has a remarkable story of student lead design and building in Second Life. The experiment that created high quality recreations of historical buildings, started from an international collaboration between the curriculums in Informatica Umanistica (Humanities Computing) of the University of Pisa and the Centre for Computing in the Humanities of the King's College in London (CCH). The students of both institutional partners work under the supervision of their teachers, following methodological guidelines established and agreed-upon. Several buildings contructed include the Tower of London, the Leaning Tower, Galileo Galilei's Laboratory and moreover the students from Pisa designed a brand "new" building, Archetipo, meant to be used as an orientation and educational center. An important benefit of the collaboration has been that they were introduced to the

methodological principles that are currently discussed by the international community interested in the reconstruction of historical buildings and environments. The experience showed that students learn, by being actively engaged in the construction. In particular they learn in a collaborative setting how to create virtual objects and environments, become aware of new usability and communication issues that arise in connection with virtual words and are stimulated to improve their culture and appreciation of history and art.

Chapter 10: Performance in Second Life

Dr. Toni Sant from the University of Hull in the UK describes the potential and interest that Second Life holds for the performing arts: performing drama, music and live art events. He claims that unlike other virtual worlds, created as games with set rules and stock characters, most of what goes on in SL is created by its users. This makes it an ideal playground for creative people. A growing number of musicians, theatre-makers, and other performers are exploring SL as an alternative stage for their ideas. Furthermore, like other similar massively multiplayer online role-playing worlds, SL is used by a large number of people for creative virtual self-presentation. These activities indicate various interesting and alternative possibilities for presenting "self". Among other possibilities, Sant presents the affordances of Machinima, which involves film-making techniques applied to characters and story-lines within virtual spaces. Machinima in SL brings together various elements of live performance in ways that are similar to performing for the camera in physical space.

Chapter 11: Collaborative Difference: Orchestrating Space for Learning and Research in Second Life

As several prior chapters have hinted at, learning and research often go hand-in-hand. In this chapter Ph.D. student James Barrett and Dr. Stefan Gelfgren from HUMlab and Umeå University in Sweden point out that those expressions of creativity are often the result of such associations. For HUMlab the interest lies in digital culture in various forms, and it aims to be a forerunner and set examples of best practice within the area of digital humanities. They also have close relation to the Humanities faculty at Umeå University, and the aspiration to influence the whole faculty. The two "legs" aren't always easy to combine – vision with tradition – but Second life has become one way of bridging this divide. This chapter describes and discusses how HUMlab has used SL in its work beginning with the establishment of virtual presence from planning a sim to the stages of involving researchers with diverse projects and interests. They point out how the use of SL has developed over time, allowing for expanding use of new technologies. They give examples of humanities research in relation to SL and also share experiences of how to use SL in education; such as students that were able to build exhibitions in SL based on their lectures and research. For example, they explain, "Gender, Nation, Religion, Ethnicity and Class are foci in the course lectures and these concepts are expected to drive the work conducted by the students in Second Life."

Chapter 12: Future Directions for Learning in Virtual Worlds

The final chapter is co-authored by Dr. Mats Deutschmann and Dr. Judith Molka-Danielsen, also the co-editors of this book. The goal of the final chapter is to identify a common thread in the case studies of this book. It is also to reflect on what we have done, to clarify what we see as the current state-of-the-art of virtual worlds in education, and to point out future directions or opportunities for learning, educational processes and research on learning in Second Life.

Part I
Pedagogic Design

Chapter 1: The New Learning and Teaching Environment

Judith Molka-Danielsen, Ph.D.
Molde University College
Britvn. 2, 6402 Molde, Norway
j.molka-danielsen@himolde.no

Chapter Overview: In September 2007 Kamimo Education Island in the virtual world of Second Life was opened to visitors. It was soon introduced to college students through regular courses. After several sessions, I asked a student, "What do you think of Second Life for learning so far?" and they asked "Well, what can I do in it?" I realized that faculty may receive more training and background information about new technologies through course planning. It is important to give this background knowledge to both students and faculty. We cannot assume that students, because many are of the NET generation, are aware of the benefits of a particular tool. This chapter will introduce what can be done in Second Life in support of learning and teaching.

1 First Impressions

For learners and educators in Second Life (SL) the possibilities for learning are very numerous and exciting. Several courses offered in SL have prompted the potential student to imagine a learning environment where they can go anywhere and do anything while interacting and sharing experiences with others. More precisely one could imagine visiting important historical places that no longer exist such as the Galileo Museum of the medieval Italy or visiting places and do things that might be dangerous in the real world such as standing in a simulation of an avalanche while skiing. The museum and the weather simulation both exist in SL. Another application of the 3D world might be to gain additional perspectives on a 3D model of a building, such that architects and designers could visualize changes to design. The disciplines of the humanities abound with opportunities to share social context through live performances. Some could be musical performances with musicians located over an entire globe coming together in a virtual space and creating a distributed but shared music experience. We describe in this book some of the communicative and relational possibilities between learners and educators. As expressed in several of the cases, educators have discovered that SL as created by its residents (who are real people) motivates learners to research events and locations, to interact and receive feedback with other learners, and to increase understanding of the real world relationships through activities in SL. This book will try to answer the question, "what can I do in it?" We can begin with a brief list of general categories of activities. Many such activities take place in SL without learning being the primary goal. SL is a general purpose platform and as such some may use it for pure entertainment. However, we will address activities in SL with learning goals in mind. The reader will soon see that the possibilities for learning are left to the imagination. We list a categorization of some possible activities in SL through interactions with context and persons to spark the imagination:

1. 3D Art experiences – motion possible
2. 3D Data visualization - multifaceted representations of images or text
3. 3D Modelling – ships, the body, buildings, campuses
4. Business meetings - pitch a budget
5. Collaboration – on shared tasks
6. Conferences and business meetings
7. Campus representations
8. Design and Building – creating immersive context, scripted tools
9. Exhibits – in sciences such as astronomy, physics, etc.
10. Job interviews – learning to participate in such
11. Libraries – interactions with
12. Museums – interactions with
13. Political campaigns, activism, social awareness
14. Performances – live or recorded, music or other
15. Re-enacted scenarios – murder mysteries
16. Reflection – while sitting on a virtual cloud or in a virtual church
17. Role play – arts, history, health, business
18. Social interactions – meet with friends, work together on homework
19. Story telling – dialogue and structure
20. Virtual offices – meeting places with students or clients

The remaining part of this chapter will explain in greater detail what exactly Second Life is. We will introduce pedagogic theories and describe how they relate to SL. We will give an initial example of a learning task. And finally we give an introduction to the rest of the book.

2 Second Life

Second Life® (www.secondlife.com) is an open access technology platform where a growing community of participants create the content of the virtual world. SL was established for public access in 2003 by the Californian based firm Linden Research, Inc. commonly known as Linden Lab. Generally speaking, Second Life may be classified as a massive multi-user online virtual environment. Recently, massive multi-user online virtual environments (MUVE) have shown undoubted potential in the ability to immerse participants in their worlds (Jenkins 2005). The platform enables participants called residents to interact through motional use of avatars or synthetic characters that can be personalized in the greatest detail. Residents can participate as individuals or as members of groups. They can socialize in a 3D virtual space through communication tools such as text chat or voice chat, using public broadcast or one-to-one private talk options. Avatars can interact with the virtual surroundings, by moving objects, or interacting with other avatars through scripts written in Linden Scripting Language (LSL). SL also has an in-world economy and its own currency called the Linden Dollar (L$). The Linden Dollar can also be exchanged with real world currencies. This has created in-world marketplaces consisting of individual and organizational run businesses. The internal marketplace also has implications for real world businesses. Real world businesses have established presence in SL for many reasons. Some incentives for them are marketing or branding, employee training, employee collaboration, demonstration of products and for revenue generating purposes. SL has inspired creation of new services that exist exclusively within the virtual world. Some services are maintaining "sims" (virtual space) or building in-world content including: terra forming virtual land, designing and building virtual structures (houses for example), and creating objects or artifacts such as clothing for avatars.

Educators can very likely capitalize on the motivational factors of these worlds to engage learners. It may even be argued that MUVE support an empathic factor in the teacher and learner relationship. Through understanding of the experiences and sharing the perspective of others through emotion MUVE offer the opportunity for all participants to step into the shoes of others; thus contributing to immersive experiences. (Molka-Danielsen 2006) (Molka-Danielsen et al forthcoming). Further, through embedding learning activities into the simulations of an online environment MUVE can offer students socially acceptable and personally gratifying opportunities to learn (Thompson & Rodriguez 2004). Examples can be taken from the gaming industry. Some of the most popular MUVE such as The Sims or World of Warcraft, feature synthetic characters with personalizing options so that the participants of these games become emotionally engaged in the both the characters and the "artificial" worlds (Hall et al 2006). More recently virtual technologies have been recognized for their potential application to learning (Nardi, Ly and Harris 2007) (NMC 2007). This book offers a roadmap to explore new opportunities and methods for learning and teaching that are actively being designed and applied within SL at present.

Educational institutions have entered Second Life. Many universities, colleges, and other educational institutions have established a presence through the rental or purchase of virtual land. The land, island or "sim" in SL is a virtual space that is simulated on a large array of servers called a Grid. So, the owner of land in SL is in actuality renting capacity on a server owned by Linden Lab. The land is sectored into regions that are the area hosted by a single server CPU. Items or objects in SL are called assets, and when they take form as 3D objects they are called primitives or prims. Each sim can support an allowance of prims that limits the number of virtual objects, including avatars that can be placed ("rezed") on one sim.

Motivations for universities to establish presence in SL vary just as they do for businesses. Some universities are present in SL for marketing purposes. These may try to replicate campuses or important campus buildings, to attract prospective students. Others institutions wish to offer courses that may support more flexible forms of education with other learning solutions; often called blended learning, and still others wish to offer pure distance courses to a broad spectrum of students. The profile of the student body can be very diverse with differing needs: some students may be geographically dispersed, while others might wish to combine work and a formal education program. Furthermore some students with disabilities may not be able to be on-campus. SL offers possibilities to serve all these groups. A third type of university entering SL is those doing active research. These are discovering new theories and methods, new "best practices" for their particular fields of research.

Figure 1. A student "blue dragon" shows the teacher the group's 3D-design of a ship.

This book will explore some of the methods and "best practices" that are under study at present. A yet unmentioned fourth category of university is also present in SL. This 4th group constitutes institutions that are doing nothing so far. This category of institution may anticipate the usefulness of SL in education, so perhaps they have purchased virtual land, but they have not decided on a plan of implementation. We hope our book will be a resource to this group. We hope it will stimulate ideas for activities of learning and teaching in virtual worlds, and in particular in Second Life. Throughout the book many of the examples given are based on the authors' experiences with the design, development and educational activities that began for us on Kamimo Education Island. Of course we include authors and experiences from several other important projects in SL. Figure 1 is a glimpse at our learning world.

3 Ways of Learning

Ways of learning have evolved in recent decades to be more focused on the Social Constructivist theory of learning as was introduced by Vygotsky (1978). The present theory centers on several main assumptions.

1. **Reality** is not discovered and does not pre-exist, but it is constructed through human activity. As Kukla (2000) explains, members of society together invent the properties of the world.
2. **Knowledge** is a product of human interaction, socially and culturally created (Ernest 1998; Gredler 1997; Prawat & Floden 1994).

3. **Learning** is a social and active process. Learning takes place when individuals partake in social activities. (McMahon 1997)

Educational or teaching models based on Social Constructivism will emphasize collaboration among learners and with educators. Based on this theory of learning, Second Life is an ideal environment for learning. As will be described in numerous examples in this book, it is a world created by its members, and the opportunities for collaboration are numerous. But even further, as will be evident in several cases, there are opportunities for enhanced production or success of the individual through collaboration. The environment is ideal for learning in social contexts as it motivates the individual to work with the contextual whole. We think in part the reason for this is that SL is an explicit and simplified world when compared to the real world. Nothing can be taken for granted, but every blade of grass or creature must be named or "created".

3.1   How do people learn?

In 1956 Benjamin Bloom introduced the "taxonomy of learning", called Bloom's Taxonomy (Bloom 1956). It is a hierarchy of learning behaviors in three learning domains: cognitive (knowledge), affective (attitude) and psychomotor (motor skills). Figure 2 gives a representation of the cognitive and affective domains. Many make reference to this taxonomy. Most have focused on learning taking place in the cognitive domain that can be viewed as a progressive mastering or contextualization of materials.

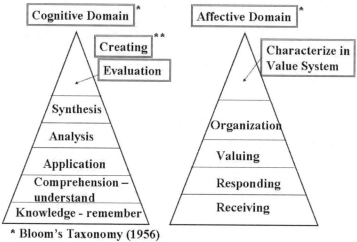

* Bloom's Taxonomy (1956)
** Anderson and Krathwohl (2001) add a category the ability to "create" new knowledge.

Figure 2. Bloom's Taxonomy (1956) in the Cognitive and Affective Domains

Fewer have examined affective learning, as is described in Bloom in (Krathwohl 1964). The affective domain addresses the learner's feelings or emotions toward the learning experience. The affective behaviours are demonstrated by: attitudes, interest, motivations, attention, awareness and self perceptions (as expression of values). According to Bloom, the affective behaviours from simplest to most complex are: receiving phenomena (awareness), responding to phenomena (active learning), valuing (attaching value to something), organization (prioritizing values), and internalizing values (characterization of values into a value system). The hierarchy of learning indicates that the simplest category of affective learning must be learned before moving on to the next category. Measuring gains in the affective domain is a difficult task; however, since "motivation" is being increasingly recognized as an important catalyst to learning, we suggest that studies are needed to measure affective learning. Some of the case studies in this book begin to examine learning in the affective domain.

4 Ways of Teaching

Ways of teaching or giving instruction based on Social Constructivism have been recommended and applied in main stream education. In particular Shunk (2000) has tested several approaches: peer collaboration, reciprocal teaching (parties switching roles as learner and teacher), cognitive apprenticeships, problem-based instruction (or Problem Based Learning - PBL), webquests (inquiry-oriented activity in which resources come from the web), anchored instruction (resembles problem based learning, PBL, but the data is usually available in a closed learning module) and other collaborative approaches that would support social learning. In addition to these other valuable approaches are Active Learning and Action Learning.

Active Learning is an approach that places responsibility on the learners and these working in pairs or groups while actively working with materials. Bonwell & Eison (1991) have suggested activities can include role playing, active discussion or debates, learning by teaching exercises, and other forms of cooperative learning. "Role play" of itself is an interesting concept. It is done for example by thespians in the theatre. But, it also can be simply defined as the turn taking of teacher and learner. Role play can also be applied in many scenarios. The three dimensional world of SL allows for realistic settings, and many researchers and educators are exploring how these settings enhance learning. It is argued that the believable environments give support to those taking on roles, that they can help the role-taker to empathize with the role, and can help all participants to become more greatly immersed in the context. Role-play was used as a learning activity in the language learning courses taught on Kamimo. Another chapter on performance in SL discusses concepts of identity and the difference between role-play and real-play. We feel that further studies of role-play are needed to understand how it supports learning.

Action Learning was developed by Reg Revans (1980). He expressed the concept by the equation $L = P + Q$, where learning (L) occurs through programmed knowledge (P) and insightful questioning (Q). Action Learning is further expressed as a cyclic process that embeds implementation in the learning process. It takes place in four phases: Explore: question a problem or issue, Plan: model ideas or hypothesis, Action: test, experiment, try out the hypothesis and Reflection: review, evaluate and form new meaning (Enderby & Phelan 1994). Action Learning has been found to embody effective professional learning criteria as reported in (Downes et al 2001). Summarizing them, some of the criteria that Action Learning supports are:

- Addresses change
- Collaborative and interactive
- Centred on communities of practise
- Experiential basis (experiment and experience)
- Inquiry based or problem solving based
- Intensive, ongoing, long termed involvement
- Open to internal or external support of context
- Knowledge is shared
- Reflective

Learning modules can be developed based on Action Learning, using a cyclic process of explore, plan, act and reflect. We suggest the design of a virtual learning program based on this approach would involve the following steps:

1. Define the learning outcomes.
2. Define a set of activities that support the outcomes.
3. Select an appropriate form of assessment.
4. Consider how people will contribute and whether turn taking is required.
5. Conduct the course sessions, with attention given to learning outcomes, and reflect on each session afterwards in debriefing sessions.
6. Conduct assessment of the sessions and participants. Possible approaches are self-assessment, peer-assessment and instructor based assessment.
7. Evaluate effectiveness of the course through feedback from learners and teachers
8. Re-design and re-organize the course according to feedback received.

Chapter 6 on Action Learning emphasizes the affordances of SL for this process and gives description of its concepts and example of its application in greater detail.

4.1 Debate of Open versus Closed Learning Environments

While the Social Constructivist will advocate the open learning environment, there is still an expressed preference by many educators for the safe harbor of closed leaning systems. Fortunately, both open and closed collaborative learning approaches are supported by the Second Life platform. It is simply a matter of application. We will explain this shortly.

First of all we find that open access is seldom a feature of the proprietary Learning Management Systems (LMS). Many of these support "restricted access" to students as allowed by administrators of the educational institution or by the teachers. These private LMSs often offer a plethora of features to support course administration, such as the ability to let students read stored notes or to submit homeworks. Recently LMS have tried to integrate social networking applications among registered users such as "instant messaging" or to integrate 3rd party tools such as "Skype" with limited success. Access to the course's full syllabus of materials are still often limited and restricted. (Molka-Danielsen 2008) With such systems external validation of student work is also limited to the resources brought into a particular closed course.

In comparison SL has the potential to offer courses with access restricted to specified groups and to specified materials or it can allow open access. Restricted access is achieved by using

SL Groups and by limiting access to parcels and objects. This would be similar to what the closed systems offer. For example, presentation tools can have set permission, so that only a designated group can control them, and land areas on sims can also be designated for use. Those that own and operate sims may set permissions to restrict who is allowed to visit their own sim, or in finer detail they can restrict who can visit a parcel. (The detailed approach for restricted access will be explained in Chapter 4.)

Simultaneously the SL virtual world is open for exploration, and has been called a 3D web. It is a world of many privately owned sims, unknown content and content developers with diverse interests. Serendipitous meetings are always possible. For example, a student can explore sims owned by your college or by unknown colleges or by a night club owner (teleporting in SL is just as easy as visiting web pages with a browser). Similar to the web, SL can be perceived as a "dangerous" place. It is an open access world by default, with limited ways to add on secured access. This said, there is no way to prevent a student from going out and exploring the greater virtual world.

Note: Because residents of SL can wander where they will, it is recommended that the main Grid in SL is used for adult only education activities. If minors should require the same benefits of the virtual world, those activities should be directed to the Teen Grid in SL.

As we began this chapter, first impressions are important. In particular, the first impressions of students in SL can be revealing and are worth capturing. They tell us of opportunity and they tell us something of the potential challenges to educators that intend to use SL in teaching. We opened this chapter with a few expressions of first impression. While we have begun to talk about opportunities, the remainder of this chapter will reiterate an experience from a small student project that relates some of the first impressions of a group of students. We reflect on the feedback of some of the things that went wrong in that case. We will suggest ways to avoid these mistakes, and ourselves redesign our learning modules for the next learning cycle, hopefully following an Action Learning approach.

5   A Student-Instructional Project

The project was a final bachelor's project for a student in an Information Management program. The student had the task of implementing a tool called SLoodle in SL and later to instruct his peers on how to use it. Briefly, SLoodle is an interface that allows for some interactive functions between users that are in-world in SL and with classroom functions that are served on a Moodle server. Moodle is an open source Learning Management System. An example of interaction between SL and Moodle is in-world text chat. That is persons in SL can type in the client window chat bar and send a text message to someone logged onto the Moodle server. This text chat function is supported in both directions. The interactive-tool that the student would examine was not this function but another that supported blogging.

The student designed his own learning objectives. The student's objectives were firstly to be able to develop the learning process as he experienced it. (He wanted to design or create a system for how he would give instruction to his peers.) Second he wished to improve his own knowledge of SLoodle, such that he could also use it himself in user education. That is he could pass on the knowledge to someone else. These goals were very insightful in that they consisted of high level learning objectives, that is "creating and being able to teach others" in the Bloom taxonomy.

The first thing the student did was to get Sloodle working. He also documented the process of installation and described the various features of Sloodle. He reported that these steps were easily achieved. The most interesting and difficult part of his project came when he designed a teaching module and taught his peers how to install and use a particular Sloodle feature. The special feature was how to send a message from within SL to make an entry on a Moodle server blog.

The instructional approach of the student was to give an in-class presentation of what Second Life is, and to explain where he went to set up an account, and to explain in general terms the systems that had been installed for this exercise. This presentation lasted 20 minutes. He then handed out materials at the end of the session and told his peer-students that he would be accessible by email for help. The students had one week to follow the instructions on the handout. That is they were instructed to make an entry on the blog that was supported by the Moodle server.

Table 1 that is outlined in the box contains the material that was distributed at the end of his presentation. The reason that his table is included here is to show how many steps were needed and to demonstrate how complex the procedure is for integrating the two IT tools. In brief, the students had to know how to sign up for two systems (SL and Moodle), they had to learn how to create a note card in SL and how to move this in and out of their inventory. It was much to be expected of students that had never heard of Second Life before this lecture.

Table 1. The help documents for using SLoodle (Source:Gangst, 2008, pp.50-52)

The help document(s)

Get a Second Life account
Go here: https://secure-web20.secondlife.com/join/
Fill out the form, should be really straight forward. Make sure you use a valid e-mail address when you sign up.

Sign up to my Moodle installation
Go here: (Link is removed.)
This is mandatory to be able to use SLoodle, as SLoodle is connected to Moodle and uses its databases as its backend. You also blog FROM SLoodle to Moodle when you deliver your answers to the virtual marketing assignment.

The Sloodle toolbar – What it is, and how you set it up.
The toolbar currently has two features:
1. An ability to blog from SL to SLoodle/Moodle, which is what you will be using in this course.
2. An ability to make gestures in the classroom.
To find the toolbar go here: http://slurl.com/secondlife/SJSU%20SLIS/21/227 (or

alternatively press the link "teleport now" under the "visit our in-world meeting point" box on www.Sloodle.org). Press "teleport now" when the webpage is loaded.

Your mission now is to find the customizable SLoodle toolbar in that area of Second Life. This is the SLoodle developers' home base in Second Life. To find the toolbar just read the posters in there, they will lead you to the customizable toolbar eventually. Do NOT download the normal toolbar as that will not work with this installation, it HAS to be the customizable one. When you find it you press touch (as it will be in the form of an actual object in there), and when prompted you save it to your inventory.

This is how you setup the toolbar:

- Make a new note card in your inventory and call it "SLoodle_config", then paste this into the note card (server address is false here):

set:Sloodleserverroot|http://home.himolde.no/~0123456
set:pwd|123456789
set:Sloodle_courseid|1

After you have done this you press save.

- Find the customizable toolbar in your inventory.
- Right click on it and select wear.
- The toolbar should now appear on your screen.
- Right-click on the new toolbar on your screen and select "edit".
- Delete the existing "SLoodle_config" in the toolbars' contents.
- Click and drag the new "SLoodle_config" note card you made from your note card inventory into the toolbar contents.
- Right click the note card, and click on "properties".
- Uncheck the "modify" box and close the window.
- Then click on the "general" tab.
- Then uncheck the "modify" box near the bottom.
- Now you could choose to rename the toolbar if you wish, but I didn't bother with that since it doesn't really serve a purpose.

You can now check if the toolbar works by left clicking on "click here to start" on your toolbar. If it works the toolbar will tell you to "please chat the subject line of your blog entry". This is rather self-explanatory and means that you are supposed to type in the subject for your blog entry. When you've done this it will tell you to "please chat the body of your blog entry", which means that you are supposed to type in the contents of your blog entry. Last but not least it will tell you to "please review your entry, and click save changes if you want to upload what you wrote to your Moodle blog". If you now press "save changes" it will attempt to send your blog entry to the Moodle/SLoodle server. If it is successful it tells you that "it has updated your blog entry successfully, and you will find your entry on your blog on the Moodle/SLoodle website. If not: You better ask for help.

Educational videos

Here are some useful links to videos where they use (and even set up) the toolbar:

(YouTube addresses are removed here.)

A student survey

Please take the time to do the student survey when you are done with the marketing assignment in the e-biz course. It's only 10 questions long (and the two last ones are optional), so it will only take 1 minute and your responses are much appreciated.

You find the survey here: (Link to the survey on SurveyMonkey is removed.)

Assessments of the instruction we will state as a summary of the comments from the student subjects themselves. The student profiles were such that they came from different learning backgrounds. Eighteen of a class of 30 students were in their second year of a Bachelor in Information Management (IM). The remaining twelve students were in second or third year Bachelors in Business Administration (BA). All students had English as a second language. The course was taught in English because students were from different European countries. It so happened that the native students were all Information Management students, and the external international students were the Business Administration students. They worked in groups of 4, and chose their own groups. There was only one group that contained a mix of native and external students. This case is also described in further detail in Molka-Danielsen (2008) and in Gangstø (2008).

After one week all of the groups that contained some IM students had completed the task of making a blog entry and none of the groups that contained uniquely BA students had completed it. The students had been asked to find popular brands represented in SL (such as Nike or IBM) and to report on what they found as the content of the blog entry. The BA students had been unable to complete the exercise because each of these groups had failed to register on the Moodle server in the "room" of the class where the Moodle blog was located. This had not been stated explicitly in the instructions, and while the IM student groups had guessed it was necessary, it was not assumed by the BA students. This was discovered on the second class meeting, and once the BA students received this instruction they also were able to make a blog entry.

6 Reflections

Through a reflective discussion with the class following the assignment we learned that those who experienced trouble had a low opinion of Second Life in general and thought the course exercise was a waste of time. Many claimed that they had spent hours trying to get it to work. But the student instructor claimed that he did not receive requests for help. Those that were able to complete in the first week thought that SL had potential for learning. This simply states that first impressions are important. While the students had access to a university computer lab with computers that had been tested and were able to access Second Life, this was not the problem. The problem was the instructional approach. More time was needed to be introduced to so many technologies. More specifically several meetings and less expected after the first experience. Also, we needed to recognize the students were from different technology ready backgrounds. We needed to identify clear user support roles so that the students would know where they could go to get help and to make it clear that they did not have to fear asking for help. This was an important learning experience for our student-instructor but also for us. We did gain insight as to how to introduce Second Life in the classroom. We were also impressed by how quickly our students could function with the SL client. It was in fact Moodle and an integration of systems that proved the obstacle in this case. As teachers, we were left with the impression that Second Life has potential. The general issues that this case study demonstrates are that SL has both potential and challenges for learning. Educators must be considerate of several factors of the learning environment: the context of access to the learning space, the dispersed and differentiated needs of the learners, the selected pedagogic approach for a given course, and the design of the learning space to meet these needs and approach. These are subjects within the forthcoming chapters.

References

Anderson, L.W., & Krathwohl, D. R. (Eds.). (2001). A taxonomy for learning, teaching and assessing: A revision of Bloom's Taxonomy of educational objectives: Complete edition, New York : Longman.

Bloom, B.S. (1956). The Taxonomy of Educational Objectives: Classification of Educational Goals Handbook 1: The Cognitive Domain. New York: McKay Press.

Bonwell, C. & Eison, J. (1991). "Active Learning: Creating Excitement in the Classroom", *AEHE-ERIC Higher Education Report No.1*. Washington, D.C.: Jossey-Bass. ISBN 1-87838-00-87.

Downes, T. (2001). "Making Better Connections. Models of Teacher Professional Development for the Integration of ICT into Classroom Practice", *A Report to the Commonwealth Department of Education, Science and Training*, Commonwealth of Australia, Canberra. ISBN 1-875864-38-5.

Enderby, J. & Phelan, D. (1994) "Action Learning Groups as the foundation for cultural change", *Asia Pacific Journal of Human Resources*, 32(1): p74-82.

Ernest, P. (1998). *Social Constructivism as a Philosophy of Mathematics*, Albany, New York: SUNY Press.

Gangstø, T.J. (2008). "IBE610 Bacheloroppgave: SLoodle", Bachelors report for Molde University College.

Gredler, M. E. (1997). Learning and instruction: Theory into practice (3rd ed). Upper Saddle River, NJ: Prentice-Hall.

Hall, L., Woods, S., Aylett, R., & Paiva, A. (2006). "Using Theory of Mind to investigate empathic engagement with synthetic characters," *International Journal of Virtual Humanoids: Special Issue on Achieving Human-Like Qualities in Interactive Virtual and Physical Humanoids*.

Kukla, A. (2000). Social Constructivism and the Philosophy of Science. New York: Routledge.

Jenkins, H. (2005). Getting into the game. *Educational Leadership*, 62(7) 48-51.

McMahon, M. (1997, December). Social Constructivism and the World Wide Web - A Paradigm for Learning. Paper presented at the ASCILITE conference. Perth, Australia.

Molka-Danielsen, J. (2006) "Empathy in the Teacher-Learner Relationship and the Potential of Virtual Gaming" in the *Proceedings of NOKOBIT 2006*, Tapir Akademisk Forlag, Trondheim, Norway, ISBN- 82-519-2187-2, pp.165-177.

Molka-Danielsen, J. (2008). "Learner Support in Multi User Virtual Environments", Proceedings of NOKOBIT 2008, in Tapir Akademisk Forlag.

Molka-Danielsen, J., Carter, B., Creelman, A. (*forthcoming*). "Empathy in Virtual Learning Environments", Int. Journal of Networking and Virtual Organisations, special issue on Virtual Learning and Knowledge Sharing.

Nardi, B. A., Ly, S. and Harris, J. (2007). "Learning Conversations in World of Warcraft", Proceedings of HICSS 2007.

NMC (2007). The Horizon Report, The New Media Consortium and EDUCAUSE Learning Initiative. ISBN. 0-9765087-4-5. Accessed: www.nmc.org/pdf/2007_Horizon_Report.pdf

Prawat, R. S., & Floden, R. E. (1994). "Philosophical Perspectives on Constructivist Views of Learning", *Educational* Psychologist, 29(1), 37-48.

Revans, R. (1980). *Action learning: New techniques for management.* London: Blond & Briggs, Ltd.

Shunk, D. H. (2000). *Learning Theories: An educational perspective (3rd ed.).* Upper Saddle River, NJ.: Prentice-Hall.

Thompson, A. & Rodriguez (2004). Computer Gaming for Teacher Educators. *Journal of Computing in Teacher Education*, 20(3), 94, 96.

Vygotsky, L.S. (1978). Mind in Society. Harvard University Press.

Chapter 2: Instructional Design, Teacher Practice and Learner Autonomy

Mats Deutschmann Ph.D.
Department of Humanities, Mid Sweden University
871 88 Härnösand
Sweden
mats.deutschmann@miun.se

Dott.ssa Luisa Panichi
Centro Linguistico Interdipartimentale
Università di Pisa
Via Santa Maria, 36 56126 Pisa
Italy
panichi@cli.unipi.it

Chapter Overview: This chapter is based on the experiences from language proficiency courses given on Kamimo Education Island and addresses concerns related to teacher practice in Second Life. We examine preparatory issues, task design and the teacher's role in fostering learner autonomy in Second Life. Although the chapter draws mainly on experiences from and reflections in the domain of language education, it has general pedagogical implications for teaching in SL.

1 Introduction and Background

During the autumn term 2007 and spring term 2008, a number of different language teaching/learning projects were carried out on Kamimo. The ambition was to see how our groups of educators could find models for using the environment in language teaching and to become familiar with the practical issues involved in using SL in a realistic teaching context. The courses, primarily addressing the needs of doctoral students, aimed to use the affordances of SL for language proficiency classes. An affordance can be defined as the quality of an object, or an environment, that allows an individual to perform action (van Lier 2004). In this sense, we wanted the students themselves with their knowledge capital to contribute to the content of the course. In combination with SL we also used the more traditional on-line video conferencing tool Marratech (tools here included web camera projection, white board, voice and text chat). Our students were exclusively adults and most of them were highly motivated. An added ambition of the test courses was to conduct research into learner attitudes and performance in the environment, and also to compare how they viewed SL in comparison with the more traditional tool Marratech. We recorded all that we did and collected additional information from questionnaires and personal interviews.

The feedback we received indicated that there were no set answers to our questions. Individual preferences made it impossible to come to any general conclusions. For example, students who had attended a course were asked to compare the difference between the video feature in the video conferencing platform and the fact that there was no live video feature in SL. Students varied in their perception of the usefulness of live video vs avatar in learning a foreign language. Some felt that video-conferencing provided more information such as gestures and facial expressions and as such made communication more effective. Some preferred the use of an avatar as it afforded them a higher level of "protection" and was perceived as limiting their "exposure" and thus increasing their sense of comfort in the environment. Some students found it more appropriate to use a video-conferencing system for education because is was felt to be more "serious". Others again preferred the freedom of movement and creativity of SL. Others stated that the lack of live video in SL actually increased their level of concentration when listening to and producing the target language and SL was thus perceived as being more beneficial than the video environment. In other words, initial feedback collection and analysis indicates so far a variety of individual responses to teaching and learning a foreign language in SL (Deutschmann, Molka-Danielsen & Panichi 2008a).

This chapter is an attempt to summarise what we learnt and to provide recommendations to others that may want to use virtual worlds such as SL in language teaching. Note, however, that we present no single best method. One clear conclusion we draw from our experiences is that further research is needed to determine the extent to which the many variables come into play in the environment. Besides the complexities of the technological environment one thing we found is that learner perception of the environment is an additional variable that needs to be taken into account when designing tasks in SL (see paragraph above). Ultimately, the degree to and the pace at which the use of SL challenges the learners' perception of learning and education, may also be an aspect that designers and instructors need to bear in mind. And, last but not least, be prepared to change your own mind set as an educator – we think it is fair to say that the use of SL also challenged our own preconceived views of what a language class is all about.

2   In Preparation – Before you get started

Careful preparation is, in our experience, a key to successful learning in Second Life. This, as a practice, is obviously applicable to all forms of teaching, but teaching in SL may offer additional and/or different challenges than those of the more traditional on-line learning environments we may be familiar with. Preparation includes many aspects: familiarising ourselves with the technical, spatial and communicative possibilities of the learning environment, preparing a course content which takes the specific affordances of SL into account, giving explicit technical and course specific instructions to our course participants, catering for the importance of initial technical guidance and allowing for socialisation. An additional aspect is accounting for the range of expectations and attitudes about SL (negative and positive) that may exist among the student group prior to the start of the course. Being a novice in this teaching context may be daunting, but can also be seen as an advantage: the challenges that you encounter are likely to be similar to those of your course participants.

2.1 Familiarising yourself with the Environment

Speaking from first hand experience, the time we invested as teachers familiarising with the environment was well spent. This process of initial familiarisation is of two types: becoming familiar with the general functions available in SL, and secondly getting to know the specific environment(s) that you will be using for your classes. In the teaching situation we operated, familiarising oneself with the functions of SL included creating one's avatar (spend some time and thought on how you, as a teacher, want to be represented visually), learning how to move the avatar in physical space (walking, flying, sitting down and teleporting) and learning how to operate the communicative tools where voice chat was of particular importance (see Chapter 4 for more detailed information on how to activate this tool).

As a teacher, it is also important to familiarise yourself with the particular environment that you will be teaching in. In our case, we conducted English proficiency courses on Kamimo island and it was important that we knew how to get to the different locations so that we could guide our course participants. We started all of our sessions at the general meeting area on Kamimo only to move on to various other locations suited for the particular task at hand. As teachers we would take the lead and the course participants would follow and it goes without saying that we had to know where we were going. Another aspect that needed some getting used to was how to operate the specific tools in the environment such as Quick Time video players, white boards, etc.

2.2 Preparing Course Content Suitable for SL

When we designed the course content initial familiarity with the environment was important. It influenced the tasks we constructed. We would, for example, conduct informal conversations around the camp fire (see Figure 2.1) on the island in order to enhance the feeling of informality, while more formal presentations were conducted in the Peer Gynt Rotunda (see Figure 2.2). Taking the physical characteristics of our learning environment into account when designing the course content is only one example of how we adapted the course to cater for the specific affordances of SL. Another aspect that we had to consider was the synchronous nature of SL. In order to make full use of this feature we had to carefully schedule the courses so that our participants could attend, taking aspects such as time differences into account (the course participants were located in various parts of the world). The specific characteristics of SL are thus of particular importance when designing different course activities, something which will be dealt with in further detail under Section 3, Task Design, below.

Figure 1. Getting to know each other around the camp fire

Figure 2. Giving formal presentations in the Peer Gynt Rotunda

2.3   Giving Explicit Instructions

We found that giving clear instructions prior to the course was of key importance, especially as we were teaching exclusively on-line with no physical contact with our course participants. The study guides we produced did not only include course goals, specific instructions for each session as well as a timetable (taking time differences into account) for the entire course, but also specific instructions on how to download the SL software, how to activate voice, how to reach our teaching location; a SLurl, a link taking you straight to the teaching location in SL, proved invaluable here. In the study guide we also provided the contact details (including Skype contacts, e-mail, telephone and SL identity) of the teachers, and encouraged the participants to schedule test sessions in SL so that they could test out their equipment prior to course start. During the course, we also ended each session with a briefing in preparation for the next session.

2.4   Technical Guidance and Socialisation

In her discussion of the teacher role in computer supported collaborative learning, Salmon (2004) lists five stages that a learner group will go through, stages which we should be aware of when designing an online course. The two initial stages of the model, which focuses on technical, social and learning processes, are of particular interest during the initial stages of a course. During the first stage, the Access and Motivation stage, the participants engage in trying to access the system, according to Salmon, and the main role of the teacher/e-moderator is to welcome and encourage course participants. The community then moves onto the second stage, the Online Socialisation stage, whereby participants familiarise themselves with each other and their learning environment. It is also here that the social culture of the community starts being established. In our courses we tried to take into account these two initial stages of Salmon's model as they were felt to be particularly critical in our teaching context and prerequisites for learning to occur.

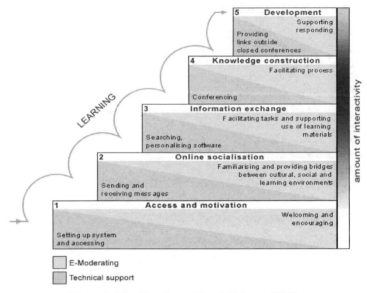

Figure 3. The Five Stage Model (Salmon 2004)

As mentioned above, it was our ambition that all course participants should have tested SL using the different communicative tools we required for the course prior to the actual course start. We used e-mail communication to arrange times for meetings and then we used Skype to guide our course participants into SL in realtime. At the start of the course we had thus managed to meet every student individually in SL and had communicated with them using voice and text. We also encouraged them to further explore the environment at their leisure. During earlier courses - when we had not taken this measure - the first meetings of the course tended to be marred with technical difficulties. These problems were avoided by taking some extra time to make sure that the course participants mastered the technical basics. An added advantage of this procedure was that we could provide a complete class list including e-mail, Skype identity and SL identity of all the participants before the start of the course. The course participants could thus meet each other in SL prior to the start of the course. Obviously this technical initiation can equally well be carried out by technical staff or even students who have experienced the environment.

Time for socialisation was worked in as an integral part of course design. In our most recent course, we actually spent the first two group sessions getting to know each other. Allowing for socialisation may at first seem inefficient, taking time from the ordinary course content but the importance of allowing this process cannot be overemphasised. In the initial course we conducted, we did not allow for this process. We jumped straight into various proficiency tasks before the course participants had had the opportunity to get to know each other, a practice which we would argue here was not so successful. The course participants tended to be reserved and embarrassed and did not communicate freely. This initial lack of socialisation affected the social dynamics of the entire course and meant that the participants never really reached a stage where they could contribute to each others' learning experience in any meaningful way. SL as an environment has many features which make socialisation easy. For example, when first meeting, the course participants are often quick to comment on each others' appearances, and initial inexperience in how to move the avatars often leads to laughter as participants bump into each other. All this helps to break the ice and creates a friendly atmosphere and a sense of group belonging.

2.5 Taking Prior Attitudes and Expectations of SL into Account

Whether SL can be considered more or less advantageous to learning will depend on a number of factors including the learners' digital competence, learner types and learner beliefs about learning and prior experience of on-line learning. Feedback from questionnaires (see Appendix) administered to our students makes it apparent that some learners associated the environment with gaming and leisure and found it inappropriate as a formal learning context, while others viewed the environment positively for learning. There are, in other words a range of individual beliefs represented in an average class, beliefs which may later affect the learning experience and the group dynamics. Such beliefs may have to be addressed prior to the course. Being explicit as to why you as an educator are using the environment and what benefits it may add to the learning experience is something that should arguably be pointed out and/or discussed at the beginning of the course. Attitudes such as the one reflected in this comment from a final evaluation – "SL felt like a game and I find it difficult to see how students will take it seriously" – can obviously affect motivation. Negative beliefs as well as unrealistic expectations can be addressed by providing examples from various pedagogic activities going on in SL and by discussing the issues involved in learning in virtual environments. Doing this will also give you, as an educator, a better idea of the group profile and the individual needs and backgrounds housed therein. These may well be important factors to take into account when designing the specific tasks of a course, the subject of the next section.

3 Task Design – What Tasks are Suited for SL

It is common knowledge that foreign language classrooms in the vast majority of educational settings from primary through secondary and tertiary levels are still monolingual (or treated as such) and opportunities for authentic communicative interaction with other speakers of the target language are few. Thus, the main advantage of SL, and other virtual environments for learners of a foreign language, is that they are able to provide realtime access to communicative events, both with members of the community whose language and culture is being studied and with other learners of the same target language from different L1 (first language) backgrounds and cultures. In addition, as an "open" platform, SL has the potential for unregulated intercultural communication and cross-linguistic fertilisation with, as yet unchartered, implications for language acquisition and spontaneous learning (i.e. Tandem language exchanges) and other linguistic developments (i.e. the development of English as an International Language – EIL and English as a Lingua Franca – ELF or the revival and maintenance of lesser spoken languages). It is with this in mind that we argue that SL also has the potential to contribute to the development in the language learner of effective communicative skills suited for multicultural, multilingual and transnational contexts.

Indeed there are plenty of platforms which enable virtual contact among students from different geographical locations. However, SL, while sharing many of the features of these platforms, is also able to provide the following affordances to the language learner and educator:

- Personal and cultural anonymity
- Visual representation of self via an avatar
- Co-construction of reality and shared culture (both via artifacts and via a community of avatars)
- Physical simulations of real life tasks

As the examples and our discussion will illustrate, these unique features have the potential to enable learners and educators to explore specific areas of language learning and cultural awareness in unprecedented ways. It is felt in particular that these features are capable of opening up the language classroom both to discussions of and play with issues of power and identity, the perception of self and "the other", and the relationship between language and culture. It is argued thus that SL provides a new scope for tasks which question assumptions about "the other", stereotypes, cultural values and beliefs all of which an integral part of learning a foreign language.

Finally, it is suggested that the physical dimension to SL (i.e. that there is movement of a kind) actually brings SL tasks closer to tasks carried out in real classrooms thus restoring the physical and kinesthetic/holistic dimension to learning which is lost in other virtual learning platforms (i.e. in the more conventional video-conferencing tools).

However, as mentioned in the introduction to this chapter, whether these differences can be considered more or less advantageous to learning will depend on a number of factors. Experience from the English Proficiency courses we conducted on Kamimo island shows that group discussion about the environment itself and of learners' perceptions of it provides not only teachers with useful feedback but also contributes to the learners process' of "adaptation" to the new environment.

Another general concern of all distance and online educational programmes (White 2003) is learner participation. Recent research (Panichi, Deutschmann & Molka-Danielsen 2008b) that we ourselves conducted during our course activity shows that learner engagement and participation in language learning in SL benefits from looser rather than stricter frameworks and that the learner community is central to the learning experience. With this in mind, the tasks listed below are ones that attempt to maximise learner interaction with the specific learning environment, encourage group/pair interaction and include a strong oral communicative component.

At this point it needs to be noted that the primary modes of communication in SL are chat mode and the recently introduced voice-chat mode. While both forms of communication offer a variety of communicative affordances, feedback from our oral proficiency students from several course occasions in SL indicate that some learners find it hard to manage both modes in their target language at the same time. One of the advantages of chat mode, however, is that it enables others to provide unobtrusive feedback about what is being said as it is being said. As with all forms of learner-learner interaction and teacher-learner interaction, the mode of communication and teacher preference will often depend on the type of task at hand, the level of language proficiency of the students and their level of technical comfort and ease within the SL environment. The model adopted in recent courses has been to use voice chat as the primary mode of communication and text chat only as a supplement or when for some reason voice chat was disabled (see section 4 below). The examples of tasks described in the section below have been created with voice-chat as the primary form of communication.

The following section will provide examples of tasks that have been designed for language learning in SL in controlled situations, i.e. as part of institutional courses. However, the potential for spontaneous unstructured language learning is felt to be huge and the examples of course based tasks provided here is by no means exhaustive.

The tasks listed below are tasks for language learning set-ups which have a class (a group of learners and a teacher/instructor) who are engaged mainly in synchronous communication as a group and as part of a course or of a series of learning encounters in SL. However, the tasks may also be deemed as appropriate for one-off learning occasions or as an extension or complement to other tasks which do not take place in SL. These tasks may be incorporated into more general course syllabi in which language instruction is provided via other modes or in more traditional environments.

Finally, while the use of SL in self-access centres or for individual learning tasks will not be examined here, we nevertheless hope that the discussion which follows will provide enough background information for those wishing to create tasks for different learning needs as well.

Tasks

In foreign-language learning a task is "an activity which learners carry out using their available language resources and leading to a real outcome." (Richards & Renandya, 2002, p.94). Our understanding of task is a learner group activity which makes use of the affordances of the specific learning context in the pursuit of a specific learning goal the outcome of which will vary according to the variables that come into play each time (cfr. van Lier 2004). The task is usually part of a series of tasks and of a greater learning unit (i.e. a course syllabus) but may also make sense as an isolated event.

The tasks illustrated here are of two types: tasks for language learning within a closed community in SL (i.e. tasks for the virtual classroom) and those tasks which create links between a specific language learning community or classes and SL as a broader virtual world (i.e tasks which encourage learners to mine SL for linguistic, cultural and artefactual information they can then take back into their virtual classroom).

SL can be used for learning and teaching activities including, but not limited to, tasks which replicate or are identical to those carried out in classroom based contexts:
-   individual, pair or group work
-   tasks focussed on one of the four language skills (listening, reading, writing, speaking and their combinations)

- learner centred tasks
- lectures and formal readings
- group/class reading and analysis of written texts
- PowerPoint presentations
- video projections
- listening of recordings
- formal debate and questions
- informal conversations

In addition to the above, however, we would like to present tasks for language learning in Second Life according to which dimension of SL they privilege most: the social-communicative, the creative-cultural and the physical. These can be divided into several categories:

1. The social/communicative/cognitive dimension:
- tasks that enable learners to share and build on their knowledge (community as source of knowledge)
- tasks that are embedded in social interaction (building/joint creation of an object)

2. The affective/creative dimension:
- tasks that explore identity
- tasks that explore cultural norms and values
- tasks that encourage artistic expression or representation (theatre and performance, artwork)

3. The spatial/physical dimension
- tasks that use SL as a source of information
- tasks that use SL as a space for navigation and movement
- task that use SL as a space for cross-linguistic and inter-cultural contact
- tasks that encourage exploration of existing artefacts

Finally, many tasks actually offer a combination of dimensions.

3.1 Task type 1 – Tasks that make use of the social, communicative or cognitive dimension

The tasks presented in this section focus on developing the learners' oral/aural competence and proficiency levels and are conceived of as "talking about" tasks. The primary focus here is getting students to practice their target language in a communicative setting in ways that are meaningful for them and their fellow learners.

Tasks that enable learners to share and build on their knowledge
Tasks that fall into this category are typically conversation tasks carried out either in pairs or in groups. Topics can range from the personal to the discussion of more complex issues. For example, students may be asked to talk about their field of studies or a project they are working on. The main aim of this type of task is to provide learners with the opportunity to

practice the target language. Students may be asked to talk about a topic and share information and knowledge with other members of their group or class. In this sense, the learner community becomes a source of knowledge. Tasks of this type will tap into the knowledge base of the learners.

In addition to this, activities can be made more or less formal by changing the location and the mode of presentation. This can be done simply by talking about the same topic around a campfire or in another similar informal setting or by asking students to prepare a PowerPoint presentation in a lecture theatre followed by a more structured question and answer session.

Examples of this type of task might be:
1. Introduce yourself to and find out about the other members of your group.
2. Present your field of studies or talk about your job.
3. Participate in a debate on a specific topic.
4. problem solving
5. comparing learning experiences

Tasks that are embedded in social interaction (building/joint creation of an object)
Tasks in this category will involve the building or creation of an object in the virtual environment or a specific learning outcome. There are two main learning objectives in this kind of task: practicing the target language and producing a joint piece of work.
Examples of this kind of task might be:
1. the recreation of a historical artefacts. This type of task is particularly suited for students who need to combine the development of language skills alongside those of digital design. An example of this can be taken from the Digital Humanites course at the University of Pisa (see Chapter 9) where students met in-world with students from King's College London to work on a joint project. Students took part in both the historical reconstruction of the Leaning Tower of Pisa and the Tower of London. Similar activities on a much smaller scale can be carried out in specific "building area" in Second Life. The island of Kamimo, for example, has a public sandbox devoted to this purpose where students can build objects.
2. creating a story
3. carrying out a joint project either for display in SL or projected into real life
4. the creation of a shared image display. This was done by Lund University in Sweden with visiting students from China. Both groups displayed images of their culture on poster boards on Kamimo and used this as a discussion starting point to share stories about their cultures.

3.2 Task type 2 – Tasks that make use of the affective/creative dimension

Tasks that make use of the affective/creative dimension of SL are those tasks which encourage learners to explore their identity through their avatar. It is suggested that SL is less culturally restrictive than other more traditional learning settings insofar as the use of avatars allows for members to play with their notion of self both in physical and cultural terms. The use of avatars allows for students to present an alternate self which, in turn, may be perceived by others in unexpected ways. The degree of cultural anonymity afforded by avatars creates a new/neutral ground for discussing issues which can be sensitive in language education. Tasks that fall into this category allow for both language practice and the development of cultural and artistic awareness.

Examples of tasks of this kind are:

1) dressing your avatar to represent a stereotypical image of your/the other's culture and discussing it with the other members of your group
2) creating an artwork that is representative of one's culture or the target language culture and discussing it
3) the production of performing art (theatre, music, dance, etc.)
4) discussion of cultural topics

3.3   Task type 3 – Tasks that make use of the spatial/physical dimension

Tasks in this category will involve movement within SL and/or the use of the environment as a source of information. The aim of this type of task is to allow for greater levels of experiential learning combined with language practice which may not always be possible in more traditional e-learning environments.

Examples of tasks in this category are:
1) asking and giving directions
2) touring SL and finding specific places
3) visits to a cultural location (i.e. a library, an art gallery)
4) attending a conference or a live performance
5) interviewing residents of SL
6) finding factual information from SL sources
7) using avatar movements to express emotions
8) participating in physical activities (playing sport, etc.)
9) doing things (shopping, playing chess)

Finally it is important to note that the affordances of SL increase the scope for authenticity. Asking someone for directions in SL, for example, is a real act of communication. The spatial environment is such that the act of communication becomes real (compare with a similar task set in a traditional classroom where you have to pretend that you are lost and pretend to follow the directions). Going off into SL to find out factual information involves going to locations and seeing artifacts' first hand (rather than just reading about them), and the people you may encounter on such explorations are real people that you can communicate with. This authentic aspect of communication in SL is, in our opinion, one of the greatest benefits of using SL in language education.

4   Teacher Role, Teacher Behaviour

Van Lier (2004) argues that "the resources of a specific learning environment become affordances via engagement". As discussed earlier, an affordance is the quality of an object, or an environment that allows an individual to perform action. Whether this action is performed or not is very much a question of engagement and ultimately the question we have to address as teachers, or learning managers, is how course design can maximize the potential for engagement. Another relevant question in this respect is what variables we actually have control over and what our own roles as teachers are in creating engagement and active participation. What can we influence and what is beyond our control? How much control should we exercise and when? Some of these issues will be addressed below.

4.1 Managing Participation

One of the main motivational forces for using SL in our courses was to bring together learners from different language backgrounds in order to increase the scope for intercultural interaction to the extent that the target language, in this case English, was the only viable option for meaningful communication. In addition, we wanted to design tasks in such a way that the information needed was contained in the knowledge capital of the student group so that the students themselves became the source of the course content. Our role as teachers was thus not so much to provide information as such, but rather to act as facilitators and to try to make sure that "things started happening".

During the first language course we conducted on Kamimo, we did not really use the potential of the student body to contribute to the course content as described above. With hindsight we realised that we had designed the tasks too rigidly not allowing for individual interests and expressions. This resulted in rather mechanical exercises where students where asked to perform certain linguistic rituals rather than using language for real communication. As teachers we spent considerable effort in giving feedback and pointing out what could have been done differently, but the result was rather unsatisfactory; the students did not participate as we had hoped and were on the whole rather inactive producing short contributions timewise (averaging only nine seconds). The teachers, in contrast, produced average turn lengths of over twenty seconds. This difference in participation was further illustrated by the proportion of the floor space taken up by the students; only 18 per cent of the floor space was in fact taken up by the students, the remaining 82 per cent being occupied by the teachers (Deutschmann, Molka-Danielsen & Panichi 2008a).

Based on the experiences of our early attempts we decided to re-evaluate both the design of the tasks and our own roles as teachers on the course. On latter course occasions our main function was that of facilitating communication between the students and making sure that all participants became active. During the early stages of the course this involved directing questions to individuals and encouraging oral production by asking questions and by giving frequent oral minimal supportive moves (ahs, uhms, encouragement, expressing interest, etc). We also made sure that we directed questions in such a manner that all students would participate more or less equally. At this point it is important to note that an environment such as SL, where there are no direct visual cues as, a question has to be addressed specifically to a certain person. Open questions such as "Does anyone have anything to say about this?" would lead to confusion. Sometimes such questions were followed by a moment of silence after which two or three students would answer simultaneously only to apologise for interrupting each other. We found that the practice of actually directing questions to specific individuals got rid of this problem. Being aware of our roles as facilitators and actively encouraging students participation dramatically changed the student activity, not only in terms of how often they contributed but also in the lengths of the turns. In contrast to the first course occasions, average student turn lengths were much longer than the teachers' turn lengths; 23 seconds and nine seconds respectively, and the students occupied 78 per cent of the floor space, the remaining 22 per cent being occupied by the teachers. Important to note, however, is that although this practice of managing turn taking was important during the initial stages of the course, our ultimate aim was to make the students as autonomous as possible, and as the group culture was established we as teachers tended to step back to let the students themselves negotiate their communication (Deutschmann, Molka-Danielsen, & Panichi 2008a).

Another aspect related to managing participation that was brought to our attention during our sessions in SL was the issue of using voice chat in combination with text chat. The use or non-use of the text chat depended greatly on how familiar students were with using SL and similar environments. Novices found it particularly disturbing when others used the chat during voice chat conversations and presentations. One student in particular felt that it was rude and distracted from what he/she was saying. Others found it stressful and altogether too much to use the text chat in combination with voice since they were fully occupied with trying to operate their avatars and speaking. In our own opinion, the text chat can be a useful compliment to the voice chat so long as the comments given relate to the activity going on at the time. Obviously a text chat running parallel and dealing with a different subject to the main voice chat can be disturbing and draw attention away from the main activity. Private IMs (Instant Messages) may be used instead of public chat for themes that should be discussed between 2 persons and not of interest to the whole group. However, we have no clear recommendations or rules of thumb on the use, non-use of text chat, but the matter can be discussed with the students. In general, we found that prior verbal agreement amongst participants on the norms for communication led to fewer misunderstandings and more efficient communication. We should also be aware of the fact that novices in SL often find too much multitasking stressful; while digitally competent students who are used to multimodal communication may feel restricted if they cannot use text in combination with voice.

4.2   Dealing with Technical Problems

On a few occasions we experienced technical difficulties. These were mainly related to the voice chat, but some students also had problems navigating their avatars and even entering SL. To give a complete list of the sort of problems which may arise and how they can be dealt with is beyond the scope of this chapter but a few general guidelines may help to avert any serious crisis. Firstly, we should be mentally prepared to the fact that computer technology can never be totally reliable. This is especially noticeable when we are using computers for synchronous communication. The problems encountered may be of minor nature technically, but the consequences may still serious in terms of functionality. If sound is not being transmitted it does not really matter whether it is caused by a firewall or the fact that you have forgotten to activate the sound on your computer; the end result is the same – you cannot communicate. Having said this, nine out of ten technical problems that we encountered were of minor nature and could quite easily be remedied. Note here that it was not really our knowledge as teachers that helped solve issues. The problem solving turned out to be a truly collective effort where we all contributed, students and teachers. Together we managed to solve most of the technical problems we encountered in Second Life.

Being mentally prepared for the fact that technical hitches may occur will enable you to be better equipped to deal with things when they do happen. Having back-up channels for communication was important during our course. We had access to all students via Skype, for example, and we also had their telephone numbers. Being prepared mentally also meant that we had back-up plans. When, for example one of our students was hindered from using his/her voice chat function we would instead use the text chat function. On one occasion the teacher communicated to a student via the cell phone and relayed the information into SL. The point here is really that a minor technical hitch is no disaster. It happens and the important thing is not to panic and to be flexible, sometimes rearranging the original lesson plan. Obviously, it is a great advantage to have a technical support at hand to help sort problems out but this is a luxury few of us have. Having noted some of the problems we also want to point out that, on the whole, the quality and reliability of the communicative tools in SL were at least as good, if not better, than those of more traditional e-conferencing tools we have used.

4.3 Feedback

Although feedback is important in a language proficiency class, we decided to restrict feedback to the end of each session in order to avoid interfering with the communicative dynamics during the actual class. These in-world feedback sessions would mainly address general communicative issues related to the session. Often these discussions dealt with how the students experienced SL itself and what they felt worked well or less well. During these sessions we also invited the students to comment on tasks and our performance as teachers. We also sent out general feedback related to language issues in the form of written comments after each session. In these letters we would try to avoid commenting on individual language difficulties but rather try to give more general advice related to the individual problems we had observed. We also offered individual consultations for those students who felt that they wanted more specific personal feedback.

4.4 As the Course Progresses – Fostering Autonomy

Although acting as facilitators and managing participation was important during the initial stages of a course our ultimate ambition was to let the participants take control of their own learning situation. As courses progressed we made conscious efforts as teachers to gradually let discussions and conversations flow naturally with minimum teacher interference. This sometimes meant accepting longer pauses in the conversations but as the groups were cemented conversations would flow more naturally. Figure 4 shows the turn taking patterns of the first and the last session of a proficiency course taught in SL. At the beginning of the course almost every student's turn (represented by the white bars) is prompted by the teachers (represented by the black bars). Towards the end of the course however this pattern is less regular and there are long periods when the students talk and respond freely without the involvement of the teachers.

Turn taking pattern first session: 268 turns

Turn taking pattern last session: 234 turns

Figure 4. Turn taking pattern at the beginning and the end of a course: white bars represent student turns (Panichi, Deutschmann & Molka-Danielsen 2008b)

5 Summing up – an Ecological Model of Learning

When designing and teaching language proficiency courses in SL; we tried to follow an ecological approach to learning. This model is felt to be extremely relevant and applicable to the learning and teaching of languages, particularly in complex environments such as SL. Language is the only subject matter in which content and mode of transmission coincide. In teaching language, the distinction between the teaching of content and teaching of form does not hold. We learn language via language but our knowledge is not only measurable in what we know but in how we perform and behave, i.e. in our language performance and our communicative skills. In this sense, the unique nature of language instruction makes it particularly difficult to identify relationships of cause and effect between teaching and learning events. In an ecological approach to learning, the subject matter to be 'imparted' or 'transferred' to the learner does not exist per se (i.e. static) but is determined through a series of interactions: subject-learner, subject-teacher, mode of transmission-learner (i.e. voice, images, signs, oral text, written text, face-to-face instruction, self-access, pair work, etc.), subject-group, group-teacher, learner-learner, etc and is as variable as the infinite combinations of these interactions. The outcome of these combinations then go onto to feed into yet further interactions between elements in the environment in a continual process of change. In this sense the subject matter is dynamic.

This dynamic nature of the subject matter became very apparent when running language courses in SL. In the latter courses we conducted, when we designed the course content on a looser framework filled by the communicative input of the participants themselves, the outcome of each course session was unpredictable. It would depend on numerable variables ranging from the technical and visual nature of SL, the make-up of the student group and how different students would interact and what roles they would take. At times technical hitches would mean that a course session could take an entirely unexpected turn, and as the groups were cemented they developed into unique communicative environments in their own right. As teachers our role was to facilitate this process so that the maximum potential could be reached during each session. The most exciting part of it all was that we never quite knew what this potential was from session to session, but the immersive nature of SL certainly did bring out the best in our students and we were rarely disappointed.

References

Deutschmann, M., Molka-Danielsen, J. & Panichi, L. (2008a). "Designing Authentic Communication for Language Learning in Virtual Space" Conference presentation *Designs for Learning*, Stockholm, March 2008.

Panichi, L., Deutschmann, M. & Molka-Danielsen, J. (2008b). "Virtual reality, real engagement? Exploring engagement in Second Life language-learning environments" Conference presentation 9th International Conference of the Association for Language Awareness, Hong Kong, June 2008.

Richards , J. C. & Renandya, W. A. (Eds.). (2002). *Methodology in Language Teaching: An Anthology of Current Practice.* (2nd Ed.). Cambridge: Cambridge University Press.

Salmon, G. (2004). *E-moderating: The Key to Teaching and Learning Online.* London: Taylor & Francis.

Van Lier, L. (2004). *The Ecology and Semiotics of Language Learning: a Sociocultural Perspective.* London: Kluwer Academic Publishers.

White, C. (2003). *Language Learning in Distance Education.* Cambridge: Cambridge University Press.

Appendix: Examples of questionnaires used in evaluation of course.

A: **Perception of the environment for learning**

Answer the questions about the lesson. Use the following standard:**1= I don't agree at all with the statement 10= I agree completely with the statement.** Add any comments if necessary.

I felt that the experience of this lesson was very relevant to my language learning. _____

Comment:

I felt that Second Life was very easy to operate. _____

Comment:

I felt very comfortable in the environment. _____

Comment:

I felt very much part of the group. _____

Comment:

I felt that Second Life was an excellent environment for x (the type of task the lesson addressed). _____

Comment:

Overall I would rate the lesson -------- out of 10 (1-terrible 10 excellent).

Comment:

B: **Factors contributing to lesson outcome**

How important do you think the following factors were to a successful outcome of the lesson (rank 1-10).

1. The participation of individual members of the group
2. The make-up of the group
3. The nature of the task
4. The environment of Second Life
5. Absence of technical problems
6. The action of the teachers
7. Any other factor you want to mention

C: **Open question**

Please comment on the lesson in terms of why it worked/did not work for you and how you experienced the session (visually, socially, technically, linguistically, teacher roles or any other aspect you want to point to).

Chapter 3: Assessing Student Performance

David Richardson
University of Kalmar
Kalmar, Sweden
david.richardson@hik.se

Judith Molka-Danielsen, Ph.D.
Molde University College
Britvn. 2, 6402 Molde, Norway
j.molka-danielsen@himolde.no

Chapter Overview: This chapter addresses the issues of assessing student performance on courses run in virtual worlds. While best practices for assessment in education in virtual worlds are not yet established, our applied practices and experiences help to develop theses. This chapter presents the practices and experience of David Richardson. He has been teaching English as a Foreign Language for 25 years in a number of countries and in a variety of contexts. Currently with University of Kalmar in Sweden, he works with flexible courses in academic English and English for Special Purposes. Since both his students and colleagues live and work all over the world, ICT has been an important tool in his work, beginning with the use of text-telephones to work with deaf students in the early 1980s, through studio video conference equipment in the early 1990s, to desktop video conferencing and virtual worlds, such as Second Life at present. David has designed a 'main-line' course that has been run thus far on Kamimo Island in spring and fall 2008, Business Talking, 3 ECTS credits.

1 Opportunities for Assessment

Virtual environments such as Second Life (SL) provide special opportunities to work on educational courses where the participants could possibly live in different geographical areas, without requiring them to attend any 'real-life' sessions together with the teachers on the course. At the same time, though, the virtual nature of these environments poses particular problems for assessment on an educational course, starting with the problem of identifying the student at the beginning of the course, and checking that it is the same individual who is given credit for performance later on in the course. By their very nature, SL-based courses invited anonymity from the participants (one of the reasons for this is that avatars do not take the 'real-world' name of the participant), but this can present problems for course administrators. Some of these problems are generic for any on-line course, but some are specific for courses in virtual environments, and this chapter discusses different ways in which these problems can be solved.

One general principle is to use 'analogue' methods to solve digital problems. Checking identity digitally can be complicated to the point of absolutely impossible, but, since courses are places where human beings interact with each other, 'analogue' information, such as personal information shared and known via other media (such as telephones or direct personal meetings) can be used to establish the bond between student and assessor on a course. This has to be done sensitively, of course, since the integrity of the personal relationships is also important.

SL-based courses are also very rarely based around text, since the point of using an environment like this is to appeal to a greater variety of sense impressions and learning styles. Text-based assessment is, however, the dominant mode of assessment in education. There are, however, alternative means of assessment, both on a group and an individual level, and these can be adapted and developed within Second Life. There are potential problems relating to the transparency of the assessments and their objectivity, but these problems can be either solved or avoided altogether. The assessment procedure also needs to be integrated into both the pedagogical aims of the course and its budget for the amount of time which can be allocated to assessment. This chapter also discusses different ways of doing this.

1.1 What parameters?

Virtual worlds, such as Second Life (SL), remove many of the limitations and constraints imposed in real life, but once you start to use the virtual world as a course environment, some of these limitations and constraints reappear. One characteristic which almost defines what a 'course' is involves assessment of student performance, and this chapter is a discussion of how this can be carried out even on a course which takes place in a virtual world. It is difficult to provide a definitive treatment of this topic at this stage in development, though. Even though Second Life (and similar worlds) have been used widely by educational establishments we're still at the 'early adopter' stage, and it's difficult to distinguish the characteristics of the environment (and courses run in that environment) from the idiosyncrasies of the early adopters who are designing and running courses in it. However, it is in the nature of early adopters to also define the environment itself, and the discussion here may give an indication about the parameters assessment in virtual worlds will take place within.

1.2 Why assess student performance at all?

In this chapter we are making the assumption that assessment of performance is an integral part of the design of a course. It may be, however, that you are running courses which do not involve assessment at all, in which case, this chapter won't be very interesting for you! Assessment, however, is usually required of course designers, by organisations which want to maintain the 'currency' of the qualifications they issue, and by students who want to be sure that their achievements are identified and notified to them according to a procedure which involves better judgements than arbitrary ones. These two sets of constraints pose particular problems for an SL course designer. Amongst other considerations, organisations want to ensure that the assessment procedures and results fit in with those of all their non-virtual reality courses, and students want to feel confident that the assessment procedure is open, objective - and rewarding.

1.3 General Principles of Reliability and Validity

Firstly, a discussion of one of the general principles of assessment is needed. There are two key concepts which are applied to the design of assessment procedures, no matter what the subject matter of the course is. 'Reliability' (in this specialist sense) is the quality by which the same answer to a question receives the same credit, no matter who the examiner or the examinee is. 'Validity' is the quality of correspondence with the real world. In other words, does the assessment actually test what it is intended to test - and is this subject matter of the assessment something which ought to be tested at all?

Perhaps the ultimate in reliable tests is the machine-marked multiple-choice test, where there can be no interference at all with the objective allocation of marks for answers. Unfortunately, and as we shall argue later on, particularly unfortunately for SL-based courses, the relative banality of the results of such reliable tests makes them of limited use when you're trying to make a judgement, as a course teacher, about the way students reason or understand procedures.

Assessments with a high degree of validity have their particular problems too. As soon as the assessment deals with more than extremely practical skills, a degree of subjective judgement is almost inevitably involved. A language teacher frequently must make judgements about a student's competence in communicating in a foreign language. Such judgements inevitably involve weighing up a number of factors (e.g. grammatical accuracy, clarity of pronunciation plus body language) and allocating relative weights to them in order to make a final judgement. Ultimately this final judgement has to be made from the experience of the teacher or teachers involved in making the assessment, and this experience is always going to be somewhat subjective.

As we will be arguing later in this chapter, the constraints of reliability and validity are not insurmountable on courses in SL. It's actually a question of doing what you do with courses in the real world - you have to create a balance between the parameters within which the assessment takes place and the pedagogical and academic requirements of the course and the organisation which is offering it.

2 Organisational Factors

2.1 Administrative Factors

One of the constraints a course designer runs into, when she designs the assessment procedure of a course in Second Life is connected with the administrative and legal framework within which she is working. The identity of the student needs to be ascertained (both for billing and the award of results), and organisations often have procedures for the way assessments are carried out. There are other administrative factors to be taken into account too, such as procedures for dealing with plagiarism and course evaluations, which are often common to both conventional, classroom-based courses and flexible courses. These are often designed with the classroom environment in mind, and have to be adapted once the physical, real-world classroom is not the focus of the teacher's and students' interaction. One of problems an SL-based course can run into, for example, is a requirement to carry out a course evaluation procedure in the classroom during the last lesson of the course. But what if: the course doesn't have a 'last lesson', and if the students are never in the same location IRL (in real life)?

2.2 Legal Factors

There are often legal requirements on course providers which need to be taken into account when designing assessment procedures. As in the case of the administrative factors, these were invariably written with a conventional classroom environment in mind, and need to be adapted and worked round when assessing SL-based courses. In Sweden and in Norway for example, university students must be given the opportunity to appeal against an assessment, to repeat the assessment, and, ultimately, to receive a second opinion from another teacher, for example. The assessment procedure also needs to be described in the course syllabus, and is one of the factors assessed in its turn when the student evaluates the course afterwards. The assessment procedures thus need to be transparent, and openly described to the students. The difference between 'transparency' and 'openness', lies in the difference between the design of the assessment procedure and its execution. A transparent assessment design is one which can be explained and justified - if it is ever examined in detail. An open assessment procedure is one where the students can actually carry out this detailed examination in practice.

2.3 Environmental Factors

The character of the environment in SL also places constraints on the types of assessment procedure you can design into an SL-based course. On the face of it, it is a very distracting environment, where outsiders can - and often do - pop up in the middle of a lesson or an assessment. The environment is also very rich, leading to potential problems in limiting the scope of the experience the students and teachers have. Thus assessment procedures in Second Life need to take these factors into account. If, for example, you need to have a 'private' assessment, you need to create a private environment within which to carry it out.

3 Assessment in the Cognitive Domain

Assessment in education has often been lead by cognitive forms of assessment. In particular institutions are interested in academic achievement and the development of critical thinking, problem solving abilities, creativity, the ability to transfer knowledge and acquisition of skills. All of these higher level cognitive outcomes have been measured with programs that use among other artifacts: standardized tests, tailored tests and domain experts to assess levels of achievements. The cognitive and affective domains were introduced in Chapter 1 (Bloom 1956). We will discuss affective assessment in the next section with a more innovative approach then by traditional means. This section addresses assessment in the cognitive domain. This begins with examination of the pedagogical factors.

3.1 Pedagogical Factors

Pedagogical factors are directly connected with the subject matter of the course. So, it is impossible to avoid a brief discussion of the kind of course or course element SL is suited for. Thus far, courses in SL have tended to use the environment either as a place of study or as an object of study. By the former, we mean using SL as a place to gather students in order to learn something that is not necessarily connected with the SL island itself. By the latter, we mean using SL as a source of teaching and learning materials. Combining these two aspects is, of course, quite easy, but, even so, the tendency is to concentrate on the one or the other.

Thus, the staging of 'A Midsummer Night's Dream' in the Gardens of Caracalla in Roma is, for me, the use of SL as a place of study, since the virtual surroundings are not a necessary part of the actual learning experience - the lesson could just as easily be run on Kamimo Island (which is very Norwegian in character, but still has water and trees around). Using resources on SL as source material for compositions on a Composition Course at the University of Central Missouri, on the other hand, is very much using SL as an object of study, since it's the resources which are the important factor in student learning, rather than the use of the SL environment as such.

'**Place of study**' courses also tend to attract students who are in widely-different locations in the real world (IRL - in real life), whilst 'object of study' courses are often studied from the same IRL location, such as a university computer room (although there is nothing that determines that they must be run like this). This, however, puts the SL course examiner in very different situations, depending on which type of course is being run. The organisational factors function in very different ways, which, in turn, leads to different designs for the assessments.

In addition to this, 'place of study' courses tend also to be run more or less entirely in SL (because of the IRL distribution of the students), whilst 'object of study' courses tend to involve SL being one element among many for the students. This allows the latter to be able to rely on more conventional assessment procedures than the former, since the assessment is often being carried out IRL, rather than in SL. This, however, is largely influenced by the current nature of the educational use of SL. As the environment becomes both more accessible for and accepted by the academic community, 'hybrid' courses will almost certainly be developed where certain 'distributed' activities take place in SL and others IRL. One course element under discussion at Kalmar campus, for example, is student oral presentation on academic courses in English. At present these take place at locations which are approximately 100 kms apart, IRL. A situation where students instead practice and develop their skills in SL but where the course element culminates in a 'performance' IRL is well within reach. Ultimately, though, we feel that 'place of study' courses and course elements present a different set of challenges to the examiner from 'object of study' ones. Hybrid courses can help to circumvent some of the organisational problems (such as the establishment of the identity of the student being assessed), but not all of them.

3.2 Establishing Identity on a 'Place of Study' Course

There is no current widely-available and -acceptable way of establishing the identity of someone on-line, which makes one of the first tasks of an SL course examiner rather difficult. Sweden and Denmark do, for example, have systems for citizens to obtain electronic IDs for themselves for the purposes of communicating with government departments, but these are not currently available to non-residents or to universities, making their existence rather moot for someone working in the university system with non-residents. However, there is a principle which can be used to circumvent this problem of establishing the identity of a student. We call it 'using analogue means to solve digital problems'. Students on courses - especially courses using SL - either submit a great deal of personal information, or have a certain amount of personal contact with the teacher before the course begins. Thus, at course launch, the teacher has a number of ways of double-checking the identity of the person whose avatar she is talking to. It could be a question of asking for one or two of the 'secret' digits of the person's personal number or a check question connected with a conversation or mail exchange the teacher has had with the student prior to the course (SL-based courses generate a lot of these, since the students tend to be neophytes - or 'newbies' in SL jargon - who need help with technical and administrative problems).

There are logistical problems involved in this process, though. Dealing with a group of newbies is going to be confusing and time-consuming (which is why SL mentors tend to have a one-to-one relationship with newbies on Help Island). One way to handle this is to stagger the arrival of newbies and to have help! The way the Business Talking course at the University of Kalmar is launched is that the new students are introduced in small groups (usually three), to an environment where a number of more-experienced students from the University of Central Missouri are waiting for them. After an identity check and a very quick orientation (so that the students know where they'll be meeting next time), the newbies are whisked away by the Americans on a tour of the Americans' favourite places in SL (a process which usually also involves the European students learning the things they need to know about navigating in SL, buying clothes, etc). What we've done, in effect, is to separate the initial introduction to the learning environment from the start of the first class, rather like what happens during Registration Weeks on conventional courses.

Figure 1. shows a Business Talking Course Launch

Once the identity of the student is established, a course with a large amount of interaction in it allows the examiner to be able to recognise both the sound of the student's voice and her mannerisms, particularly in a foreign language. This assumes, of course, that the course involves a large amount of interaction ... however, courses which do not involve interaction between teachers and students, and students and students, are, perhaps, best not run in SL.

'**Object of study**' courses often do not run into this kind of problem, since identity is established in the conventional way when the student enrol at the university, and is maintained through IRL contact between course participants.

There is, however, a tendency to set a higher standard for the establishment of personal identity on net-based courses (such as courses in SL) than there are for conventional campus courses (often because so much of what campus courses involve is taken for granted, whilst net-based courses are subjected to detailed examination, simply because they are so new). Imagine, though, that I am a Russian with a brother who is a mathematical genius with time on his hands. If we wanted a qualification in mathematics from a Swedish university, it would not be too difficult to send him to Sweden in my place with a piece of my ID (which he would need during the time it took him to get a Student Union card in my name). You could argue that it is difficult to imagine who would go to such lengths, just for a qualification from Sweden ... but the same argument applies to net-based courses. In reality, the greater obstacles to success which are found on SL-based courses (there are technical issues, for example, but also issues connected with the self-discipline required to study via a medium like

SL) probably make it less likely that a potential fraudster would choose an SL-based course, since the possibilities of discovery are that much greater.

3.3 Assessment of Performance

If we assume that courses which use SL as a place of study are going to be performance-rich, rather than information-rich, then a whole set of assessment and examination procedures which examine performance, rather than the reproduction and manipulation of information are going to be required. This does not, of course, rule out the student's information-rich reflections on her performance, but it probably requires these to be a minor, rather than a dominant part of the assessment procedures. Few, or no, essay-type or single-word-answer responses are required, in other words.

For a communicative language teacher, the assessment of performance is something they rather familiar with from the conventional classroom, and transferring the assessment techniques from that environment into SL is not too complicated. Even within other disciplines, the SL learning environment lends itself to courses involving presentation, group work and group discussion, even if the focus is not specifically the students' language. The environment contains tools for displaying information (on PowerPoint slides, for example) and playing back both sound files and videos, so the basic toolbox of presentation techniques is available for students, teachers and examiners. Situations involving real-time discussion and negotiation are also readily available, now that the audio chat facility has been improved.

There are currently two aspects of communication which can cause problems: firstly, the presence of a large number of avatars all talking at once can be difficult to cope with (especially if you're a newbie); and secondly, your avatar has an extremely limited range of body language and facial expression. The first problem can be alleviated by simply moving people who're talking to each other away from other groups (there's plenty of room on the average island, for example, to send people far enough away so that they do not distract each other). The second problem is more difficult to cope with, but people tend to become used to the 'deadpan' nature of other avatars quite quickly and fill in the missing body language and facial expressions from the sound of the other avatar's voice and the content of her message.

Given these constraints, there's still a great deal an examiner has at her disposal in SL. There are, firstly, plenty of varied environments within which performance can be assessed, some of which are collective and some of which are much more individualistic. On Kamimo Island, for example, we have 'lecture theatres', comfy armchairs set around a crackling fire, an open-air grill, and rooms 'up in the sky' and behind a waterfall, which are only accessible if you know they are there. Thus, a whole range of assessment situations are possible, from individual presentations to guided group discussions and negotiations.

Assessment situations like this have a high degree of validity; since students feel that their avatars are participating in something 'real' (such as a business negotiation, where the outcome is absolutely up to the avatars involved). The difficulty is to achieve a similarly high degree of reliability. The Royal Society of Arts in the UK once ran an examination of spoken English called the Communicative Competence Examination (RSA CoCom) which has inspired a great deal of Richardson's own practice in the examination of performance. One feature of the RSA CoCom exam is the separation of the role of 'facilitator' and 'examiner' in guided examination discussions. A generic problem in assessing someone's ability to speak English is the difficulty of creating situations where there can be spontaneous communication with other people under examination conditions (so that the student's ability to do more than deliver a prepared speech can be examined, a higher order cognitive skill). The RSA CoCom examination involved examining a number of students at the same time, and the facilitator would participate in the discussion if one of the examinees was, perhaps, failing to take the floor, or, alternatively, dominating the proceedings. The examiner, on the other hand, sat as an outside observer, but the final grade was set after a discussion between the facilitator and the examiner, since they would have slightly different perspectives on the performance of the examinees.

In an ideal world (which a university teacher is sometimes allowed to inhabit), there is enough money in the course budget for both an examiner and a facilitator on courses run in SL, but even when there is not, this separation of roles is a very important principle in SL-based examinations. One of the examinations on the Business Talking course is the role-play examination, where students have a problem to resolve, according to the specific details on the character card of the character they have to play. One situation is that of discussing whether traffic should be banned from the centre of town, where the characters involved represent different interest groups in the local community. Each character has a set of points upon which she is prepared to compromise, and another which she is not (rather as would happen IRL). To increase the reliability of such an examination, the examiner needs to have a set of criteria for which to allocate marks. These criteria need also to be explained to the students in advance and they need to have practiced fulfilling them. The criteria also need to fit with accepted practice amongst language teachers and examiners, so that, for example, a re-sit examination could be conducted by another examiner.

During the actual role-play, if the teacher has a facilitator available, she can join in the discussion as, for example, a neutral council officer with technical expertise. Given the fact, though, that a role play exam like this will have a maximum of six different roles, an experienced teacher/examiner should be able to switch between the roles of facilitator and examiner fairly easily.

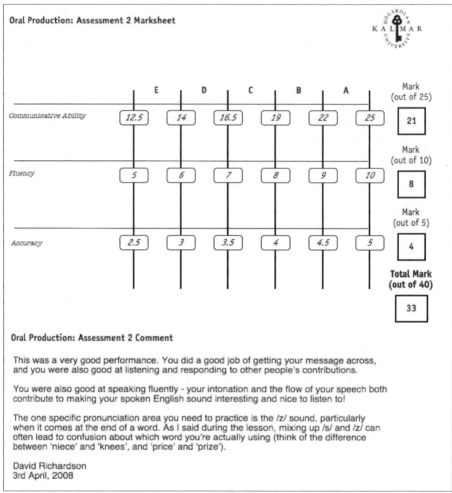

Oral Production: Assessment 2 Marksheet

	E	D	C	B	A	Mark (out of 25)
Communicative Ability	12.5	14	16.5	19	22	25	21

							Mark (out of 10)
Fluency	5	6	7	8	9	10	8

							Mark (out of 5)
Accuracy	2.5	3	3.5	4	4.5	5	4

Total Mark (out of 40)

33

Oral Production: Assessment 2 Comment

This was a very good performance. You did a good job of getting your message across, and you were also good at listening and responding to other people's contributions.

You were also good at speaking fluently - your intonation and the flow of your speech both contribute to making your spoken English sound interesting and nice to listen to!

The one specific pronunciation area you need to practice is the /z/ sound, particularly when it comes at the end of a word. As I said during the lesson, mixing up /s/ and /z/ can often lead to confusion about which word you're actually using (think of the difference between 'niece' and 'knees', and 'price' and 'prize').

David Richardson
3rd April, 2008

Figure 2. Shows the mark sheet the SL-based teacher/examiner uses during the role-play exam.

The categories of 'Communicative Ability', 'Fluency' and 'Accuracy' are all well-established in the language teaching world, and we can specify in a high degree of detail what you have to do to pass and what you have to do to fail. Fluency, for example, involves being able to keep the 'flow' of the foreign language going, with a minimum amount of time spent searching for words, and communicative ability involves the ability to transmit and receive messages with a high degree of success. Thus, a student who persistently fails to even understand what another participant in the discussion means (as opposed to not 'buying their argument') will score low marks for communicative ability. As can be seen from the relative weighting of the marks awarded for each category, grammatical accuracy is less important when communicating in speech, but it is not totally unimportant.

The vertical subdivisions act rather like the measurements on a long-jump sandpit. When the teacher is judging the actual performance of each student, she needs to decide where they have 'landed', which, in turn specifies the grade that they have achieved. Fail grades, by the way, need less specification, since there are fewer of them in the grading system we use. The teacher is faced with a series of decisions to make firstly about whether or not a particular student performance was acceptable or not, and subsequently about the degree of acceptability. These judgments have perforce an element of subjectivity in them, but they are not entirely subjective. Thus the balance between reliability and validity is struck in this particular case.

For the teacher on an SL-based course, this method of the assessment of performance has two other important features: the examination can be administered easily, and the results and feedback can be conveyed quickly to the student to inform her later performance on subsequent examinations. SL-based examinations sessions are hectic and it is easy to miss something, so during the examination notes can be made with a pen on a paper version of the mark sheet. After the examination, though, an electronic version can be made which can be immediately mailed to the student as a .pdf document. Moreover, since this is a database layout, the marks entered in the various fields go to make up the main course database subsequently used to report marks to the administrators and students. This also takes care of the elementary mathematics involved in the addition of the marks, so that the teacher under stress does not find herself having to amend mark sheets afterwards.

Oral Production, 3 hp: Course Result			Kurs kod: EN1055			K A L M A R
		Assessments				
	1	2	3	Total	ECTS	Course Grade
	14	33	35	82	B	VG

Figure 3. An anonymous example of mark sheet from April 2008

3.4 Examining the Performance of Individuals

Sometimes, however, individual performance needs to be examined. Once again, we are making the assumption that 'object of study' courses may conduct their examinations IRL (thus falling outside the scope of this chapter). If, however, they conduct their examinations in world, then they will be subject to the same constraints as 'place of study' courses. The procedure for the conduct of the individual assessment is largely the same as for the previous example from the point of view of the examiner. However, from the examinee's point of view, budgetary and time constraints come into play which could make it better to introduce group elements even into individual assessments (so that, say, six groups of four students can be examined, rather than 24 separate individuals). Creating a group activity also has the effect of creating a situation where communication between presenters and audience feels much more natural (since presentations usually have audiences).

The specific form taken on the Business Talking course was to give each group the task of preparing a joint presentation around a common theme, made up of n individual presentations (where n=the number of students in the group). What the group had to do, however, was to produce transitions between the individual presentations so that one presentation flowed in naturally to the next one. One group used 'tessellation' as its common theme, with a mathematician presenting the mathematical theory of tessellation, a graphic artist showing how tessellation applies to patterns on cloth and the shapes of tiles, and finally a social worker showing how patterns of behaviour are often transmitted from generation to generation.

4 Assessment in the Affective Domain

Assessments in the affective domain have been less frequently applied to the evaluation of individuals in courses. They have been more commonly used to assess stakeholder acceptance of new technologies. We think that affective assessment should be a part of course design and redesign. The perceptions of students and their experiences with courses could be measured through affective outcomes. These are demonstrated, for example, by course participation, engagement in work, interest to continue participation in course activities, and through increased motivation. Often the factors that are measured are the learners: attitudes or interests towards a special topic, expressed motivations and self-perception of ability.

Affective assessment contributes to the modelling of a learning environment, because it also contributes to the meaningful measurement and assessment of the cognitive outcomes. Affective assessment does this because it allows course designers to explain differences in the users (to explain learners from different backgrounds) and it allows us to track for whom a designed environment is most effective. In so doing we are able to replicate a good learning environment in other settings. For example, affective assessment can contribute in a longitudinal study to understand not only the initial acceptance of a particular "classroom setting", but to examine the acceptance after a period of use. Data may be obtained through surveys, interviews or reflective discussion on factors of interest and engagement and self perceptions. More specifically, the students that first enter Second Life may find one type of classroom to be comfortable and easy to use on initial experience. However, they may crave a more interactive and changing virtual classroom after they gain experience.

4.1 Affective Assessment Factors

Affective assessment can be done through the measurement of several factors. Here we present some definitions of factors that have been applied by others. We suggest that an affective assessment to improve course design should include some of these measures.
- **Attitudes:** The premise is that a positive attitude or high level of interest towards a factor (such as a virtual classroom) leads to higher individual investment, continued and persistent use over time and to enhanced performance (Wigfield, Eccles & Rodriguez 1998). Longitudinal studies that reveal attitudes over time will identify the "wow factor" within a particular application. That is sometimes participants are initially over enthusiastic, and such studies will help to identify the weaknesses in approaches. Another use of attitude assessment to see how well pedagogical goals meet the students' understanding of these goals.

- **Motivation**: The definition of motivation can be derived from several cognitive theories that focus on individual attributes for performance and expectations for success (Weiner 1994; Brophy 1999). These find that high levels of motivation lead to higher levels of performance on a particular task for an individual's range of ability. Others have found that task performance goals are seen as external forces while mastery goals of individuals are seen as internally impacted. The mastery goals depend on the internal focus and high motivation is associated with higher commitment and focus. Thus motivation can explain mastery goals (Ames 1992).
- **Self-perception of ability**: This measure can make use of several definitions. Self-perception is based on individual perceptions of self-concept, self-esteem and self-efficacy.
   - o **Self-concept** is a rating by the individual that is usually externally based. The rating is based on past academic achievement or performance and can have an impact on future achievement or performance (Marsh 1990). Schunk (1990) describes a bi-directional relationship between performance and self-concept. He states that achievement can contribute to a better self-concept or self-worth, and that this in terms leads to further achievement. This is a positive spiral, but negative spirals are also possible. In recognition of this factor, it may be important in Second Life to show students how their former achievements can be used positively in a new learning environment.
   - o **Self-esteem** is an internally based factor. It is how an individual feels about one's ability in a particular area. Studies that measure self-esteem often look at low levels of such and can have impact on issues such as performance, depression, social ability, and locus of control (Harter 1983). We think, it is difficult to relate this factor to learning or achievement and instead recommend the measure of self-efficacy.
   - o **Self-efficacy** is the rating of an individual's confidence or comfort level with a particular activity (Ertmer et al 1994). This factor can be used to measure technology readiness because it is the individuals self perception that all the necessary skills are in place to perform the larger pedagogical task.

We provide an example of an affective assessment that was given in the welcome area of Kamimo Island in the fall of 2007. The survey still stands there and the collected data may be used within time intervals that are significant to a particular teaching activity. We evaluated the data collected over a six week period in the fall of 2007 to determine the comfort level of students and teachers who were participating in the course "Social English for Doctoral Students". The results of this study are reported on in (Molka-Danielsen et al 2007).

Table 1. Affective assessment of self-efficacy. (Molka-Danielsen et al 2007)

Survey Goal: This is a self evaluation of self-efficacy to measure user acceptance and usability of Second Life (SL) as a virtual world for learning.
1. Please provide your avatar name and real-life address, age and gender.
  • Name of your avatar
  • Address, City, Country; Age; Gender (female or male)

2. In the Essay box: please state your roll(s) on the Kamimo sim. For example: Teacher, Student, Observer, etc. And if you are a student, state your educational program. (For

example: Doctoral student in Logistics.)

3. Is English your First language? (Please state: Yes/No)

If not, how many years of formal education have you in English? (Please state: number of years.) Do you use English in work? (Please state: Often/Sometimes/AlmostNever/Never.)

4. When did you begin using Second Life (give a Date) and approximate how many hours you have been in Second Life since you started (give number of hours).

5. How often do you go in-world in Second Life?
- Everyday
- Visits on several days in a week
- 1 visit/week
- 1 visit/month
- Almost never
- Never

6. How much time do you spend in SL (include in this average only the days you enter)? (Choose one)
- <1 hour/day
- 1 to 4 hours/day
- 5 to 8 hours/day
- 8 to 12 hours/day
- >12 hours/day

7. Self-efficacy skills in Second Life: Use the following 5-point scale below to describe your skills in using Second Life. (Select the rating that most applies to you by selecting the bullet for each activity.)

(1) "I do not know if I have done this," (2) "I have never done this," (3) "I can do this with some help," (4) "I can do this by myself," (5) "I can show someone how to do this." (Select the rating that most applies to you and put the rating in front of each bullet.)
Activities in Second Life (SL):
- Find and access the Second Life Login page
- Create an avatar
- Walk your avatar
- Fly your avatar
- Chat using text messages with your avatar
- Chat using voice with your avatar
- Private voice call with your avatar and one other avatar
- Find a vehicle and test drive it.
- Use Instant Messaging (IM)
- Save text-chats or IM that take place
- Change my avatar's hair
- Change my avatar's clothes
- Change my avatar's race or gender
- Join a Group
- Find virtual Rome
- Teleport to virtual Venice
- Take a photo of your avatar

- Find a library in Second Life; take a snapshot of yourself reading a book.
- Take a snapshot of yourself doing at least 3 different dance moves
- Get a snapshot of a non-human avatar.
- Purchase something
- Use a public white board or bulletin board to leave a message
- Build a chair

8. How do you like Second Life for learning so far?

The purpose of the affective assessment in Table 1 was to understand the comfort level of the students with the learning environment and to recognize the differences between the individual learners. This particular survey did not assess affective outcomes for a particular the pedagogic area. It was directed towards improving a learning space that was designed to be used with a variety of courses to be taught on Kamimo Island. This means that further questions would have been needed to link a general self-perception of learning in SL to a particular instance of learning within a pedagogical area for a given course. That is we could have asked how students liked assignments given in Second Life for learning English. We could have asked about attitudes on improved language performance. For example: Please rate on a scale of 1 to 5 with strongly agree(1).. to strongly disagree(5): "I like asking questions in class." Numerous other questions could be asked to relate to factors of attitudes and interests: I find it easy to pay attention in the SL meetings; I feel like the teacher is speaking directly to me in SL; I learned more from speaking English in SL than in the regular class; and so forth. Lessons learned from these assessments could identify weak points of particular meeting places or of a particular course design. Surveys directed towards single courses would go further in improving specific course design.

5 Summary

We started this chapter by setting out the problems of conducting assessments in SL: establishing the identity of the examinee; producing an assessment process with a high degree of both validity and reliability; preparing transparent and open assessment procedures; and conforming to the administrative and legal requirements of the organisation within which you are working. The pedagogical value of the assessment is contained within the discussion of the validity of the assessment - if the course has been put together pedagogically, and if the assessments have a high degree of validity, then they will also have pedagogical value (as the examination process should also be a pedagogical experience too!).

We have used examples from one of the course that we involved in ourselves to show how identities can be checked in SL, with a reasonably high degree of accuracy, by separating the introduction to the learning environment on SL from the start of the 'formal' teaching on the course. The highly-interactive nature of the SL environment is also an asset in the assessment procedure, provided that the assessments are shaped to the features of the environment. Finally, it is important to use multiple forms of assessment to achieve validation. We have pointed out the advantages of performing assessment in both the cognitive and affective domains. In summary, it is important to create assessment procedures which both generate the information about student performance the examiner needs, and allow for ease of operation, both during and after the examination itself. Setting up definable criteria by which performance can be judged is no revolutionary idea, but can relatively easily be applied in SL to produce assessments with high degrees of both validity and reliability.

How an individual teacher in another subject area applies these principles to her own courses is going to vary greatly depending on the circumstances within which she is working and the specific skill sets and experience she brings to the course. However, we feel that it is possible to produce both cognitive and affective assessment procedures of high quality even when the entire course is being conducted in SL.

In the future, however, this process may be made even easier. The SLoodle interface to Moodle (a open source learning management system), as mentioned in Chapter 1 has potential to assist course facilitators to perform examinations and assessment from within SL. It may well be that LMS assessment capabilities become available in SL. At present, however, SLoodle is insufficiently developed to make it a practical tool. Similarly, means of electronic identification are likely to be developed to allow 'place of study' courses the same degree of the security of establishing identification as 'object of study' courses (which use the IRL procedures the university is, presumably, satisfied with). The main force acting on the development of assessment procedures, however, is going to be the creativity and experience of teachers and examiners working in SL.

References

Ames, C. (1992). Classrooms: Goals, structures, and student motivation Journal of Educational Psychology, 84, 261-271.

Bloom, B.S. (1956). The Taxonomy of Educational Objectives: Classification of Educational Goals Handbook 1: The Cognitive Domain. New York: McKay Press.

Brophy, J. (1999). Toward a model of the value aspects of motivation in education: Developing appreciation for particular leanring domains and activities. *Educational Psychologist*, 34, 75-86.

Ertmer, P.A., Evenbeck, E., Cennamo, K.S. & Lehman, J.D. (1994). Enhancing self-efficacy for computer technologies through the use of positive classroom expereinces. Educational Technology Research and Development, 42(3), 45-62.

Harter, S. (1983). Developmental perspectives on the self-system. In P.H. Mussen (Gen. Ed.), E.M. Hetherington (Vol.Ed.), Handbook of child psychology, (Vol. 4; pp. 275-385). New York: Wiley.

Marsh, H.W. (1990). A multidimensional, hierarchical model of self-concept: Theoretical and empirical justification. *Educational Psychology Review*, 2(2), 77-172.

Molka-Danielsen, J., Richardson, D., Deutschmann, M. & Carter, B. (2007). Teaching Languages in a Virtual World. In Habib, L. (Ed.), NOKOBIT 2007, pp. 97-110, ISBN: 9788251-922616: Trondheim: Tapir.

Schunk, D.H. (1990). Self-concept and school acheivement. In C. Rogers & P. Kuntnick (Eds.), The social psychology of the primary school (pp. 70-91). London: Routledge.

Weiner, B. (1994). Integrating social and personal theories of achievement striving. *Review of Educational Research*, 64, 557-574.

Wigfield, A. Eccles, J.S. & Rodriguez, D. (1998). The development of chldren's motivation in school contexts. *Review of Research in Education*, 23, 73-118.

Chapter 4: Sim Creation and Management for Learning Environments

Judith Molka-Danielsen, Ph.D.
Molde University College
Britvn. 2, 6402 Molde, Norway
j.molka-danielsen@himolde.no

Linn-Cecilie Linneman
Design Container AS
Maridalsveien 87, Bygg. 5 – 0461 Oslo, Norway
linn-cecilie@designcontainer.no

Chapter Overview: This chapter gives advice on many practical issues that will be encountered by those wishing to use Second Life for educational purposes. Some of those issues are: choices in creation and design of a learning space, parcel management, group management and preparing residents to use the space for learning activities.

1 Virtual Land

Many institutions will find it necessary to privately own or manage a virtual space as a platform for their educational activities. The virtual space can be referred to as "virtual land", "parcel", "island" or "sim". Virtual land is a visual representation, something that looks like land in Second Life. A parcel can be one part of larger piece of virtual land, like houses in the real world are usually located on privately owned parcels. The word "sim" is short for "simulation". A sim is equal to one island, and appears as one square on the map that is called the Second Life grid. A parcel can be a smaller part of a sim. One sim can be divided into one or several parcels. All sizes of virtual land are actually server services (processor capacity) that are purchased from the company Linden Lab. An "island" more specifically visually appears as a virtual land area of size ~65,500 m^2.

Real world education institutions that verify their non-profit status with Linden Lab will receive at present a 50% discount on land purchase and annual "land use" fees. If a land area is a new order (not previously owned), it will have a start appearance of one of several standard shapes (new island shape) and the owners will need to modify the terrain of the land, to their personal needs. The terraforming and building on the virtual islands can be done by the owner, or it can be outsourced to those that specialize in SL design and building. To introduce tools for the support of educational activities is part of the task of design and building of the sim. For example, a 3D display screen for the presentation of slides or video can be placed on an island. People can watch the screen while their avatar is sitting on a chair that is located on the virtual island. Other tools may not be permanently manifested on the sim, but held in the inventory of one or several avatars and accessed through a "heads up display" (HUD). This chapter will not tell the reader how to terraform sims or script the tools or structures on the islands, but it will outline the choices that must be addressed in order to do this, to create a working virtual space for education.

Sim creation is followed by the need to manage the newly formed virtual learning environment (VLE). Management means allowing the right users to share the developed resources, to provide security and privacy where it is needed, and to allow openness where desired. It may also be desirable to allow others besides the island owner or maintenance team to add content to the sim in terms of information content or objects (that are made up of primitive processing elements called "prims"). The "rights" needed to create, and do other actions on the sim are administered through the creation of SL Groups and the SL rights system. We will discuss how to set up and manage SL Groups.

Finally, after establishment of a working platform of services, groups and rights, the users will need to be educated about how to access and use the VLE. That is both teachers and students must go through a learning process of how to get into SL, how to create an avatar, how to use voice chat, how to join groups and so forth. Sometimes help documents can be prepared to answer some of the anticipated new resident questions. But, there are also suggested approaches to preparing your learners and teachers before the first meeting of the course.

2 Sim Creation and Parcel Management

Several motivations were given in Chapter 1 as to why academic institutions enter Second Life. However, for the individual learner, either as teacher or student, to truly get started in SL it is important to have a virtual home, a place of one's own to learn and experiment. This place could be in many forms and sizes, depending on need. First the goal or vision of what is to be achieved in SL must be recognized. Figure 1 shows the welcome area of Kamimo Island. It has been our place to learn and experiment.

Some try out SL for social reasons, for example to establish a place for your group to meet other persons in the same academic or professional field. Others may just want to learn to build things, create objects or information content. In preparation of the design of a virtual space one should define or identify:

- Project goals
- Stakeholder groups and their needs
- Form of deliverables (i.e. shared classroom)
- Scope of deliverables (how many will use a space)
- Direction of deliverables (is the activity or development in SL for internal private groups or external organizational communication purposes)

Figure 1. Kamimo Island is a virtual campus, a place to learn and experiment.

Project goals are usually described as academic learning objectives. In identification of stakeholders and their needs, one should ask if the designed space is to be used for administration, education or marketing purposes. The form of deliverables can be quite varied: abstractly it may be providing a virtual space for "sharing a discussion" or more concretely, sharing a "3D object" that is used in a discussion – i.e. a virtual leaning Tower of Pisa. The scope of the activity must consider how many will be served and how long will the project last. Before all development, it will be necessary to construct a budget to estimate the amount of time and funding needed to achieve the initial ambitions of the project. Consideration of costs lead to the initial question: should one rent or buy virtual land in Second Life?

2.1 Rent or Buy?

To rent a land has some advantages and many disadvantages. It is great for a small project with a rather short timeline. It is a low cost and in this sense is a good way to get started. The disadvantages is that as in the real world there are many unserious estate managers, and you could easily be fooled if you don't know who you are talking too and how much you should expect to pay. The best advice if you want to rent, is to spend time talking to people and companies "in world" (in SL) that already rent land. Also get prices from various estate agents and read the contract thoroughly. Some sims have a set of rules that you have to obey. For example are some sims only for residential use and the owners do not wish to rent out to commercial use and vice versa.

Another aspect that you have to think through is your neighbourhood. This goes for both renting and buying. If you are renting a space on a sim that is not fully developed, make sure you research the kind of neighbours you could expect. If you want to use your place for corporate meetings, education, seminars and so on, you probably do not want a strip club as closest neighbour.

Equally if you buy one sim, make sure you get a location that will allow you to expand. At present, the owner of a sim (island) can request to purchase an adjacent vacant plot (quadrant) from Linden Lab. However, permissions must also be given from all other adjacent sim owners to be able to develop on that quadrant. For this and other reasons it is necessary to visit and know who are the owners of the neighbouring sims.

There is a big difference in performance on the sims as well. Some of the sims are placed on older servers, which will slow down performances. Check out this as well before purchasing a sim. You can always get it relocated later, but this is an extra cost and also extra work for you.

Buying a sim has many advantages. You are free to decide the use of the whole sim. You get listed in the search engine on the map, so people will find you easier, and you have enough prims to make the sim look as you imagine. Most rented places have a very limited amount of prims. Also you do not risk getting thrown out, getting neighbours that do not fit in with your ambitions and so on. As sim prices have dropped the last year, the initial cost is no longer so much higher than that of renting. So if you intend your SL presence to last for a while, and do not have a strict time frame on your project, it would be recommendable to buy a sim. This is done for general purpose purchases by going to the Land Auction for existing land or to the Land Portal for purchasing new private regions. (http://secondlife.com/land/index.php) From the date of order it normally takes from two-four weeks until your land is delivered.

Educational sims are half price that of regular sims. To achieve educational status, you need to be able to prove that your company or institutions are in fact an educational institution. Private persons cannot buy this type of land. Documentation is done by faxing documents to Linden Lab directly. The educational sims are not sold or purchased through the regular land portal. Educational sims cannot be used for commercial purposes.

2.2 Initial Design

In this section we present several practical usage issues such as:
- How do you wish your sim to look such as should it be a replication or a representation, or should it be something completely new?
- How many participants will be meeting at once? Is a large classroom needed or just meeting rooms?
- Do you need a public place to build such as a public sandbox?

First, you need to decide which style you want and which functions you need. We normally do not recommend making an exact replica of a real life place. This can unnecessarily limit navigation in-world as avatars do not normally move the same way as people walk in real life. Secondly, absolute replication is a hard task. Replication of every detail can be costly in prim usage, and each person will perceive different imperfections from the original. We feel it is harder to achieve satisfaction of stakeholders by using a "replication" approach than by creating something that is completely new. Sometimes the essence of a real place can be reproduced, with some familiar queues, artefacts or visual landmarks. It is safer to declare the historical site as a historical representation, rather than a replication. But, the most fun and challenging approach is to use your imagination, to try to think outside the box, and to try design spaces that would never be possible in the real world.

For both development and later use purposes, it is helpful to have a theme or style that binds it all together. People like to begin from something they know, so if there is something to metaphorically tie or associate known to the unknown, it will contribute later to the affective use of the space. That is people will intuitively be able to function in the space. But don't be afraid to experiment. When this is said, it could be a good idea to have some recognizable effects or smaller areas. This really depending on the use and the users you are expecting. Make sure all the builds and buildings have large rooms and are easy for new users to move around in. Make the landscape exciting by putting in surprises or secret areas for the users to explore. As with web-design, it could be a good idea to hire SL designers or developers for this task. You can use the SL in-world directory by using the Search tab in the client to find SL developers in your country or area. Figure 2 is an example of a surprising place that can be discovered on Kamimo Island. It is not visually apparent when first landing on the island that a cave exists behind the waterfall. So, visitors can feel a sense of excitement or accomplishment when discovering it.

There are also many practical issues with design. You want to make the design work for your planned activities. Just like a real architect would think through the use before building, a SL developer will do the same. One example is for meetings. How many will meet at once, and what will they do during the meetings? If you expect a very large crowd, you need to devote the most of the sim to this. Most sims take around 70 avatars before it slows performances down. If you need to be able to cater for even bigger crowds, you should consider to buy two or more sims and link them together, so you can create your meeting area in the cross-section of these sims drawing server power from all. If you only are meeting with a few people at the time, it could be more suitable with a more imaginative environment. The environment is very important in SL. People relax more and have more fun if the environment is suited for the purpose. It may sound ludicrous to make sure you have enough seats, but most people like to sit down during a meeting so they do not have to worry about the avatars movements. It also seems more comfortable for all parties. Also social norms will show that some people will not want to sit their avatars on the ground, even though they can!

Figure 2. There is a secret cave behind the waterfall on Kamimo Island.

Figure 3. A class meeting held around a campfire.

When using SL for teaching it is an advantage to have special custom solutions. Make sure you have at least one traditional classroom with access to a multimedia screen where you can show Quick Time movies, pictures and text. This will help you during your classes. When using Quick Time movies, each student needs to have this installed on their individual PCs. So if not all students are able to see the film this might be why. Sometimes, the traditional classroom is not the right setting. Other types of rooms may be used for smaller group discussions. Alternatively, no room at all may be chosen, but an object as a focal point can be used. Some class meetings on Kamimo Island were held around a campfire as seen in the Figure 3.

It is also recommended to use voice. This allows you to communicate more directly with your students. Even if your students do not have voice installed, they will be able to hear you if they have speakers. Ground rules for using voice in a class with many people will be the same as on a telephone or video conference. Make sure to mute your microphone when you are not speaking.

There are some e-learning tools that are incorporated in SL already, such as SLoodle that has some features of learning management systems. In-world survey tools exist to get feedback from students. Alternatively pointers can be made from objects in SL to link with external webpages and resources.

2.3 Tools to Support Learning and Teaching

Since the summer of 2007 voice was enabled in Second Life. However, there are still a large number of residents that either do not want to use voice or they do not have an integrated headset. When holding a group learning experience in SL, it is necessary to decide beforehand if voice is going to be used. Usually it is desired. If SL is being accessed from a university network, it is advisable to try out voice before the start of the scheduled meeting. It may be necessary for additional ports to be opened on university firewalls. These port numbers can be located on the SL website. Secondly, anticipated users should be told to have an integrated headset, and to run through the Voice Chat Setup under the SL client, that is found under Edit and Preferences. Some teachers may have tried out voice, and instructed students how to use voice, but when the course meeting begins it still may not work for someone. There can be several reasons, but often the problems originate from an individual's computer or access line or equipment. It is therefore a good idea to have a procedure about what to do when "one" participant (or several) cannot use voice. Here it is recommended to use private IM to help those in trouble, or if you have an assistant to have this person work with the individuals to find out the problem, while the group work continues. Also, it is possible to save with permission all written text, private and public, so that this may be sent to participants later. This is done by choosing under the client window Edit and then tabs for Preferences and Communication, and to finally check the boxes Log Chat and Log Instant Messages. If it is the first time a class is meeting, it is also recommended to hand out a Note card with instructions to the attendees. Give example about how to turn on voice, how to sit down on a chair, and how to watch films, who to contact using instant messaging (IM) if trouble and so on. The "How to" guide for new residents at (http://www.ict4lt.org/en/Euro08PCWSL.doc) is actively maintained by Graham Davies of EuroCALL.

Figure 4. The Norwegian radio station NRK P1 can play in the welcome area on Kamimo Island by adding the url for streaming audio under the Media tab.

Figure 5. Demonstration of a video clip on a display in a Kamimo Island classroom.

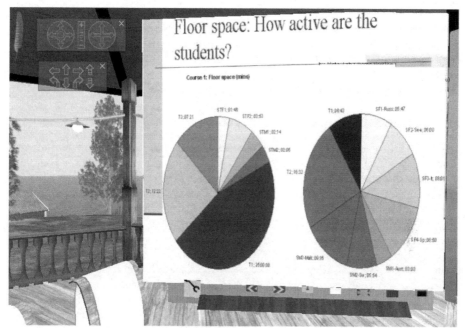

Figure 6. Example of an image on the Meta Lab Whiteboard.

Besides simply speaking with others in SL, there are a multitude of presentation tools for experiencing text and multimedia. At the top centre of the SL client window there is the name and location of the present land that the avatar stands on. If this is clicked on, it opens a window that explains various settings called "About Land". One of these settings is called Media. The owner of the land, and perhaps several others with rights to change media of particular parcels, will be able to change the media that is video or audio that can be viewed on a display on the parcel or heard through a residents headset when the streaming audio is turned on by the user. Figure 4 shows this media setting panel.

Figure 5, demonstrates how video can be shown in one of the classrooms. Of course the exact content can be selected to meet your needs. The format is type .mov and the actual screen can been zoomed in to fill your entire computer display. Audio accompanies the visual display.

There are also tools for displaying and sharing static images in SL. If you want to show PowerPoint slides, you will have to convert each slide into a jpeg and upload them all to your inventory beforehand. Then just drag and drop them to a display screen. The Meta Lab Interactive Whiteboard is an example of a display tool. It allows avatars to display slides and to write on the board. In this way a presentation can be prepared and presented as it would be done in a real classroom. Figure 6 is an example of an image that was dropped onto the classroom whiteboard on Kamimo. Just search for "media display" in the SL Search to discover where to obtain display tools.

3 Groups, Parcels and Rights Management

This section addresses: who will use the sim; what rights they need (teachers, students, researchers, guests, others); how to set up parcels for different uses, how to protect copyrighted materials, how to keep outsiders from interfering with the planned session, how to allow outsiders for spontaneous input (placement in the SL search engine); what prims are and how to reclaim them; how to find hidden objects; and getting help from the Lindens.

3.1 Managing Participation

When having meetings in SL, be aware that you can get uninvited guests. You can easily manage access from your management module. So for larger events, make sure you know how this works, so you can easily get rid of uninvited people or so called "griefers". A griefer is a person that wants to destroy or disturb your sim and/or event. This is a problem that easily can be handled, just make sure you know how before hosting the events.

Access to Land
To control access to land again go to "About Land" and see under "Access" as shown in Figure 7. If you tick off "Allow public access" anyone can visit your land. To restrict this to one group or certain avatars, simply uncheck the box and add the names of the allowed avatars under "Allowed Residents". If you want to allow anyone to visit except a few avatars, keep the box "Allow public access" ticked and add the names of the unwanted guests under "Banned Residents". You can also ban an avatar by right clicking on them and choose "Ban".

Access to Objects
In the same box there is a fan named "Objects". Here you can see who owns objects placed on your land. If someone has placed unwanted objects on your land, go to this window. Click "Refresh List" and a list with names of all avatars with objects on your land will appear. Mark the name of the person whose items you want to return and press "Return Objects". This cannot be undone, so make sure you choose to return the right objects and not those objects you want to keep on your land.

Rights to Create Objects
Under the fan "Options" you can control who is allowed to build and leave items on your land. In most cases it is recommended to unclick "Create objects" "All Residents" and choose "Group". If you allow all residents to build on your land, you will be an easy target for griefers. The same goes for Edit Terrain and Object entry.

Figure 7. The "About Land" control panel can be found by clicking on a virtual land's name in the top centre of the client window. Here the land's name is "Guru Meditation".

Figure 8. Selecting parcels in necessary before subdividing or joining land.

Access can be controlled individually on different parcels. If you want to have a public sandbox, you want everyone to be allowed to build there, but nowhere else on your land. This is managed by dividing your land into several parcels. By creating a parcel, it allows for a section of land to be managed separately from other sections. You can then use a parcel for special projects with specified users. You right click on your land, choose "Edit Terrain" and draw up the area that you want to divide. An example is shown in Figure 8. You will see yellow borders when choosing this option. You then get the options "Subdivide" or "Join". If you choose Subdivide this parcel will be an individual parcel that you can have a different access level on, different media settings and different parcel name. It can also be rented out or sold.

On communication, if you do not have restricted access in theory anyone could listen in to the conversations on open voice or text chat. Do not discuss sensitive topics in public. Also do not discuss topics you would not be comfortable using regular e-mail or other online conference tools on. Private voice and text chat may be used in 1-to-1 conversations only. All text dialogue can also be saved on any client computer. This is done as stated earlier by going into a client's "Preferences" under "Communication" and checking the boxes for "Log Instant Messages" and "Log Chat".

Besides restricting access it is important that you also restrict building rights. This cannot be stressed enough, and worst case scenario if this is not managed correctly is that your builds and area could be destroyed. It would again make you an easy target for griefers.

Figure 9. The public sandbox is a popular free building parcel on Kamimo Island.

One of the reasons it is so important to manage who can build or create things is that each virtual land has a limit on the number of primitive building blocks or "prims" that are used to represent anything that can be seen. The standard island or sim of size 65,536 m² can support 15,000 prims and when these are used up, no more objects can be rezzed or made visible. Still, many institutions will want to allow guests to build or create things. There are several ways you can do this in a safe environment. If it is only a limited regular crowd that you want to allow building rights, you can manage this through a group. More will be told about groups in the next section. If the crowd will vary and you want people to be able to experiment even when you are not there, it would be a better solution to create a public sandbox as shown in Figure 9. This is an area (parcel) designated with open build rights and auto-return on that returns objects to the owners inventory after a fixed period of time. Make sure you inform with a sign or similar that left objects will be returned. The number of minutes before items are returned is established by filling in the box "numbers of minutes before other residents' objects are returned" that is located under Land Use and under the tab for Objects.

3.2 How to Manage and Use Groups for Communication

A sim can be subdivided into parcels, with different parcels having different user rights. The best way to manage who is allowed to do certain activities on a parcel is to set up a Group and to assign the ownership of the parcel to the group. At present it costs 200 $L to start a group. A group can have one founder but multiple owners. Owners have full rights over the administration of the group. The group is further divided into roles where avatar names are assigned to roles, and rights are assigned to roles. For example, the role of "builder" may be created. Rights assigned to the role "builder" are designated by the group owner. Examples of rights are the ability to create, enter or move objects that are owned by the group. In addition to objects, parcels can be assigned to group control. If parcel-X is assigned to group-Y, and a member of group-Y has a "builder" role as discussed, that avatar can build on parcel-X. Sometimes, people wonder why they cannot build where they have assumed their avatar have been given the rights to build.

A common problem is that the avatar must wear the Group Name over their avatar or activate the group. To change the group name that is worn, right click on the avatar, select Groups from the menu and then select the group that has rights on a particular parcel. Select "Activate" and "Apply" to activate the selected group. In summary, by using groups, one or several avatars will be able to manage a parcel, allowing them such rights as: rezzing objects on the land, adding avatars to the group, sharing messages with the group. The control panel for groups is displayed in Figure 10.

While the philosophy seems relatively simple, there can be challenges to managing groups. For example, sometimes the rights to send messages to the group are given to too many avatars. If those in the group with the right to send messages become too many (in groups containing several hundred avatars), it could mean that all members of the group are interrupted very often by receiving IMs (instant messages) in their client windows. The manager of the group might consider not giving the right to send IMs to the role of "everyone".

Another issue is when the owner of the group wishes to change the purpose of the group or the rights of its members, because maybe the expected use of the parcel has changed. For example, if you are using a parcel for a building course, when the course is complete, a teacher may wish to revoke rights from students so the next group can use the parcel. In such a case it is advised to communicate the intended change to the group members so they do not feel like they have done something wrong.

Figure 10. After selecting a group a control panel reveals rights and roles.

3.3 Preparing Residents to Use SL in the Classroom

This section addresses the issues: where the users will access SL from – school labs, office, library, home; technology obstacles of access, for example; where help can be found; how to introduce SL to your faculty; and how to prepare students prior to the first course meeting.

Minimal System Requirements

Technology readiness is a split responsibility. On the one hand the educational institution should provide the equipment and network access if students are required to use Second Life for course work. For example, if it is an official meeting place for the course, such as a real world classroom, the institution should provide a means of access. It is a good idea to provide a lab where computers have been tested for their ability to access Second Life. It cannot be assumed that any computer will work or that the institutional firewalls are set correctly to allow the SL traffic to pass. The IT centre should be warned ahead of course start to visit the Second Life website for system requirements. Attention must be paid to:

- Processing power of the client computer
- Video card used on the client computer
- Available RAM on the client computer

- Firewall settings (several different ports for text and voice are used)
- Shared Internet connection – if the Internet connection is slow, and many students log onto the same Internet access point, it can create problems. Even for single user access broadband Internet access of 2Mbps or higher is recommended.

The minimal system requirements that are listed on the Linden Lab support page (http://secondlife.com/support/sysreqs.php) are systems that have been tested, and there is a wiki page that one can read a dialogue of experiences.

Sometimes students already own a private computer that is seemingly not powerful enough to enter SL and they may wish to know if there is any way they can use their present system. One suggestion is to open the SL client in full screen mode. This will dedicate more of the processor to the SL application. Another suggestion is to leave even laptop computers plugged-in the entire time while using SL. It is also possible to reduce graphical demands by going into the Preference and reducing the distance that objects are viewed, or reducing the detail on the objects that are viewed. Finally, for anyone purchasing a new computer for use in SL, it is a good idea to test access (in shop) even if the specifications are listed as acceptable.

Support from the Lindens
The Second Life support page contains a tab for "Knowledge Base" and this is a very good resource for finding answers to most user questions including answers to FAQ, and videos. The link at present is: (https://support.secondlife.com/ics/support/default.asp?deptID=4417).

Residents that own an entire island are considered Concierge Resident. To receive support they login on the Second Life main page with their avatar account. They can then receive support by telephone, by Live Chat, or by submitting a ticket. The Live Chat will usually generate a Support Ticket also. Even after your questions are resolved it is possible to look back on the transaction history. From experience, all closed-ticket support has been followed up with a survey from Linden Lab about the support service received.

Preparing Faculty for Second Life
The majority of your faculty may have never heard of Second Life, although this majority becomes smaller with the passage of time. At Molde University College, we have repeatedly presented how we use SL in education. We have presented our designs and implementations of courses at conferences, and internally within the college. In the fall of 2007 when our island had just been opened, we presented our project in-house. The reaction was that it was interesting, but that it was hard to just try it out for one lecture. Those that wanted to try it needed help to get started.

We recommend having the support of the IT media centre, to set up the equipment needed for a single lecture. The set up should be requested as would an arrangement of a "video conference" or the "presentation of a video" in lecture. As with a video conference, it might be necessary for the whole class to move to another room such as the computer lab for access. If it is only the faculty member that is going into SL they might display the client screen containing their avatar using a projector. It is best however, that the entire class be involved and entered into SL from their own terminals. This is by experience the most engaging approach.

Prior to the course meeting the faculty member has to create an avatar account. Anyone can do this by going to the Second Life main page (www.secondlife.com). Only the owner of the virtual land needs a premium account. All other accounts of users in SL can be free accounts. Each person needs to spend time in SL to understand the interface. It may be that on the first visit that several hours are needed on the Help Island. Every avatar that is created will first enter on one of several Help Islands. They will learn the basics of how to change appearance, how to move and use transport to different locations, how to communicate by text or voice, how to search for items, people or landmarks, and how to manage inventory. There is also usually a "free store" that offers many useful, fun and free objects. This offers training of how to open and receive objects into one's own inventory. (Additionally, basic help is discussed in Graham Davies "How to" that was mentioned earlier in this chapter.) Of course it will take time to master all of the SL skills. It is recommended that the new user of SL should use the Search engine, to discover and visit places in SL, to talk to other residents. It is usually an enjoyable and rich learning experience.

Preparing Students for Second Life
While students must go through the same learning curve as teachers in Second Life, they may not have the same preparation time that the teachers have for gaining knowledge about SL before the course starts. The teachers will be responsible for making the learning curve easy and fast, so they can begin with the main theme of the course. The teachers can help students by putting out information sheets on websites or course support systems about what must be done before the first course meeting. Suggested content for the information sheets are:

- Basic equipment needed by individuals to participate, such as an integrated headset. (As most universities do not pay for books in courses, they also often do not pay for headsets.)
- Requirement that students create their avatar before the first meeting, and that all avatar names are sent to the teacher.
- Teachers should create a group for their course in SL. (Linden dollars can be transferred from any one avatar to any of the teachers' avatars. So it is still only necessary for the landowner to have a premium account. Teachers can have free accounts. And, once the teachers are allocated Linden dollars for their courses, they can also transfer dollars to other accounts. L$ are needed for example to upload textures that may be used in the building of object. Of course there are many objects and textures that can be found for free in SL.)
- Post information on a course resource page outside of SL that describes minimum computer hardware requirements, and where public university computers with these requirements as well as the installed SL client software can be found.
- Post information about how to activate voice and describe how you would like the students to use voice or text messaging under class meetings.
- And most importantly, be available in Second Life to assist and help the students when they get started.

Part II
Learning Projects

Chapter 5: Serious Fun and Serious Learning: The Challenge of Second Life

Dr Clare Atkins
Nelson Marlborough Institute of Technology,
Nelson, New Zealand
clare.atkins@nmit.ac.nz

Mark Caukill
Nelson Marlborough Institute of Technology,
Nelson, New Zealand
mark.caukill@nmit.ac.nz

Chapter Overview: This chapter describes the learning that was gained by both a student and his supervisors during the conduct of a student project in Second Life in Semester 2 2008. In particular it highlights the potential for creating 'authentic tasks' for learning in an immersive environment but cautions against the use of SL as an environment for impromptu tutorial style learning. Attention is drawn to the importance of the SL core competencies as a guide to the requisite skills for learning and teaching and to the need for a methodical process and standards for the development of SL builds.

1 Introduction

Nelson Marlborough Institute of Technology (NMIT) is a tertiary education institute in New Zealand which offers a range of degree and sub-degree programmes. In December 2006, it joined the growing number of educational institutes exploring the potential of multi-user virtual environments (MUVEs) for enhancing adult student learning by renting a small plot of land on EduIsland in Second Life (SL). In March 2007 the first students, enrolled on a final year Bachelor of Information (BIT) course, were informally introduced to SL. Although not a requirement of the course, all the students participated in the Second Life activities and several became intrigued by the immersive environment that it provided.

Encouraged by the student response, staff interest and a belief that education in immersive multi-user virtual environments was likely to become a major delivery mechanism, NMIT decided to buy its own space or island in Second Life in June 2007 followed by a second in July 2008. The first island was named Koru {http://slurl.com/secondlife/Koru/156/122/27}, as the koru, or unfolding fern frond, is a symbol of the unfurling of new ideas, re-birth and the acknowledgment of slowly emerging potential. The purchase of Koru provided virtual space in Second Life for both students and staff from NMIT, and other New Zealand institutions to pursue individual projects related to education and one of these was the student experience on which the observations and reflections in this case study are based.

2 Background

All students enrolled on the Bachelor of Information Technology programme at NMIT are required to complete a major 450 hour project to complete their degree. Although an undergraduate course, the project provides students with the opportunity to undertake a significant piece of independent work supervised by an academic staff member. Students are generally free to choose a topic of interest to them provided that they can demonstrate both a reasonable chance of completing the work successfully, an acceptable level of intellectual challenge within the work and they can secure the support of a supervising staff member.

One of the students introduced to Second Life in Semester 1 2007, put forward a proposal to investigate the environment further for educational purposes by building some form of learning activity that could potentially be used by students in the first year of the degree. This proposal coming directly from the student was both intriguing and unexpected. However, it coincided with a burgeoning interest of these two authors, one of whom was interested in a general investigation of MUVEs for adult learning and the other who was experimenting with ideas around using 3D objects to construct activities to explain abstract concepts that the students traditionally found difficult to grasp. The student himself had not only enjoyed time in-world during the original first semester class but had also appeared to benefit in terms of an increasing self-confidence and self-belief which had improved his relationships with other students and had made him uncharacteristically bold in suggesting the project in the first place.

Although initially somewhat ill-defined, a project within Second Life seemed to offer an exciting opportunity for both the student and his supervisors, although some of the challenges would not become immediately apparent. The primary challenges for the student were to become sufficiently familiar with Second Life to become an adequate builder of SL objects, including texturing, sound effects and scripting, to understand the subject of subnetting sufficiently to be able to create an activity to explain it, and to build something which other students would be able to use for learning. In retrospect, one of these challenges would have been sufficient for the purpose of the project and as the student remarked later, somewhat tongue-in-cheek, "...programming and subnetting; the two things I hate most in the world..." (Bateman 2007). However, the work also provided some exciting and sometimes unexpected challenges for the supervisors too whose understanding of the potential and drawbacks of teaching in Second Life were largely unexplored. It is these challenges which provide the basis of the discussion and observations in this chapter.

3 Educational Possibilities in Second Life

The potential of education in immersive virtual environments is discussed in more detail in other chapters but it is relevant to touch here on the aspects of pedagogy that influenced the authors. These primarily concern the authors' belief, largely unsubstantiated at the time that

Second Life provided a unique environment for situated and experiential learning by providing for the creation of authentic tasks in an immersive environment. Lombardi (2007) indicates that students are often motivated by realistic challenges and often express a preference for being in action instead of passivity. In addition, she indicates that many educators deem "learning-by-doing" the most potent way to learn. This has recently been confirmed by educators involved in creating a learning space on Koru for students at Massey University who in describing an initial educational foray into Second Life remark that, "....the provision we had was too passive and … more creative participation was what we needed to support" (Parsons et al 2008)

One of SL's great strengths for what Lombardi (2007) calls "authentic learning", lies in the ability to create interactive virtual 3D objects which can be built into activities to involve the learner and explain abstract concepts that can otherwise be difficult, or at the very least restrictive, for both a teacher to describe in 2D space or expensive or impossible to model in 3D space and for a student to understand. In a MUVE there are opportunities to use colour, sound, movement, and interactivity, to create in a 3D space almost all aspects of a real life activity with understandable but not dire consequences of failure for students who are thus able to learn from their mistakes. Not only activities that are too difficult, too expensive, too dangerous or too resource intensive for real world experiences but also those which are impossible or metaphoric explanations of abstract phenomena can be built (Atkins, 2008). "By using Second Life as a platform for experiential learning, we create a radical expansion of the problems that students are able to address. This increase is in two areas: problems that are infeasible due to a lack of resources, and problems that are impossible because of the limits of the physical world." (Mason 2007).

Sustainability is also an important factor to consider when looking to implement any MUVE based teaching artefact. As with any work done on teaching materials, being able to reuse the object for successive courses is important. Once the groundwork is done, the object can potentially be modified and adjusted to keep it up to date and fresh for the students with only a fraction of the original workload. An ecological sustainable set of teaching tools is considered by the authors to be a valuable asset and using Second Life to create interactive virtual scenarios and artefacts appeared to provide a means to save on the use of physical resources. Although it can be argued that the computing resources necessary for SL are far from ecologically sustainable, there is the ecological advantage of SL that it may well lighten the load on the petrochemical transport requirements of the current, generally centralised, education system.

4 The Student Project

4.1 Project Concept

The chief aims of the project in which this student was enrolled are to provide students with a significant piece of work, an environment in which they can develop their problem solving skills to a high level and develop their expertise in one or more specialised areas of information technology. In this case the student initially proposed to explore Second Life's educational capabilities and assess if it was capable of supporting effective teaching. The supervisors conceptualised this project as a task that would suit the student's strengths and weaknesses. He had used Second Life on a previous course, was familiar with a number of online games (MMORPGs) and very much took to and understood the virtual world concept. His creativity showed with the design of his unconventional avatar which seemed to allow him to 'expand' himself in his first life. Creating a teaching and learning artefact in SL would allow him to immerse himself in the world and discover whether one could use this commercial MUVE to teach effectively. In order to undertake his build the student was provided with a plot of land on NMIT's Koru island and became an active member of the Kiwi Educators group of in-world educators who provided both formal and informal support and encouragement to him.

The means the student chose to do this was through the building of an activity to demonstrate the principles of IPv4 (Internet Protocol version 4) subnetting. IPv4 subnetting is the practice of taking a network address range and dividing it up into smaller (sub) networks which allows for hierarchical structuring and easier management of the network. As illustrated in Figure 1, it is analogous to the geographical hierarchy of a country through to a house division where each sub-part (eg: a city) can be both a sub-part (eg: of a district) and have sub-parts (eg: streets) with many other parts existing independently. The original intention was to test how feasible it would be to build a teaching 'artefact' and whether and in what ways it might be aid in teaching and learning. An IPv4 tutorial was chosen as this was a topic that first year degree students traditionally found difficult to conceptualise and understand. The artefact that was chosen was a 'build' to demonstrate an Internet Protocol v4 (IPv4) subnetting tutorial. At the time of the project, the research done showed that a tutorial of this type had not been done in SL.

Internet Protocol Addressing (IPv4)

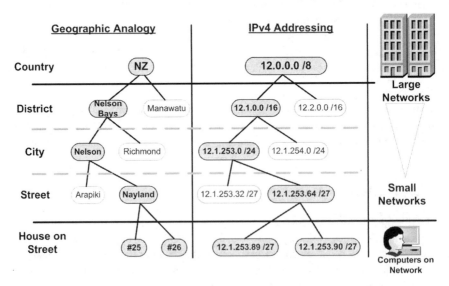

Figure 1. A graphical representation of subnetting using a geographical analogy

The idea of using Internet Protocol v4 (IPv4) subnetting was deemed worthy as this was a difficult learning issue for the student himself and it was felt that he could combine a deeper knowledge of the topic with his growing understanding of the SL environment and the Linden Scripting Language (LSL) scripting that would be necessary. Having a poor knowledge of subnetting was seen as an advantage in this situation as it was hoped the student could potentially gain new insight into a subject that had caused him problems in the past, and combined with a virtual environment, allow him to create a tutorial that crossed the bounds between the conceptual and virtually created 'real' interactive objects. In essence, he was unbound by not knowing what or how it couldn't be done. He was also encouraged to use colour and sound in what he built to assist future users of the activity with their learning of subnetting.

4.2 Project Outcomes

This project then was based around a student-created artefact. As stated above, the student involved had a dislike for both programming and subnetting which created some initial exasperation and frustration for both the student and the staff. However, the student persisted, perhaps because as Lombardi (2007) suggests, "students involved in authentic learning are motivated to persevere despite initial disorientation or frustration, as long as the exercise simulates what really counts...". As this artefact represented creating a tutorial to help others with a real-life networking activity, the student did indeed work through his frustrations and learned where otherwise he may not have. Although successful on this occasion, it must be said that projects which require sophisticated building skills in Second Life could create an almost insurmountable obstacle for non-IT or technologically literate students. The initial learning curve of SL is acknowledged to be steep and while all users of Second Life need to have some understanding of basic building techniques, if only how to open a box and copy items to their inventory, the level of building complexity and sophistication can escalate rapidly as a student begins to experiment and this could prove too high a barrier for some.

In order to successfully create the learning activity the student also needed to determine some form of systematic process for both recording the requirements of the activity and for developing the necessary objects and behaviours. Beginning with some real life storyboarding to try out various ideas on paper and in the face of a total lack of guidelines on how to create 'builds' methodically, the student retrenched to a position of trial and error and also paid little attention to the naming of objects which on occasion caused confusion on which were the latest versions. Although both the supervisors and student acknowledged that time was wasted and mistakes made because of this, no obvious solution appeared during the project.

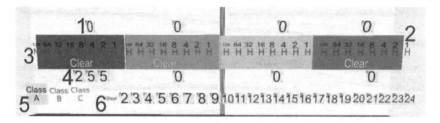

Figure 2. A close-up view of the student's IP subnetting tutorial interface

The final artefact that the student created was very different from that originally envisaged by any of the project participants being a sophisticated binary number manipulation machine which demonstrated the creation of subnetting addresses but did not attempt to explain how or why such manipulation was done. A close-up view of the subnetting interface created by the student is illustrated at Figure 2. However, this was not seen as a failure but a recognition that the project objectives as originally articulated were significantly more complex than had been identified. It also represented an important new area of understanding for the student who chose to construct a visual display of a complex algorithm even though it involved the programming which he had spent almost three years trying to avoid. Ultimately it demonstrated to him that not only was he capable of complex programming if the motivation was sufficiently high but also that he could grasp mathematical concepts that he had previously struggled with.

An additional and unforeseen benefit to the student was the improvement in his ability to socialize and communicate with a wide variety of people both in second and real life. He took great delight and pride in describing and explaining to visitors to his building site on Koru what he was doing and what he was trying to achieve. Although initially a little overawed by the thought that many of the visitors were educators from institutions all over the world, the student gradually came to understand that they were not only genuinely interested in his opinions but also impressed with the work he was doing. This contributed to his already growing self-esteem and manifested itself in real life as a much more positive attitude to all his study which was noticed and remarked upon by other staff and students. In many respects it re-energised his interest in study and in IT and everyone who attended his final presentation of his project was impressed with the fluency and enthusiasm with which he described his work.

4.3 Project Issues

While the student initially continued researching and learning about virtual environments in general and Second Life in particular, one of the initial steps that the supervisors needed to overcome was the difficulty the student had in understanding the subnetting process itself. It seemed intuitive in the circumstances to use Second Life as the medium to use especially as it allowed interaction between the student and staff member from a distance and in the evening but it soon became apparent that there were barriers to overcome. The teaching and learning attempted here was of an impromptu tutorial nature. In normal circumstances multiple sketches would be done on whiteboards, alongside the binary and decimal maths, and gesticulation would be prominent and examples chosen that were relevant to the specific student in the moment. In other words this was a type of teaching that could not be readily planned and which required easy access to a combination of flexible tools in Second Life.

Initially, note cards and in-world instant messaging (IM) were used for giving step by step instructions. These text tools are very serial in nature as well as being restrictive by not easily allowing functions such as superscript and mathematical formulae. But as with any interactive lesson, the instructions can be misinterpreted and questions asked between instructions, so for IM, this 'in-band' method of teaching instruction was interfered with by the simple process of communications. After finding IM restrictive, the voice component of SL was attempted in conjunction with notecards. This reduced the complexity of mixing direct instructions with 'teaching conversations' somewhat but as it was very intermittent audio, it added to the difficulty of the situation. The audio aspect in this case was possibly influenced by the network situations at both ends of the cloud, so was not necessarily an SL issue. The notecards were now the bottleneck in teaching so an SL whiteboard was trialled. This turned out to be very restrictive and time consuming so it was not used any further.

Being that we were faced with barriers to teaching within SL, but wished to keep the lessons online, other tools were sought on the 'flat web' (Livingstone and Kemp 2007) to enable the teaching to continue. Previous experience led us to use Skrbl (http://www.skrbl.com) and Skype (http://www.skype.com). Skrbl (pronounced 'scribble') is an online, synchronous whiteboard that allows freehand drawing and typed text. Other than the slight restriction of having to draw with a mouse as there was no digital pad available, it provided a very useful interface to teach on. A tool similar to this within SL would have been very useful and would have made unplanned, impromptu teaching in-world far more plausible. Skype is software that allows voice calls over the Internet. This service at the time was better quality than the inworld voice capability supplied although this has now improved considerably. As a side note, teaching this student subnetting was eventually taken to first life as their resistance to understanding the subject was great. In the end, four different colours and flavours of liquorice were used with eventual success!!

5 Lessons Learned

5.1 Organisation

As with many things in life, being organised is important in getting a successful outcome and teaching in Second Life, is no exception. In face to face teaching, working with students and maintaining the educational value of group work takes some planning and some simple tools but in SL, where communications can be overwhelmingly confusing, intermittent and even absent, it takes a high level of pre-organisation combined with very good in-world abilities. In the real world, students come into a room and know how to sit down, ask a question without interrupting others and how to focus their eyes on a whiteboard; however none of these apparently straightforward abilities can be assumed for students reasonably new to Second Life. Anticipating and accommodating these basic needs and questions is an essential pre-requisite to a successful experience as Steven Warburton discusses in a recent blog posting (2008). Despite being an experienced Second Life resident who was well prepared he was surprised by the difficulties he faced. He provides both a humorous and heartfelt description of his experiences and also some suggestions for how to avoid some of the more obvious problems.

5.2 Competency

Although teaching in Second Life can be very rewarding, it is not for the faint hearted. A lesson learned in the initial phase of this particular project is that in an in-world course it is not currently possible to decide on a whim to teach in-world and have anything less than poor quality results. Both staff and students need to be competent in their use of Second Life if rewarding activities are to be designed and effective learning is to take place. Most technology tools require a level of competence from their users before real learning can take place but for many their previous computer experiences will allow them to rapidly become effective. This is not the case with SL. Anecdotally, both students and educators may need up to a minimum of 10 hours before they begin to feel remotely comfortable with the prospect of undertaking purposeful activity. Of course this can be accelerated somewhat by ensuring that the activities of those first few hours are carefully tailored to the imperative 'need to know' SL skills. A great deal of effort is being placed in creating appropriate orientation activities for both staff and students and even the standard SL orientation experience has improved considerably over the last years.

A group of educators at SL Education UK (Swaine 2007) have constructed a hierarchical framework of core competencies that is an excellent list of operating skill-sets and understandings. It is suggested that: "to be an effective educator in Second Life requires the acquisition of three sets of core competencies" which are further described as "

- A set of core skills / competencies to become an effective SL resident.
- To be an effective learner requires the resident core skills, plus a further set of skills / competencies which would enable the use of tools and functionality to support their learning within Second Life.
- To become an effective practitioner requires both resident and learner core skills, plus a further set of skills to enable them to identify and setup tools, as well as using appropriate and pedagogically sound approaches to learning and teaching, which support the personalisation of learning." (Swaine 2007)

The framework is instantiated with the various skills and skill levels that are required within each competency and work is underway to create a series of activities to teach and ultimately test each one.

5.3 Systematic Process for creating SL builds

One aspect of the development that the student project highlighted was the need for some guidelines on how to manage the design and implementation process of a build to ensure that useful artefacts were created. There is a need to adopt some form of consistent practice in order to maintain some control over the storing, re-use, testing and versions of the objects and code that are built. Consistency will also allow several developers to be involved in building activities concurrently." (Atkins & Cochrane 2008).

Atkins and Cochrane (2008) suggest that adoption of some of the principles and use of some of the techniques of the Agile methods of software development may well be helpful as "these methods are well suited to risky projects with dynamic requirements" which the majority of SL builds will be. The primary principles they identify are "

- customer satisfaction through early and continuous delivery of useable artefacts,
- welcoming changing requirements at all stages of development,
- developers and lead educator working closely together,
- frequent and open high quality communication between all team members,
- continuous attention to technical quality
- regular team reflection on the effectiveness of the process and willingness to adapt the process as required."

In addition, a high level process is suggested and in particular the importance of adopting standard naming conventions, developing a strategy for backing up and storing copies of the 'build' and the value of adopting a coherent strategy for the control of versions of the build are emphasized.

5.4 Bridging the Gap: Serious Fun vs. Serious Learning

Assuming that by using SL we are not after the old 'chalk & talk' or Pavlovian conditioning approach to teaching, it seems intuitive that creating fun and possibly game-like interactive situations and artefacts is a sensible way to provide authentic learning for our students. Incorporating aspects of learning through playful activities where incremental success is rewarded and failure is merely a step towards ultimate success encourages the student to persevere in collaborative, co-operative or individual learning. Although our student's project did not take full advantage of the possibilities of play it would not have taken significant effort to adapt the tutorial effectively.

A common feature of popular online games such as World of Warcraft and Anarchy Online, that in order to successfully complete a task or 'quest', the player will be faced with any number of failures through which to learn how to ultimately succeed. The translation of this aspect into a 'game-style' education approach such as can easily be achieved in Second Life, may well help to keep the student focused and motivated enough to attempt a task several times despite the frustration of repeated failure. This has a dualistic role in that the student is gaining valuable technical experience relevant to the real world, and at the same time developing the meta-cognitive skills necessary to enable them to cope with the process of becoming an expert, or at least a knowledgeable beginner, through, what we are terming the 'practice of failure.'

As Kay wisely remarked, "An education system that tries to make everything easy and pleasurable will prevent much important learning from happening." (1991). Through the creation of appropriate activities in Second Life, we believe there is the opportunity to provide students with challenges that have them strive for success through the practice of failure.

5.5 Technical Considerations

Second Life by its nature is a somewhat bandwidth hungry application and seems to be very aggressive at taking the bandwidth that is available. This is due to the fact that the user created content and surrounding geography, flora, fauna, and communications, must be sent to individual users and constantly streamed in as the user moves around and interacts with the environment. Second Life is not compatible with dial-up internet, satellite internet, and some wireless internet services so on a slow or highly filtered connection, the performance of the application can suffer badly even to the extent of not allowing fluid communication or avatar movement (Second Life 2008a). In addition, although SL tends to work through the NMIT firewalls without much problem or lag, at the time of writing, the campus ISP was packet shaping the traffic from the Internet and access to SL was not possible.

The issue of SL not working on dial-up connections is of some concern within NMIT as a trial campus survey conducted in the same academic year as the student project indicated that a significant proportion (37%) of surveyed students had no access or only dial-up access to the Internet. This dropped slightly (to 34%) when only Business and Computing student numbers were considered.

It might also be worth noting here that the New Zealand rural sector - a population that has a use and need for online access to remote learning facilities - predominantly only has access to dial-up or point-to-point wireless Internet connectivity. This effectively eliminates this sector from the benefits of these kinds of MUVE based educational activities although they may well be the most in need of them. It is suggested that a user should "start with 300 kbps as your default" (Second Life 2008b) bandwidth setting in the SL application and that "your bandwidth [will] idle at around 20-50 kilobits per second, and peak in the hundreds of kilobits per second while moving around or in a crowded area." (Second Life 2008b) Anecdotal bandwidth usage at NMIT was approximately 250Kb/s to 500Kb/s per computer dependent on user settings. So between five and ten students reduced the available school bandwidth down to almost nothing when being used in a third year class at the end of the 2008 academic year. Not only does this place constraint on-campus class sizes but has repercussions on the remaining general network population. Considering only 'network-affecting' issues, adjusting your bandwidth and cache size may help (Second Life 2008c) and experience also suggest that that initially limiting the draw distance (which in turn affects the cached data) to the lowest setting of 64 metres and then increasing it to the minimum required for any specific location, helps to improve the SL experience.

6 Conclusion

In retrospect both the student and the supervisors have agreed that the student's project was an exciting and challenging experience. Without a doubt it was seriously fun and all three participants were encouraged to persist even in the face of failure believing that the ultimate success was waiting at the end of the tunnel. It was also a vehicle for serious learning. For the student, both personal growth and increased technical knowledge in a variety of areas were the outcome. For the supervisors the learning was more unexpected but equally diverse. Choosing both the most appropriate activities for learning, the most appropriate tools for teaching and being well prepared for unanticipated problems and changes in direction were without doubt some of the most valuable lessons that were learned. All three emerged from the project with a strong belief in the value afforded by the Second Life environment, a strong sense of the apparently limitless possibilities for education and a very clear understanding that we are currently on the edge of a major shift in educational delivery for which the maps are only in the very early stages of development.

References

Atkins C., and Cochrane, T. 2008. Principles for Design and Implementation of SL 'Builds'. Online at http://slenz.wordpress.com/slenz-project/project-processes/design-and-implementation-of-sl-builds/ Retrieved Nov 12th 2008.

Atkins, C., 2008. Virtual Experience: Observations on Second Life. Proc of International Conference on Computer Mediated Social Networking, Dunedin, New Zealand, July.

Bateman G., 2007 Exploring the Potential of Second Life for Education, Unpublished Project Report, Pii, Available from Library Learning Centre, NMIT, Hardy Street, Nelson, New Zealand.

Burleson, W., Picard, R.W., 2004. Affective agents: sustaining motivation to learn through failure and a state of stuck. In: Frasson, C., Porayska-Pomsta, K. (eds.) ITS04 Workshop on Social and Emotional Intelligence in Learning Environments, Maceio Alagoas, Brasil. Online Proceedings: http://www.cogsci.ed.ac.uk/%7Ekaska/WorkshopSI/

Kay, A., 1991 Computers, Networks and Education. Scientific American, v265 n3 spec iss p138-48.

Livingstone, D. and Kemp, J. (eds.) Proceedings of the Second Life Education Workshop at the SL Community Convention, Chicago, August 24th 2007. Retrieved from: http://www.simteach.com/slccedu07proceedings.pdf on 10th November 2008

Mason, H. "Experiential Education in Second Life", in Proceedings of the Second Life Education Workshop at the SL Community Convention, San Francisco, August 24th, 2007. Retrieved from http://www.simteach.com/slccedu07proceedings.pdf on 10th November 2008

Lombari, M. "Authentic Learning for the 21st Century: An Overview" in Educause Learning Initiative, May 2007. Retrieved on 11th November 2008: http://www.educause.edu/ir/library/pdf/ELI3009.pdf

Parsons, D. Stockdale, R. Bowles, J. and Kamble V., (2008) If we build it will they come? Creating a virtual classroom in Second Life. Proc 19th Australasian Conference on Information Systems ACIS2008. Christchurch, New Zealand. Dec.

Second Life, 2008a Online at http://secondlife.com/support/sysreqs.php, Retrieved Nov 11th 2008.

Second Life, 2008b Online at http://wiki.secondlife.com/wiki/Help:Lag#Bandwidth retrieved Nov 11th 2008.

Second Life, 2008c Online at http://wiki.secondlife.com/wiki/Help:Lag#Network retrieved Nov 11th 2008.

Swaine, C., 2007. Core Skills Competency Framework. http://www.sleducationuk.net/vle/file.php/2/Education_UK_Island_core_skills_competency_framework.pdf retrieved on 9th March 2008

Warburton, S., 2008. Liquid Learning. http://warburton.typepad.com/liquidlearning/2008/11/herding-cats.html retrieved on 14th Nov 2008

Chapter 6: Action Learning in a Virtual World

Lindy McKeown

PhD Candidate, University of Southern Queensland, Australia
lindy@lindymckeown.com

Chapter Overview. After a brief explanation of how Action Learning works and why it is such a widely used learning strategy, this chapter will explore how to use a virtual world as a location for Action Learners. We will explore ways to address content, the Action Learning Process and course management.

1 What is Action Learning and why use it

Action Learning is a method of teaching and learning that was developed by Reg Revans (Revans 1982) in the 1930s to address the professional learning needs of managers. Since then it has been used as an effective strategy for bridging the knowing-doing gap (Pfeffer & Sutton 1999), the gap that develops between what people "learn" during formal courses or professional development programs and what they put into practice in their workplace. This gap renders much professional learning a waste of time and resources because people revert to their previous behaviours when they return to their workplace.

The Action Learning Cycle consist of explore, plan, act and reflect (see Figure 1). It is an iterative process that engages learners in an authentic task which they have generated from their work. They may want to solve a problem, improve a process or take advantage of an innovation or opportunity. It is the process of making learning relevant to the workplace and applied soon after acquisition that makes Action Learning such an effective learning and teaching strategy.

Figure 1. The workplace project is central to the Action Learning Cycle

A physicist by profession, Revans expressed learning as a formula of L = P + Q where L was learning, P was programmed knowledge (what is already known and published about a topic) and Q was insightful questioning (asking what relevance P has in the context at hand where it is to be applied). It was the marriage of the existing knowledge to the project at hand that makes the learning authentic and provides the structure to immediately put the learning into practice.

1.1   Explore content and context - Informed data-driven decision making

Exploration involves two processes. Firstly exploration of content related to the project and secondly exploration of the work site of the project and data gathering to identify the local conditions in relation to the relevant factors in creating a plan to implement. In some Action Learning Programs, such as a formal tertiary course or a workplace professional development program created by a new process or policy, there may be mandated content. In a community or environmental project, the problem, issue or opportunity may point to relevant content based on the needs of the project. In all cases the workplace project provides the context for the content which can be customised to meet the needs of specific projects, either by the teacher or by the participants themselves.

1.2   Plan and Act – Learn and implement learning

The plan is informed by the context, the experience of the Action Learner and the programmed knowledge. Once a plan is formulated based on applying the relevant content to the project context to make informed decisions, it is put into action. There is usually reflection about the plan before implementation begins in order to identify any potential flaws in the data collection, to surface the underlying assumptions or to assess critically the robustness of the plan itself prior to implementation.

1.3   Reflect – A social process for deep reflection

Reflection in Action Learning is a social practice going beyond but including personal reflective practice. Social reflection occurs in small groups of 4 to 8 called Learning Sets. The sets meet regularly (perhaps once every 3 weeks) to reflect and learn from each other after each stage of the plan is implemented. The group uses questions to deepen reflection, surface assumptions and identify blind spots. Learning Sets can be working on a single, shared project or on quite different individual projects.

To ensure a fair share of time for each participant, these meetings may follow a formal protocol such as this one based on a round robin process described by Krystina Weinstien. (1999) (See Learning Set Protocol for Round Table below) During the presentations, other group members assume the roles of scribe and time keeper to ensure the meeting runs to schedule and the speaker gets an accurate record of the points discussed.

Learning Set Protocol for Round Table

- The following steps are repeated for each member of the Learning Set
- 10 - 15 mins maximum for each person (negotiated by members)
- One set member acts as the time keeper
- One set member acts as scribe so that all the ideas are collected for the presenter

1. The set member shares their project / idea / progress with rest of group – uninterrupted.
2. Clarifying questions from the other Learning Set members – two questions per person.
3. Responses to questions.
4. Sum up.

It is expected that the participants will share not only what has gone well, but also what not gone as well as was expected and to surface areas of uncertainty that may require further exploration of existing knowledge. Trust and discretion are essential elements in the effective functioning of a Learning Set. What is shared during a set meeting should not be discussed with others outside of the Learning Set.

It is important to note that in this process, it is the use of the questions from the other set members that aids the learning of the person presenting their progress report. Participants should avoid offering suggestions and ideas for alternative ways of approaching the issue except in the form of a question. For example, instead of saying, "You should try this", the learning set member might ask, "Would this technique used where I work be of any use in your context?" As this is often a new experience for learners, scaffolding questions with list of question starters may be helpful.

The program facilitator acts as the Learning Set Adviser providing guidance to the Learning Set members and helping develop their skills so they can become an independently functioning group.

This cycle is repeated with new data collected about the environment, new content explored in relation to topics identified during reflection, adjustments to the plan and further action taken. Over the course of the Action Learning Program, there will be several iterations of this cycle.

2 Why use Action Learning in a virtual world

With the ever increasing need for lifelong learning because of the rapid pace of change in our society, people are seeking more and more opportunities for learning in both formal courses and initiating personal learning opportunities. (OECD 2004) Coupled with the rapid pace of technological change and widespread access to the Internet, many individuals and organisations are taking advantage of online access to learning opportunities. The reasons for choosing online learning vary from geographic remoteness from the learning provider's location, to cost saving, lifestyle choices and family commitments. Learning online also allows learning to occur in small time chunks within the workplace or home without the loss of time spent travelling to another location to participate.

Facilitators of Action Learning programs have been exploring the use of various online technologies to support the processes within their programs for many years. The two key elements that can be supported online are the exploration of content and the reflective meetings of the Learning Sets. Content has been developed and delivered asynchronously via the worldwide web and this can be very successful. However for some it can be a lonely and isolating experience missing the richness of the face-to-face learning environment. (Russell 2004)

Learning Sets have been conducted in asynchronous discussion forums over an extended period of time as a means of trying to replicate the Learning Set meeting. This process has had more mixed results. It is understandable that there may be a reluctance to put failures or challenges in writing that will be recorded on the forum site leaving a paper trail of sensitive point-in-time material.

3 Conducting Action Learning in Second Life

During 2006 and 2007, Lindy McKeown was involved in conducting Action Learning programs in ActiveWorlds (Sanders & McKeown 2007) and Second Life as part of her PhD research. The first of these was a formal course of study at Appalachian State University conducted by Dr. Robert Sanders with Lindy in the role of Action Learning mentor and adviser to this course development and delivery. The Second Life programs were conducted by Lindy as program facilitator and were professional development courses for teachers. Outlined here are the processes and tools used and a description of the new technologies and features that have been developed in Second Life since that time that would be useful additions.

Two elements of these programs occurred in the virtual world. These were the exploration of programmed knowledge (content) that related to the courses or projects and the Learning Set meetings. The project plans were created and carried out by the participants in their workplaces. These two phases of the cycle, planning and acting, were discussed in the formal Learning Set meetings that occurred in the virtual world and in informal chats between participants.

Embodied as an avatar in a virtual world, people get a sense of physical presence. They feel like they are there in the virtual place as opposed to sitting at their computer at their current location. When they meet the other avatars in their group, they get a sense of social presence. They feel like the others are there with them. There is enough willing suspension of disbelief to allow people to have a strong sense of being with the other people allowing them to interact as they would if they were in close physical proximity.

3.1 Conducting a Learning Set Meeting in Second Life

To conduct a learning set meeting you require a location where a small group can sit together and have an uninterrupted discussion in private. Each participant will give a short presentation about what they have achieved towards their planned project and share successes, challenges, failures, outcomes, delaying factors and opportunities that have arisen. In Second Life there is no shortage of suitable locations to hold this kind of a meeting. With a massive land area of millions of square meters and less than 60 000 avatars logged in at any one time, it is easy to find places to hold a meeting.

Figure 2. Learning Set Meeting on Terra Incognita Island, Second Life

The island of Terra Incognita in Second Life was established for Lindy's research group with a lot of small group areas to allow several simultaneous Learning Set meetings. Some locations had tables and chairs for a more formal and traditional setting but some had beach towels or floating rings for a less traditional, more relaxed approach (see Figure 2). The group locations vary from a board room to the torpedo room of a submarine.

Building choice has implications for users especially in the complexity of camera control needed to see other avatars. For beginners, open buildings with few if any walls make camera management simple because the default camera position is looking from behind the avatar in the third person position. Enclosed rooms force the avatars to manipulate their camera position to enable them to maintain an unobscured view of their own avatars and those of the group. In very small spaces, avatars can use the first person view which is looking through the eyes of the avatar as opposed to looking from behind the avatar. This is also called "mouselook" in Second Life .

3.2   The conversation

Second Life allows the use of voice or text chat and both are suitable for this process. Voice is certainly easier than text chat but it does not provide an automatic transcript the way that logging text chat can. If using voice, notes can be taken by the scribe using the built in note card system. The notecard can be passed to the speaker's avatar at the end of the meeting as a record of the discussion.

3.3   Turn taking

In the absence of the gesture cues available when in face-to-face settings, the built in voice indicator brackets above the avatar's head indicate who is speaking.

3.4   Visual materials

A range of screens in Second Life allow learning set members to display photos, show video or presentation slides can be useful presentation aids but are not essential and many learning set presentations are just verbal. It is also possible to show a web page in Second Life so participants can show a YouTube video, Google document or other web page for their presentations.

It is important to train participants in using these tools and the interface effectively to meet their needs so they can interact effectively.

4   Conducting a class on a topic related to the Action Learning projects of the participants.

Reg Revan's called everything we already know about a subject "Programmed Knowledge" but was adamant that it was asking insightful questions about content as it was applied to the context at hand that was what made programmed knowledge useful to action. One way to access programmed knowledge, especially in formal courses of study that use Action Learning, is to conduct a class in much the same way as you might in a face-to-face setting.

To effectively link this content to the Action Learning projects, it is essential, however, to include a structured activity as part of this class in which participants consider the relevance of the content to their projects. Action Learners could consider what insightful questions need to be asked in the light of this new knowledge and how the content they have encountered can be applied to inform and modify their plans.

4.1   Roles for Virtual Worlds

There are 5 key roles for virtual worlds in learning, 6 if you include combinations of the others. (McKeown 2008) Each of these should be considered in relation to the role the virtual world might play in the exploration of programmed knowledge (content) in the "Explore" phase of an Action Learning cycle. They are:

1. Location

2. Context

3. Content

4. Community

5. Material

6. Combinations of any number of these roles

Exploration of relevant programmed knowledge (content) can include individual research but also extends to Learning Set groups organising their own learning events and whole group activities organised by the program facilitator where appropriate.

4.1.1 The Virtual World As A Location

4.1.1.1   Clever classrooms

In addition to providing a location for the learning set meeting, content (programmed knowledge) may be delivered in the form of class lessons or group learning events in accordance with the requirements of the course or program of professional development. To do this a range of tools and venues are available in virtual worlds to facilitate a range of pedagogies.

Second Life has a programming language that allows objects to be scripted to perform tasks on command. One example of how scripted objects that can not exist in the physical world can be developed and used in the virtual world is the Decka's Decks Conference Facility.

Using the affordances of the virtual world, a group classroom that can start out with a large group and fly apart into small break out rooms for discussion was created to make managing the avatar movement automatic and instantaneous (see Figure 3). In this way the small groups of avatars were flown out of range of each other's 'noise' as they chat in either voice or text. The facilitator can recall the groups using a control panel.

4.1.1.2   Portable classrooms

Each avatar has an inventory which holds all their possessions. It is possible to store a range of furniture in the inventory. This can include individual items as well as furniture arrangements suitable for a group or class to use. The teacher can then place these items on demand when needed for a learning experience. Note: The only limitation being that the "build" facility must be allowed on the land where you intend to place the item. Some land owners disable this facility preventing any other person taking items from their inventory and placing them on the ground.

It is also possible to have a "holodeck" device that can store and then place entire arrangements of furniture at the touch of a button. This "room" can provide a diverse range of furniture arrangements to suit an equally diverse range of teaching situations. For example, the holodeck might contain a board room table and chairs, a lecture hall, a set of tables and chairs for discussions and a panel and audience configuration. It may also contain simulation set ups for role play.

Figure 3. Decka's Decks - The classroom in large group mode

Figure 4. Hand show chair with animation (Created by Angrybeth Shortbread)

4.1.1.3   Audio visual tools

Screens for slides, images or video and whiteboards are useful additions and serve the same purpose in the virtual world as they do in the physical world. Web pages can be viewed in Second Life with new levels of interaction between virtual worlds and digital resources hosted outside the world under constant development.

Like many other features, this too changes over time as development in these innovative new learning spaces is an ongoing process of rapid change and technological advancement paralleling the advancement of the World Wide Web. Some of these developments are created by the education community in Second Life and are available for free or for low cost. There is also commercial development of these tools underway for enterprise application that may be charged on a par with other corporate licensing rates but this is yet to be determined. Organisations who can afford more sophisticated tools will be able to incorporate these into their Action Learning programs.

However, just as in the physical world, Action Learning can be conducted very successfully without these tools as it is the quality of the insightful questioning and the plans put into action that from the basis of the learning in Action Learning, not the sophistication of the tools to support the set meetings.

4.1.1.4   Animation

The ability to control animations in Second Life allows the creation of realistic non-verbal communication. This can be used to add to the natural look and feel of the environment such as speaking gestures, animated sitting poses and casual movement of the avatar to a range of standing poses. Specific gestures can also provide effective cues and non verbal communication. For example, an animation to raise the avatar's arm triggered from a single keystroke such as the page up key can also be used to indicate the need to ask a question. These can be controlled either from the keyboard, (see Figure 4).

4.1.2   The Virtual World As Context

Some subjects lend themselves to being contextualized in immersive environments more readily than others. Language learning, customer service, criminal law and interview techniques are amongst the diverse range of topics that can take advantage of the opportunities for simulation and role play afforded by virtual worlds. Learners can participate in costume in virtual environments that replicate the physical world. You can either create a range of locations to use, visit existing public locations in Second Life with everything from an oil rig to an art gallery available, or use a 'holodeck' to use a single site that can be changed from one arrangement such as a board room to another such as a court room quickly.

4.1.3   The Virtual World As Content

Because of the enormous diversity of Second Life, there are many opportunities to find content within the virtual world itself depending on the topic. Many universities, institutions and interest groups have publicly available models, kiosks, demonstrations, interactive displays and information centres within the virtual world. An immersive experience with these interactive tools or static displays can be very realistic and support or replace learning offered in other environments such as text based web pages.

4.1.4   The Community In The Virtual World

With over 5 million users (2008), there are opportunities to use the individuals and the groups within Second Life to find one of Reg Revans' preferred sources of wisdom, the lived experience of people in the field. Opportunities exist to use avatars or even to stream video presentations of guest presenters, practitioners who use the stuff you are teaching about, members of professional associations or to create expert panels.

The other role that the population of Second Life can play in the Action Learning process is as audience especially for ideas and performances or as customers for business ventures in Second Life.

4.1.5   The Virtual World As A Material – Making Movies (Machinima)

Virtual Worlds can provide simple and cheap sets to create film, a process called machinima. There are two ways to use film made this way in Action Learning programs. Firstly the film can be a resource for teaching the content. Secondly filming Learning Set meetings can be a useful way to capture the discussion but also to aid further personal reflection by the Action Learners. There are many free and commercial screen capture programs available to record the video and audio from your computer.

5   Effectiveness as a learning environment

There is, as yet, little research to show whether this type of location is any more or less effective than using web based tools to host online classes. Many educators point to the embodiment of people as avatars as having a profound effect on the social presence and sense of being there together. Recent research in the medical training simulation in virtual worlds (Heinrichs et al 2008) provides evidence to support the position found previously with other distance learning technologies that "an overwhelming number of studies showed that when the course materials and teaching methodology were held constant, there were no significant differences (NSD) between student outcomes in a distance delivery course as compared to a face to face course. In other words, student outcomes in distance delivery courses were neither worse nor better than those in face to face courses." (Russell 2008)

One key difference between virtual worlds and other synchronous technologies used in education such as Eluminate, WebEx or Wimba is that because of the persistent nature of virtual worlds, allowing students can come before and stay after class or meet at other times to interact with other students or the facilitator/teacher.

6 Administration tasks

6.1 Group management

Managing the administrative task for your Action Learning groups can be completely conducted in the virtual world or with a blend of email, web and in-world communication and tools. Second Life uses a system of groups that can be created by the facilitator and all the avatars can be invited to join. This allows notices about events, voting, sharing of landmarks, images and 3D objects needed for classes or Learning Set meetings to be distributed efficiently to all members. If group members are offline when these are sent, an email alerts them that there is an item awaiting them in the virtual world when they next log in. Learning Sets can have their own groups to allow them to self organise. Groups can also be used to control access to land, allowing you to give groups privacy through exclusive access to locations you own in the virtual world.

6.2 Document Management

The only documents that can be created inside Second Life (at the time of writing) are in the form of simple notecards. These do not allow a lot of formatting but can include embedded images and landmarks to locations inside Second Life. Distribution and storage can be automated using scripted tools and group notices.

Distribution systems for course materials in the form of notecards include tools that will send the materials to all and those that require the participants to collect the items they require. A notecard giver can provide items when touched. These can be in the form of familiar items such as a filing cabinet or attached to a sign inviting participants to collect items. Notecard distribution systems can be scripted to only allow access by your class members rather than public access.

Images can be created and uploaded into Second Life for a small cost (10 Linden dollars each which is equivalent to about 4 cents US$). These can be displayed on slide screens, display boards, embedded in notecards or distributed directly to Action Learners through group notices.

7 Learning Journals

Although not a mandatory element of Action Learning, the use of journals can aid organisation and personal reflection. Inside Second Life the only documents easily created are notecards, a simplistic text document stored in the inventory. These can be used to from a series of journal entries but can not be accessed outside the world. Blogs can be a useful alternative as the learning journal. It is possible to blog from within Second Life using scripted devices available for free and for sale in Second Life . The blogs can then be accessed and added to outside the virtual world as well as from within it. Using a display screen, journal entries can be made visible inside the virtual world if needed.

8 Blended learning environments

It is also possible to blend a range of technologies, including face-to-face events, into the overall course or professional development program conducted using an Action Learning process. For Action Learning, Second Life provides a great environment as a location for Learning Sets to meet. This key element of the Action Learning Cycle sits so comfortably in Second Life especially for geographically separated learners. It provides the physical and social presence that can let the Learning Set members make the kind of connection that allows for a frank and open social reflective practice. Other web-based technologies could be used to deliver programmed knowledge in support of the Action Learning program and Second Life can be one of these sources. Second Life can also be used as the "home" of an Action Learning program providing a 'resource centre' metaphor by either linking to resources outside the virtual world including text, images and video based material or retrieving them for display in-world.

9 Future of Action Learning and Virtual Worlds

Because Action Learning is such a useful and effective method for applying learning in the workplace, it will continue to be used as a strategy for organisations wanting to get return on their learning investments. As more virtual worlds appear and the tools within them become more sophisticated and integrated with tools that exist on the web and in corporate systems, Action Learning will become even more effective in virtual environments.

References

Heinrichs, W. L. Youngblood, P. Harter, P. M.Dev, P. (2008) Simulation for Team Training and Assessment: Case Studies of Online Training with Virtual Worlds. World Journal of Surgery; Special Issue, 32(2008)161-170

McKeown, L. (2008) Technical and social affordances of a virtual perpetual world designed for use with an Action Learning Model of professional learning. University of Southern Queensland. (Unpublished PhD thesis)

OECD, Organisation for Economic Co-operation and Development. (2004). Policy brief: Lifelong learning: Organisation for Economic Co-operation and Development.

Pfeffer, J., & Sutton, R. I. (1999). The knowing-doing gap: How smart companies turn knowledge into action. Boston: Harvard Business School Press.

Revans, R. W. (1982). The origins and growth of action learning. Bromley, UK: Chartwell Bratt Ltd.

Russell, G. (2004). The distancing dilemma in distance education. International Journal of Instructional Technology and Distance Learning, 1(2).

Russell, T. (2008). No significant difference. Retrieved 16 November, 2008, from http://nosignificantdifference.wcet.info/faq.asp

Sanders, R. L., & McKeown, L. (2007). Promoting Reflection through Action Learning in a 3D Virtual World. International Journal of Social Sciences, 2(1).

Weinstein, K. (1999). Action learning: A practical guide (2nd ed.). Aldershot, Hants. UK: Gower.

Chapter 7: Enhancing Virtual Environments

Bryan W. Carter, Ph.D.
University of Central Missouri
English
MARTIN 336
Warrensburg, MI, 64093
USA
BCarter@CMSU1.CMSU.EDU

Chapter Overview: Since it's inception in 2003, Second Life has offered educators an opportunity to engage students on a level never before possible in a traditional classroom setting. Through the creation of historical or futuristic environments, interactive assignments and multiple ways to communicate and collaborate, Second life is the pedagogical compliment for which many educators have been waiting. Early adopters of the platform have constructed fantastic builds such as Renaissance Island, reminiscent of early British culture, 19th Century America where visitors may meet Abraham Lincoln or Mary Todd, or Virtual Harlem/Montmartre where the Jazz Age is highlighted and experienced. Within these environments, classes are taught, conferences are held, meetings take place and collaborations occur between old and new colleagues. Second Life encourages engagement, communication and interaction with both the environment and other residents on the same level if not more so than that which occurs in the real world. How, then, might an environment designed in such a way, be enhanced to increase that which is already at such a high level? The current state of technology suggests two very real possibilities, one of which is already deployed on Virtual Harlem. Artificial Intelligent Agents and performance are two compliments to Second Life that may offer educators an additional way to engage students both in-world and out.

1 Notions of Identity

To explore and experience Virtual Harlem only through the lens of performance and how it can be enhanced to increase the overall experience really takes away from the overall aim of the project. Virtual Harlem was originally intended to not just encourage student engagement with a period that many felt (and still feel) very distant, but more importantly, to explore notions of identity. Creating an Avatar and interacting with an intelligent agent is, on a much deeper level, what brings Virtual Harlem to life and really gives the environment meaning far beyond that which some believe is the intent of the project. Virtual Harlem is not just about the creation of 1920s Jazz era Harlem, New York and Montmartre, France, it is about how multiple identities were created, performed and engaged during a period in American history when racial politics were at best cordial, and at worst, so violent and demeaning that some would rather "pass" than have their opportunities limited.

2 History of Virtual Harlem

In the Fall of 2006, the National Black Programming Consortium funded $15,000 for the development of Virtual Harlem in Second Life, a 3D online virtual world. Later that year the Government of Norway awarded a grant to a collaborative group of scholars from Molde University College, Norway, Kalmar University, Sweden and the University of Central Missouri in the US. The grant covered the development of two additional educational environments in Second Life; a teaching space with virtual classrooms and additional multimedia integration capabilities, and Virtual Montmartre. Virtual Montmartre, a representation of parts of the 18th Arrondisement in 1920's Paris, provides the perfect learning complement to Virtual Harlem, and both utilize the teaching space. The College of Arts and Humanities at the University of Central Missouri also awarded a grant $5,400 for further maintenance of these environments. The University of Paris IV - Sorbonne provided in-kind contributions.

A first injection of funds to develop Virtual Harlem and Virtual Montmartre in Second Life enabled a proof of concept supporting the reliability of the medium for historical re-enactment and cultural learning. This early stage project brought together an international collaboration of academic, private, cultural and government participants. It also permitted the capture of know-how related to content and knowledge migration into virtual worlds. Starting in Fall 2007, post-secondary students were brought into the environments as part of their formal learning program. They were tasked with the creation of historically accurate and interactive content supplements to the environment. From a learning and teaching perspective, this has been a conspicuous success. Outputs have included an art gallery that uses audio, visual, and textual content to highlight the major artists of the period, a photographic studio that showcases the work of one of the most famous photographers of the period, a clothing store based on the fashion of the period and that became popular with other residents of Second Life, a theatrical production on the stage of the Apollo Theater, and several cabarets where students run operations and also incorporated historical content to document the specifics of the music, the entertainers, the ownership and also information related to racism in that period and context. In other words, the end-users of this virtual world cultural and learning environment naturally become content makers within it, in keeping with the aims of the long-term project.

Virtual Harlem, at present, is a digital representation of 1920s Harlem, New York, at the height of the Harlem Renaissance, and comprises its key landmarks such as the Cotton Club, the Apollo Theater, Small's Paradise and the Savoy Ballroom. Since its inception, the environment was designed to house re-enactments of key moments in its cultural life, provide opportunities for students to learn and to test their knowledge, and offer opportunities for scholars to bring their historical research to life, and to communicate their findings to learners, to other scholars, and to the general public. By the same token, Virtual Montmartre is a representation of a small portion of the 18th Arrondisement in Paris, France; Montmartre where the intent is to add an international dimension to the overall project through collaborative activities with students from the University of Paris IV-Sorbonne. This is where Jazz was introduced to an eager audience in France after World War I ended.

3 Enhancement through Performance

Performance has always been one of the pinnacles of Humanistic experience. Ballet, poetry readings, theatre, opera, or even that which we find more commonly like street corner orators, preachers and performance artists are expressions of our collective experience that few other disciplinary studies can offer. Performance is also one way in which we document and in a sense, archive periods in history. Performance, however, is multi-dimensional when experiencing it through a racial lens. On the surface, it includes all of the forms mentioned above. However, when race is included in the equation, one must always keep in mind that performance is a part of the African American experience, both consciously and subconsciously. Virtual worlds and the creation of avatars now enables others who are not members of groups that have been traditionally oppressed to both consciously and subconsciously experience that which many African Americans experience on a daily basis.

More traditional modes of performance made possible through virtual environments have added an interesting level of excitement among those who teach theatre and performance theory. As our reality expands into virtual environments, I believe it is crucial to incorporate similar experiences into a world increasingly inhabited by residents craving more than most online communities currently offer. To date, there have been a limited number of virtual world performances. There are plays by Shakespeare; there is a ballet company in Second Life and venues where one may hear/experience concerts or other musical performances. Most of these endeavours are done by professional or semi-professional companies who are seeking to expand their visibility, or gain experience in virtual world performance.

On Virtual Harlem, we endeavour to explore live performance in a very different way. First, we plan to employ students as the primary performers within a contextual environment. In other words, not only will students be the performers, but performances will take place in an historically contextual setting which adds to the overall effect of the performance. Secondly, to supplement the traditional fare of performance mentioned earlier, students will also role play as a part of the larger performance or trope which will supplement the overall effect of the various performances taking place, each feeding off of one another. For instance, a theatre group from the university performs a portion of the 1936 version of McBeth, which was the first featuring an all African American cast. Members of the audience, after having studied the reception of the initial performance, role play that of an enthusiastic audience using similar vernacular. Outside the Lafayette Theater, where the performance was held, there is a street corner orator with an audience of his own and across the street at a local cabaret, say Small's Paradise, Jimmy Lunsdford is performing, while residents of Second Life move between performances. The first performance can be recorded and archived, played back at anytime and enjoyed by one or many anytime after the "live" performance has actually taken place, while regular secondary performances can be scheduled throughout the term. Other examples include historic speeches, interviews, radio broadcasts, conversations and other types of stage performances and lectures, all of which have an historical foundation to inform the performance.

Figure 1. Virtual Harlem in Second Life.

Figure 2. Virtual Montmartre in Second Life.

In addition to students controlling avatars as the basis of the performances done in-world, there is also the possibility of motion capture where the movements of "live" actors are mapped onto those of avatars in Second Life. Motion capture when added to live performance adds to the accuracy of movements when necessary and also encourages more natural movements instead of relying on keyboard initiated gestures.

What a project like this does is to further blur the line between real life and that which some consider the virtual. What we may ultimately discover is that which we experience in Second Life is really an extension of reality that we are only now discovering.

Figure 3. Dancing at the Cotton Club on Virtual Harlem

4   Engagement through Artificial Intelligent Agents

Artificial intelligent agents are not a new technology. We have, over the years experienced them in a number of ways to include fictional versions like HAL in 2001 A Space Oddesy, The Terminator and iRobot as well as real life agents, from the small computers we find in almost every device made, to the recommendations we get from Amazon when we shop online. Similar to the agents that recommend further purchases to us through complex algorithms, learning from our every move, the agents deployed on Virtual Harlem have the ability to do very complex tasks, learning more as they continue to interact with "real" residents of Second Life.

In early 2008, the College of Arts, Science and Humanities at the University of Central Missouri awarded a Creative Activities grant to purchase three AI bots. These bots were purchased from iVersity, a company based in Kansas City, Missouri. What prompted the purchase of these bots was a demonstration of their capabilities. To understand how they work, we must first understand the technology behind their operation. The system is called CINDI, a centralized intelligence system developed by iVersity, which utilizes a sophisticated combination of the latest in A.I. (Artificial Intelligence), Cognitive Systems, Data Interpretation/Storage, and Bio-Feedback technologies. The system features:

• Dynamic creation and storage of AIML (Artificial Intelligence Markup Language) knowledge base and reasoning data based on advanced, proprietary "truth" algorithms. The current knowledge base is at approximately 35,000 patterns for use in its natural language processing.

• Open API (Application Programming Interface) for universal accessibility of Centralized A.I. interfacing utilizing any one of the standardized methods supported. (Currently in beta)

• Advanced Speech Recognition / Text to Speech combination (Currently in beta)

What captured our attention was the ability of the bots to translate languages, offer directions, perform calculations and search for information via popular search engines. We were also intrigued by the ability of the bots to both remember those with whom they encounter and "learn" on a continual basis.

4.1   Performance through AI Bots

Combining performance and AI Bot technologies a very interesting set of possibilities emerges. Imagine visiting Virtual Harlem and being greeted by a persona resembling an historic figure of the period who can not only offer you directions to the Cotton Club but also offer information related to the Harlem Renaissance when asked. Furthermore, the bot has the ability to recite poetry, search for information on the Web and understand those whose language may not be English. AI bots deployed on Virtual Harlem will not only be of assistance to visitors but also become an integral part of performances held on the Sim. The bots can learn scripts, respond to one another based on key words and navigate a space based on pre-scripted instructions. Attending an event performed completely by AI bots is one of the goals of this project that we believe is possible in the very near future.

5 Performance Theory and Virtual Environments

Postmodern theorists suggest that elements of race are performative in nature. When mated to the cyberworld, this "technological domain readily becomes a world of its own, dissociated from the complexity and gravity of the real world" (Robins 1995, 143). Brenda Laurel refers to cyberspace as a virtual theater where we can "satisfy the age-old desire to make our fantasies palpable, [providing] an experience where [one] can play make-believe, and where the world auto-magically pushes back" (Laurel 1990, 262-3). Joyce McDougall refers to this same space as a "psychic theater" that involves individuals who are "acting out of more basic and primitive instincts and desires" that might even include unconscious fantasies (Robins 1995, 143). Robins refers to virtual space as "constituting a protective container within which all wishes are gratified" and where the "frustrations of the real world auto-magically deferred" (143). Peter Weibel, however, describes virtuality, regardless of it's being textual or visual as a "psychotic space" where he/she existing there:

> stage-manage reality in hallucinatory wish-fulfillment, uttering the battle-cry 'VR everywhere'.... Cyberspace is the name for such a psychotic environment, where the boundaries between wish and reality are blurred (Weibel 1990, 29).

Interestingly, quite a number of literary works produced by African American authors of the late 19th and early 20th centuries portray "passing" protagonists who refer to their existence in the "white" world as a bit schizophrenic, being a part of one world, appearing to be of another, yet being fully accepted by neither.

In this psychotic space, the reality of the real world is disavowed; the coherence of the self deconstructed into fragments; and the quality of experience reduced to sensation and intoxication. It is what is evoked in the fiction of cyberpunk, where the speed of thrill substitutes for affection, reflection and care, and where, as hallucinations and reality collapse into each other, there is no space from which to reflect (Csicsery-Ronay 1991, 190-192).

Gerard Raulet refers to this sort of "schizophrenia or neo-narcissism as [a] sense of unrestricted freedom and mastery [belonging] to disembodied identities [and that] such a fantasy, when it is socially institutionalized, must have it consequences for a real world of situated identities (Robins 1995, 144). Three prominent African American authors, Jessie Fauset, James Weldon Johnson and Nella Larsen describe the serious effects of what may befall those who decide to "pass" from an existence of objectification and discrimination to one with limitless possibilities. What, then, do these three authors suggest those consequences might be? Fauset believes that the individual "passing" will ultimately see the "error of her ways" and come back to the family and that all will end happily ever after. Larsen, on the other hand, suggests that there is no return to the fold and that any attempt to do so will meet with hostility and ultimately death of some sort. Johnson, however, suggests that the decision will ultimately be that of the individual and that most will decide to remain anonymous, and materially secure but psychically unhappy and unfulfilled. All three suggest that it is society that creates the stage and is the author of the script that their characters must act out, regardless as to whether they choose to "pass" for economic, social, or material reasons. The social institutionalization of certain ideas has left the characters in their novels few choices.

As we move further into the twenty-first century, we can easily see how virtual environments enable us to "pass" in many ways through performance, exterior design of our alternate personae and through our interaction within worlds that exist in parallel with our first lives. We suggest that in the very near future there will be even more emerging ways to practice the art, that, in the digital age, offer more choices for those who wish to take advantage of various opportunities, be accepted by various communities, or even alter their surrounding environment in ways that are almost futuristic.

The inspiration for this essay comes from multiple sources, beginning with an interest and subsequent study of Jessie Fauset. Of primary interest was her under representation as a writer and critic of the early twentieth century. Through several graduate seminars in African American literature, an appreciation was developed for her writing, her background, and her positive and negative criticism of the period we now know as the Harlem Renaissance. Also of interest was Fauset's keen interest in the notion of "passing," although she could not do so herself. She does, however, encourage alternate interpretations that can be associated with the term that indicate she was "passing" in other ways. Thus, this study was narrowed to the idea of "passing" as represented by Fauset.

In addition to the work of Fauset, there are other African American writers who have written "passing" novels. Walter White, James Weldon Johnson, Nella Larsen, Charles Chesnutt, and others have all contributed to the genre. Additionally, although all three focused some of their work on "passing," and the subsequent performance associated with the act of passing, they approached the notion from totally different perspectives. Instead of adhering to the tragic mulatto theme, each constructed a new way of using the metaphor of "passing" as a vehicle to introduce more crucial issues inspired by the period such as those related to gender, identity, class, performance and, of course, race.

In 1996, an article was published in the faculty newsletter about a new organization on the University of Missouri-Columbia campus that was experimenting with advanced visualization and multimedia for use in the classroom. The director of the program, said that they were primarily interested in virtual reality (VR), and were soliciting proposals from faculty members to create projects using this new technology. The idea, related to this essay, was to re-create a portion of Harlem, New York as it existed during the 1920s, or the period known as the Harlem Renaissance, to use as visual support for classes taught on 20th century African American literature. The goals of this project continued to expand as more was learned more about virtual reality and the possibilities of visual media with relation to student comprehension and learning. These goals included fostering curricular and pedagogical reform, making more productive use of networking resources, incorporating a degree of faculty development which emphasizes the inclusion of advanced technologies, developing a national and global dissemination plan, and to develop relevant curriculum within several disciplinary areas for use within a virtual reality learning environment. While researching what exactly virtual reality was and to what extent other universities were using the technology, it was discovered that the University of Missouri was one of only a handful of universities developing the use of virtual reality for the classroom, among an even fewer number using it in an American Literature setting and the only one developing a project in the area of African American literature.

The Virtual Harlem project allows students not only to visualize the setting and context of several fictional texts in a computer-generated environment, but also enables them to interact with it by navigating through streets, interact with historical characters through questions and audio queues, and participate in its design. As students "build" a spatial context for their reading of the text, it is anticipated that their enthusiasm for research would skyrocket. Approximately ten square blocks of Harlem, NY, as it existed in the early 20th Century, have been reconstructed in a virtual reality learning environment. This environment gives students an unprecedented view of the cultural wealth and history of one of the most productive periods in African American culture -- the Harlem Renaissance, circa 1921-30. Currently, student research materials help to refine and expand upon this base, as students have the pleasure of not only navigating but also performing interdisciplinary research on the time period, providing extra dimensions to the learning environment. Interaction of this sort is only possible in a virtual environment because the goal of VR is to simulate the real world along with the non-linearity associated with navigating real-world situations and settings. To this end, one must also consider that the period that was re-created no longer exists in the form that it did during the 1920s and 30s. Historic figures are no longer living, buildings have been torn down, moved or have decayed to the extent that they are no longer recognizable, and the style of dress and use of language has changed over the years. It is anticipated that by placing users in the context in which a work of art or literature was created that the depth to which their research is focused will deepen and be more comprehensive.

As my interest in this advanced form of visualization increased and I became more knowledgeable about the technology behind the creation of computer generated environments, I began to focus my attention on how this project, which was becoming international in scope, might be somehow incorporated into this study. The connection between "passing," "performance," and in computer generated environments is not in VR technology, but found in the "avatars" that inhabit virtual worlds. Norman Badler, professor of computer and information science at the University of Pennsylvania, suggests that our generation "may be the last [one] that sees and readily knows the difference between real and virtual things" (Badler 2001, 33). Further, Badler suggests, "visual portrayals of human figures will achieve uncanny accuracy in skin, muscle, bone, hair, and exterior physiology. Humanlike models will allow the seamless transition between virtual and real images" (Badler 2001, 34).

Based on these ideas, it is not difficult to imagine virtual worlds populated by computer generated figures, that are controlled by computers or "real life" users who may or may not actually resemble the avatar they control. Additionally, with recent advances in computer processing power, it is not difficult to imagine these same figures controlled by some sort of artificial intelligence. Whomever is in control might make certain decisions as to what their avatar looks like based on the community in which they wish to be accepted, or because they feel a differing comfort level with the visuality associated with their new online persona. This differing comfort level, and the association with expanded opportunities of acceptance, relates to the notion of "passing." Granted, there are many other factors related to "passing" that are not necessarily related to avatars and cyborgs, such as racism, violence, and miscegenation, but there are some interesting connections that can made. Considering the many possibilities associated with online personae and how we soon may "be able to insert (or delete) ourselves from practically any interactive content...[viewing] ourselves and others in customized guises

– as we are, as we were, as we wish to be and likewise with other people," it is not impossible to imagine how "passing" still exists in 21st century computer generated environments (Badler 2001, 34). The possibilities for connections are endless regarding how one can configure him or herself in a computer generated environment and the reasoning behind why people decide to "pass" in real life.

This essay extends the notion of configuring oneself to realms outside of the computer so that more concrete connections can be made with the real world. Imagine one day being able to merge ourselves, in various ways, with advanced computing systems. These systems might include nanotechnology, neural networks, or advanced bionics. The merge will be seamless as we already are doing it in many ways. There are people with artificial organs, prosthetic limbs, and artificial eyes. When more is learned about human physiology and how it can be more effectively merged with advanced computing systems, we will see a rise in the development of the cyborg, or an individual who is part human and part machine. When this occurs, there is the possibility that humans will be able to configure themselves based on situational context, available opportunities, or for fun. This move will be made possible through what John von Neumann, mathematician and computer scientist, refers to as Singularity, or "the point when human progress, particularly technological progress, accelerates so dramatically that predicting what will happen next is futile" (McCullagh 2001, 1). The definition deepens to include "whether mankind will approach Singularity by way of machine intelligence alone or through augmented mental processes" suggesting that technology will assist us with our eventual move to new levels of understanding of the universe (McCullagh 2001, 1). These ideas are not totally detached from the original notion of "passing" discussed earlier. As those who "pass" seek to find acceptance within a world that often rejects them for various reasons, the reasoning behind the practice might be justified. If, however, someone is not born with the physical attributes to "pass" what are their options? Might technology, particularly that dealing with advanced computing systems, and our increasing knowledge of human anatomy and physiology, be used to supplement that which we were not born? Might someone, regardless of their racial or physical characteristics, be tempted to "pass," in whatever way they might, in order to make a better life for him or herself? The connection between technology assisted notions of "passing" and that which is purely biological appears clear. Through a literary examination of three novels of passing, a discussion of visual theory and technology, it is possible to not just blur the line between the study of the humanities and technology but attempt to demonstrate that they can and should be dependent upon one another in order to achieve our next level of human evolution and interaction with one another and our environment.

6 Future Explorations of "passing" within Virtual Worlds

In 2001, Tiger Woods became the first person to win four major pro golf tournaments in a calendar year, surprising many golf analysts who never believed someone as young as Tiger could accomplish what many considered impossible. When he began his ascendancy to greatness, Tiger, during one of his many interviews made a point of not being "labeled" African American. He instead indicated that he was actually a multitude of ethnicities, including African American, Asian, German, etc. Many in the African American community, however, were a bit dismayed with Tiger's hesitancy to embrace his African American heritage. On the surface, he "looks" black, and his father is obviously of African American heritage. Additionally, it is well known in the Black community that regardless of what you consider yourself, if you "look" black, you will usually be considered so by the rest of the world. What is it that motivates Tiger not to want to be identified as an African American? Could be partly because of the social dynamic of the game of golf, a primarily European sport, which has historically banned African American athletes, segregated them, or discounted the ability of blacks to play the sport well? In the back of Tiger's mind, could he believe that by not embracing part of his heritage that the golf community may accept him "differently"? Was Tiger, unbeknownst to his detractors, performing the ultimate trope of "passing" although he did not adhere to the historical definition of the term?

The practice of "passing" occurs in various ways. One can "pass" within or without of her race, gender, class and eventually, out of her humanity, regardless of her outward appearance. If one is not fully knowledgeable about the practice of passing and some of the subtleties associated with it, confusion, questions, and sometimes frustration can occur.

How is it then that we are able to guide those who are unfamiliar with the performance associated with "passing" to more fully understand the motives of those who choose to "pass" in various ways? When studying how people are able to "pass," the most obvious delineator is being able to "look the part," which is also one way to link the actual practice with that represented in works of literature. Visual cues are one of the tools that are used to explore various themes within a text. Those who are visual learners are often drawn to the visual nature of a text and try to construct within their minds the environment the author is trying to convey. One way to assist visual learners to more fully comprehend and thus enjoy a text is to teach them how to visualize the words on the page. Reading is an act of both visualization and identity making. According to Dennis Sumara in his essay, "Fictionalizing Acts: Reading and the Making of Identity," students are often encouraged to both visualize and to identify with various characters within a text. By doing so, they are sometimes more able to understand both the context in which the work was written as well as experience the setting from a perspective other than their own. Through visualization and identification with characters, students are able to experience and critically evaluate decisions characters must make while forming various identities within the textual environment (Sumara 2000, 15-17). These examples serve as models for students who in some way may see themselves similar to the characters about whom they are reading. Sometimes, however, this strategy is not used when dealing with displays of "passing" like that of Tiger Woods.

How, then, might the practice of "passing," whether it be current-day and real life, or that found in the fictionalized work of various authors, be best understood, synthesized and contextualized by those who don't understand the motives behind the act? How might this performance be incorporated into that which occurs within virtual environments? Some choose to "perform" some portion of their own backgrounds to further their understanding and subsequent relationship with an avatar. Some use the examples they observe in real life or read about as models for their own identity formation, using both visual and textual cues to recreate the person or character within their virtual persona. Others may choose to use the same information within only a portion of their lives, that which is concealed from "view" from the rest of the real world. In what ways do those studying the performance of "passing" choose to represent themselves within virtual worlds? How are those decisions made and what information do they have to draw upon when making choices about representation? There are no easy answers to these questions, but there are ways that we can begin to explore the motivations behind how residents of virtual environments interact with one another, which, in the long term, enhances the overall experience of everyone.

References

Badler, Norman. "Virtual Beings." Communications of the ACM 44.3 (2001): 33-35.

Csicsery-Ronay, Istvan. "Cyberpunk and Neuromanticism" Ed. Larry McCaffery, Storming the Reality Studio. Durham: Duke University Press: 1990, 182-193.

Laurel, Brenda. "On Dramatic Interaction" Ed. Gottfried Hattinger et al. Ars Electronica, vol. 2. (1990): 259-63.

McCullagh, D. Anonymity at any Cost. 1997. Web site. The Netly News. Available: http://cgi.pathfinder.com/netly/opinion/)1042,1594,00,html November 24, 1997.

McCullagh, D. "Making HAL Your Pal" . 2001 Web Site. Wired News. Available: http://www.wired.com/news/print/0,1294,43080,00.html April19, 2001.

Raulet, Gerard. "The New Utopia: Communication Technologies." Telos 87, (1991): 39 58.

Robins, Kevin. "Cyberspace and the World We Live In." Cyberspace, Cyberbodies, Cyberpunk: Cultures of Technological Embodiment. Ed. Mike Featherstone and Roger Burrows. London: Sage Publications, Inc., 1996.

Sumara, Dennis. "Fictionalizing Acts." Engaging minds: learning and teaching in a complex world / Brent Davis, Dennis Sumara, Rebecca Luce-Kapler. Mahwah, N.J.: L. Erlbaum Associates, 2000.

Weibel, Peter. "virtual worlds: The Emperor's New Body". Ed. Gottfried Hattinger et al. Ars Electronica, vol 2, (1990): 29.

Chapter 8: Role Play study in a Purchase Management class

Bjørn Jæger, Ph.D. and Berit Helgheim, Ph.D.

Molde University College
Britvn. 2, 6402 Molde, Norway
bjorn.jager@himolde.no, berit.helgheim@himolde.no

1 Introduction

This chapter summarizes the results of a pilot study investigating the use of the 3-dimensional virtual world Second Life for distributed role play exercises in a purchase management class. In practice purchasing decisions are made based on both explicit and tacit knowledge. The purpose of the role play exercise is to give students an introduction to the purchasing decision process including the importance of teams, the use of explicit and tacit knowledge and at the same time give the students an introduction to the basic characteristics of Enterprise Resource Planning (ERP) Systems. (Giunipero, Dawley and Anthony 1999) found that approximately equal amounts of formal data and tacit knowledge were used in buying decisions made by purchasing managers. Tacit knowledge relates to personal experiences, it represents knowledge that is used in evaluation, points of view, commitments and decisions. This type of knowledge is difficult to articulate or codify. In contrast, explicit knowledge is knowledge that has been codified. Explicit knowledge in the form of vendor web sites, on-line library resources, trade publications and marketing publications only takes a purchase manager half the way to make a decision. Students and inexperienced purchase managers typically break social norms and misunderstand subtle cues that experienced buyers take for granted. When teaching purchase management we would like to introduce students to the importance of tacit knowledge in making purchasing decisions. Role plays have been found to be a useful technique in teaching people-facing skills including training purchasing and sales people (Aldrich 2005). Introducing a team oriented role play to convey tacit knowledge require a rich medium capable of conveying multiple cues expressing this knowledge. Videoconferencing used for our distributed class is not a suitable tool for team oriented role plays. Given the promising results from our early experiments in using Second Life (Molka-Danielsen et al forthcoming) we decided to use Second Life to run the role play. In order to strengthen the real world relevance and motivate the students we invited experienced buyers from real business firms to participate in the role play in Second Life.

2 Role Play

Role play used for educational purposes has been a characteristic of student-centred learning environments for many years. It has been widely employed to support specified training needs like military, surgical, medical and business training (Aldrich 2005, De Freitas 2006). (Bloom

1956) argues that a role play can engage both the affective and cognitive domains. The content addressing the cognitive domain consists of the explicit material provided, hand outs, books, exams and other tangible artefacts. The affective domain relates to our attitudes, emotions, feelings and interests. Through role play learners engage in stories that are either open ended or defined by a manuscript. Role play can be described as a social activity in which players act or take on specific roles presented to them. In doing so, players get the opportunity to both share their knowledge and to extend their knowledge by learning from others. Recent developments of virtual worlds like Second Life have enabled the design of more sophisticated on-line role play environments which both mimic real world environments more closely than before, and which go beyond what is possible in real world domains (Aldrich 2005, Jones 2007). Role play has a high learning value in educational domains where skills such as critical thinking, group communication, debate and decision making are of high importance. Business education being an applied discipline is one such domain: "Business education involves studying applications of mathematics, economics and behavioural sciences to problems in the production and distribution of goods and services." (Carter et al 1986). Role playing, simulations and games have been taken up by those involved in business education to produce training scenarios needed to learn an important part of the skill sets that business leaders need. In Purchase Management, where the emphasis is upon choices, role play exercises focusing on decision making are ideal for supporting an educator's training needs (De Freitas 2006).

2.1 Role Play Case

The role play selected is Response to Request-For-Proposal for an ERP-system. This is a well developed and much used role play in Business and Management Information Systems classes described in the book Enterprise Resource Planning by Mary Sumner (Sumner 2004). The request-for-proposal has been developed to meet the needs of a fictional mid-sized manufacturing company, Wingate Electric. Wingate Electric currently has a set of computer applications handling their information management needs. However, their applications have become fragmented over time, they do not use an integrated database and they are difficult to maintain, therefore the company considers buying an ERP-system. The new system should have functions supporting its financial and accounting processes including general ledger and accounts payable/receivable, with the option of adding modules for production planning and manufacturing later on. In the role play there are three competing ERP-vendors who are responding to the request-for-proposal; Oracle, Microsoft and SAP. The class is organized into four teams, one team for each vendor and one purchasing team representing a panel of managers from Wingate Electric. The purchasing team was given a set of selection criteria and a scoring method to evaluate the three alternative financial and accounting modules. Each vendor team is required to make a sales presentation based on some given sales material and pointers to other vendor resources. Other material provided were: company background of Wingate Electric, the request-for-proposal, team directions with a list of roles with job titles and background of each role. Each vendor team gave a presentation and the Wingate managers used the selection criteria and a scoring method to decide upon a winning vendor. At the end the managers provided feedback to each vendor with respect to the how effectively each presentation addressed the selection criteria before they announced the winner.

3 Role Play in Second Life

Second life being a non-gaming virtual world imagined and created by its users can be used for conducting role plays. The primary interaction object in Second Life is an avatar which is a representation of a user in Second Life. The term was made popular by Neal Stephenson (1992) in his novel 'Snow Crash' but the word originates from the Sanskrit word Avatāra which means descent. It is used in Hinduism to describe incarnations of Vishnu the Preserver who many Hindus worship as God, this can bee seen as a form of role play. An avatar in Second Life has human characteristics, including speech and facial expressions which enables transfer of expressions in the affective domain. In the section below we present four arguments to justify bringing role playing from the real world into the virtual world. The first argument is actually a set of arguments that follows from Media Richness Theory from the Management Information Systems field, the second is cost efficiency, the third is the advantage of using external professionals from real companies in the role play, the fourth argument we claim that virtual worlds are superior to videoconferencing for role play in distance education, and the last argument is the ability to record Second Life activities to play back the role play.

3.1 Media Richness Theory

The researchers Daft and Lengel proposed that communication media have varying capacities for resolving ambiguity, negotiating varying interpretations, and facilitating understanding (Daft and Lengel 1984). Media Richness Theory has been successfully used to describe the suitability of a communications medium to communicate certain tasks. The main assumptions of Media Richness Theory are that individuals, groups, and organizations process information to reduce uncertainty and unequivocality and that some communication media are more suitable for certain tasks than other. Uncertainty is the difference between the amount of information required to perform the task and the amount of information already possessed. Equivocality is defined as the ambiguity inherent in the task caused by conflicting and inconsistent interpretations and expectations. Richness is characterized by the four properties: 1) multiplicity of cues, 2) ability to provide feedback, 3) the ability to provide personal focus, and 4) the variety of languages usable. When tasks entail processing highly equivocal information, as is required for example in the negotiation process in purchasing, then the medium that supports communications and information processing must be rich. For the task of processing of unequivocal information such as filling out a standard form then a less rich medium such as an email is suitable. A face-to-face meeting is "rich" because gestures, facial expressions, surrounding contexts, and other sensory cues provide rich supplementary information beyond spoken or written words.

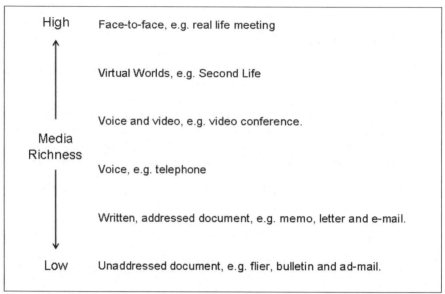

Figure 1. Media richness hierarchy and virtual worlds.

The four properties of Media Richness Theory are seen to support the use of Second Life for role play as follows: *1) multiplicity of cues.* Cues can steer participants towards issues that help makes real progress in a role play, and away from distraction ones. Cues can inform the avatar in action (purchaser or vendor) where he/she is in the process i.e. what has been delivered and what remains. Cues can monitor and report reactions of the purchaser to the vendor, and visa versa. The avatar appearance is a cue that can help to create realistic role plays (Jones 2007), as can the group memberships of an avatar. Group membership is a fundamental social structure in Second Life stored in the avatar's Profile shown by right-click on the avatar. *2) Feedback Capabilities* is supported in two ways in Second Life. First, the virtual environment supports instant feedback from other avatars and from constructs within Second Life. Secondly, feedback can be supported by using recordings. Second Life, being a mediated technology, has the intrinsic property of mediated technologies that they can be recorded, stored and played back with little effort and small costs. Recording is not an inherent option in Second Life, instead one can use screen recording programs that records all activities and the sound into a movie file for later playback. Popular recording tools are (Camtasia 2008; Fraps 2008). Recording and playback enables a post-exercise reflection of the virtual-experience and a debriefing of the experiences which is important for the learning outcome (De Freitas 2006). *3) Personal Focus* is supported by the use of avatars and the communication possibilities included in Second Life. Users can communicate via instant text messages or voice chat. Both can be used for all users, a group of users or between two users. This is not feasible to do in real life or other traditional distance education media like videoconferencing. Personal focus is also supported by the strong feeling of presence users experience when acting via their avatar in virtual worlds (Gorini et al 2008). *4) Variety of languages* is supported in Second Life through the chat facilities.

3.2 Cost Efficiency

Second Life has the capability to create a wide range of learning environments in a cost efficient way compared with real life environments. A real life role play would be substantially more expensive due to the costs of co-locating participants, allocate or rent professional meeting rooms, changing the appearance of the academics into a business style, and setting up studio recording capabilities.

3.3 Invited Professionals and Experts

One unique feature of virtual worlds is the possibility to invite professionals to participate directly in the educational situation at virtually zero monetary cost. Professionals being experts in their field can give guest lectures, advise students and participate in interactive discussions and role plays. The students can interact directly with experts letting them express individual concerns and discuss issues with less time and place constraints than required by real world meetings. In the few studies that have reported involvement of virtual guest experts in mediated teaching environments the studies have found that students were excited by the opportunity to hold discussions with the guest hosts, and vice versa; the guests were positive to spend time doing the interaction (Kumari 2001; Wearmouth et al 2004).

3.4 Virtual Worlds are superior to video conferencing for Role Play in distance education

Video conferencing is a common and contemporary technology for lecturing in distance education. At Molde University College is used to teach Purchase Management in three cities. This works fairly well for traditional lectures and exercises, but it does not support team oriented projects like a role play that depends on a medium able to convey a set of environmental and sensory cues related to interpersonal communication being part of the tacit knowledge. This can be illustrated by an example where nine persons each at a different location participate in a video conference. A typical screen seen by each participant shows a set of talking heads with each persons head sitting in front of the video camera as illustrated in Figure 2.

Figure 2. Example of a typical multi-party video conference screen showing the participants as a set of talking heads. The Image is used with permission from Mats Deutschmann.

The video server collects separate video streams, orders them into one video stream showing each of the nine environments separately as a video-in-video, and distributes the stream to each of the participants. The ability to show group membership and coordinate activities between participants is very limited in this environment. Now consider having the same meeting in Second Life. By using the possibilities of virtual worlds to create a common virtual environment for all to experience one can create realistic environments familiar to the participants. All participants observes the same virtual environment in which they can easily group themselves according to team membership and their role in the meeting in the same way as in real life. Acting via an avatar also means that they see themselves in the setting which is not possible in videoconferencing. At the same time they have a range of communication facilities at their hands including full voice chat between all participants like in videoconferencing in addition to group voice chat and instant text messaging. This is illustrated in Figure 3.

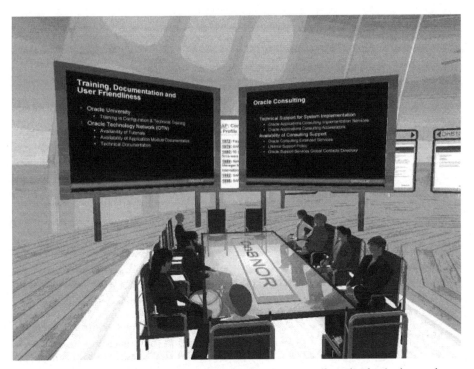

Figure 3. Meeting held in Second Life. The image is from our pilot role play in the purchase management class at the DnB NOR site in Second Life.

We conclude that the four properties of Media Richness Theory, the cost efficiency, the possibility to invite guests from real businesses, and the advantages of using Second Life over video conferences all strongly support the use of Second Life for role playing.

4 Pilot Role Play Study

Molde University College teaches the course Purchase Management in three different cities; Molde, Ålesund and Kristiansund using videoconferencing equipment. Purchase Management would like to run a role play related to the process of buying large complex products that affects the whole organization. Videoconferencing is not well suited for this since it is hard to get several people at several places to discuss/talk simultaneously as is required in the role play. Distributing multi-party voice and video to all participants require network support beyond what is usual in typical Internet connections not only due to the substantial bandwidth requirements, but also because of the lack of quality-of-service guarantees in the contemporary Internet. Based on our early experiments in using Second Life (Molka-Danielsen, J. et al forthcoming), we decided to use Second Life to run the role play. This required a new setup with three classes at three locations. We had no experience in running Second Life in three locations simultaneously with a class with several students at each location. We needed technical equipment, time for training participants, and time to make the learning material. It became clear that running a full-scale role play in Second Life would be a highly risky attempt, thus we decided to do initial investigations by running a Pilot Study in

March 2008 to test logistics and gather information prior to the full-scale test to be done in March 2009. The role play selected for the pilot test, "Response to Request for Proposal for an ERP system" is used by another standard on-campus course as well, BØK700 Enterprise Resource Planning with SAP, which gave us additional information. Our path to integrating the role play in the course is illustrated in Figure 4.

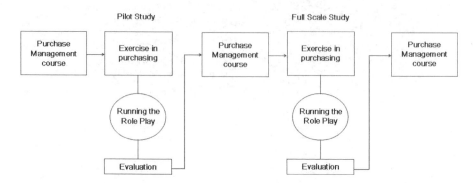

Figure 4. The role play is embedded into the Purchase Management course by going through a pilot study and a full scale study.

4.1 Guest Experts

For the study four professionals in four Norwegian companies were asked to participate in the role-play. All of them were enthusiastic and would do the guest appearance pro bono for the course. The professionals had experience from using ERP-systems and from buying and selling large complex software systems. The four companies asked were: DnB NOR (DnB NOR 2008), Ernst and Young, The Norwegian Labour and Welfare Administration (NAV) and Wise Consulting (Jæger & Helgheim 2008). The professionals were excited to be using Second Life to get in direct contact with students/academia. Reasons mentioned were: it might help in recruiting new employees, enable new innovative business opportunities, and use Second Life as a collaborative tool for team work. Due to the limited scope of our pilot study we only used DnB NOR in the test. DnB NOR are familiar with Second Life through the use of their own island in Second Life, and DnB NOR provided the professional meeting room in Second Life that were used for the role play illustrated in Figure 3.

5 Conclusion and future work

The results of the pilot study and the theoretical evaluation indeed shows that Role Play in Second Life has potential to enhance learning outcome of educational efforts when learning concepts in Purchase Management and large complex software products like Enterprise Resource Planning systems. In the full scale study we will adjust the role play as described above and in (Jæger & Helgheim 2008). A particular interesting topic we will seek to explore is the use of external experts and their identity in the role play. Questions raised are: Should they be anonymous, semi anonymous or identifiable? To what extent should they participate in or be allowed to affect the role play? To what extent should the students interact with the experts? Another issue we would like to try out is the use of MODs: Moderators. MODs are much used in computer games to ensure a fair game and that the game is run in accordance with the owners wish. A form of moderator role should be investigated for educational purposes as well, especially regarding the dynamic in-the-situation use of remunerations and penalties to help steering students to achieve the learning goals.

References

Aldrich, C. (2005). Learning by doing. San Francisco. CA. Pfeiffer.

Bloom, B.S. (1956). The Taxonomy of Educational Objectives: Classification of Educational Goals Handbook 1: The Cognitive Domain. New York: McKay Press.

Camtasia. (2008). Last retrieved 15th September 2008 at: http://www.techsmith.com/

Carter, P., Hickman, J., McDonald, P., Patton, R. & Powell, D. C. (1986). Memorandum on Applied and Experiential Learning Curriculum Development. St. Louis: American Assembly of Collegiate Schools of Business.

Daft, R.L., and Lengel, R.H. (1984). "Information richness: a new approach to managerial behavior and organizational design". In: Cummings, L.L. & Staw, B.M. (Eds.), Research in organizational behavior 6, (191-233). Homewood, IL: JAI Press.

DnB NOR. (2008). DnB NOR. Last retrieved 15th September 2008 at: https://www.dnbnor.com

Fraps. (2008). Last retrieved 15th September 2008 at: http://www.fraps.com/

De Freitas, S. (2006) Learning in Immersive worlds. Joint Information Systems Committee (JISC) e-Learning Programme, UK. Last retrieved 15th September 2008 at: http://www.jisc.ac.uk/media/documents/programmes/elearninginnovation/gamingreport_v3.pdf

Giunipero, L., Dawley, D., and Anthony W. P. (1999). "The Impact of Tacit Knowledge on Purchasing Decisions," The Journal of Supply Chain Management, vol.35, no. 1, pp. 42-49, 1999.

Gorini, G., Gaggioli, A., Vigna, C., and Riva, G. (2008). "A Second Life for eHealth: Prospects for the Use of 3-D Virtual Worlds in Clinical Psychology", Journal of Medical Internet Research, 10(3):e21, Last retrieved 10th October 2008 at: http://www.jmir.org/2008/3/e21/

Jones, S. (2007). "Adding value to online role plays: Virtual situated learning environments", Proceedings of Ascilite, Singapore 2007.

Jæger, B., and Helgheim, B. (2008). "Results from a Role Play Exercise in Second Life for LOG505 and BØK700," Working Paper/Arbeidsnotat 2008:11, Molde University College, Norway.

Kumari (2001). Connecting graduate students to virtual guests through asynchronous discussions – Analysis of an experience. Journal of Asynchronous Learning Networks, 5(2), 53-63.

Molka-Danielsen, J., W. Carter, B. W., Richardson, D., and Jæger, B. (forthcoming). "Teaching and Learning Affectively within a Virtual Campus," Int. J. Networking and Virtual Organisations, Vol.x, No.x.

Stephenson, N. (1992). Snow Crash, Bantam Spectra Book, New York.

Sumner, M. (2004). Enterprise Resource Planning, Prentice Hall, 2004.

Wearmouth J., Smith, A.P., and Soler, J. (2004). Computer conferencing with access to a 'guest expert' in the professional development of special educational needs coordinators. British Journal of Educational Technology, 35(1), 81-93.

Chapter 9: Learning by creating historical buildings

Marco Bani, Francesco Genovesi, Elisa Ciregia, Flavia Piscioneri, Beatrice Rapisarda, Enrica Salvatori, Maria Simi

University di Pisa, Italia

e.salvatori@mediev.unipi.it; rapisard@df.unipi.it; simi@di.unipi.it

Chapter Overview. This chapter will provide an account of an educational experiment made at the University of Pisa in the 2007-2008 academic year, and that will continue next year. This experiment consists of the use and exploitation of Second Life as a teaching/learning platform in the context of a multidisciplinary and international project spanning several courses. In a few months students were able to achieve high quality recreations of historical buildings, while learning about history, multimedia production, and 3D modelling in virtual worlds in the process.

1 Introduction

The current generation's university students are "digital natives" (Prensky 2001), i.e. they have great familiarity with new technologies, being raised in an environment in which games and the web are ubiquitous and information technology is easily accessible.

Moreover, the increasing diffusion and success of easy-to-use multimedia authoring tools, together with libraries of digital assets and community sites have enabled the creation of an ever increasing number of amateur multimedia products, whose potential for communication among the new generations is incredible (Bardzell 2007). Among the new platforms supporting these new forms of creativity, Second Life (SL), a multi-user participant-created 3D world, has achieved a great diffusion, by offering off-the-shelf components (avatars, scripted objects, and animations) that can be easily modified, reused, and bought.

Classrooms and traditional education can hardly keep pace in this world. Betting on a tool like SL, to be used side by side with other more traditional ways of learning, can be a winning move in improving the learning process, for it puts instruments that are varied and innovative within an easy reach, enables teachers to engage in educational experimentation regarding both the learning environment and its content, and focuses on the interactions between teachers and students.

The potential to offer a learner-centred educational philosophy, sharing many similarities with constructivist and active learning paradigms, makes SL an advanced place (or better, a *no-place*) of training, where learners are faced with real life problems and challenges, which allows them to develop strong skills of relevance, critical thinking and reflection (Mason 2007).

When students are asked to design an immersive experience that effectively communicates a message, they are required to research and reflect in depth. If they can construct an item or repurpose existing content into a new experience that teaches others, they will also acquire deep understanding.

The teachers' role is to give participants the tools to engage actively in the construction of their experiences and to learn how to create far greater levels of interactivity, not just between users, or between users and the Internet, but between complementary online services and Web services, virtual worlds, and Web 2.0 tools.

For users unfamiliar with online gaming, the initial introduction to virtual worlds can be particularly confusing, since learners are co-learners and co-authors, making the educator identity more complicated; indeed, the roles of teachers and students can at times be inverted.

The ramifications are that teachers will have to reinvent themselves (Joseph 2007). It is not essential to know everything about SL in order to use it in teaching – more important is to know how to connect students with people who do know. In a social network, information and people are ever-present and affordable; educators who can use these networks and train their students to do the same need not rely on being the expert imparting knowledge, but become facilitators connecting students with sources of knowledge and skills. As teachers become facilitators and students specialize and improve their skills, learners are able informally to teach one another when required. Rather than isolate learners from one another, or discourage side conversations, the interactions between students can be where some of the best learning takes place, for all involved. Thanks to the ability to easily create digital reports and the provision of tools to encourage collaboration, SL is a great way to facilitate teamwork.

A sandbox is always a popular place in SL, because it is where residents often hang out and simply play by building things together. A solitary educational task in SL can be turned from dull to exciting when done by a team.

Combining elements of current, asynchronous, and synchronous learning environments you can create virtual classes; these are starting to become increasingly common as more and more schools offer online courses in SL. The virtual environment makes it possible to create an endless number of different situations and interpersonal relationships, in which students learn different styles of linguistic interaction and behaviour appropriate to their perceived immersion in an alternative world.

Class can meet both face-to-face and inside SL. Logs of their experiences, and class discussions can be analyzed, making it possible to identify patterns of perceptions, frustrations, and solutions that occur as students learn new skills.

Teachers, who have to face the lack of an efficient way to locate, share, or evaluate the many educational builds available, could give students opportunities to use tools within and outside of the SL environment to present information, in order to afford the experience of a range of tools, thereby expanding the learning experience.

In this experimental context, an important field being explored is the use of virtual worlds for teaching and learning about history, art, and cultural heritage. Several projects aim at creating a virtual counterpart to historical buildings of the present or of the past. In the reconstruction of historical buildings, especially for educational purposes, it is important to follow specific rules in order to ensure that such work is intellectually and technically rigorous (Ryan 1996). In this chapter, we report on a teaching/learning experience performed as part of the study programme in *Informatica Umanistica* (i.e. Humanities computing, now on InfoUma) at the University of Pisa: in particular students were involved in the construction of the Leaning Tower of Pisa, Galileo's laboratory, and a meeting centre, called Arketipo, in SL.

InfoUma offers an interdisciplinary curriculum where students receive a solid education in humanities together with the technological skills and methodologies to master the tools for processing cultural contents in different digital forms. Most of the students involved in the project specialize in a graduate level curriculum called 'Graphics, Interactivity, Virtual Environments'. Given their specific background, students have the necessary competences to be the main actors in the construction of artefacts in SL.

The project has been carried on with an international partner so that students have the opportunity to learn about different cultures and acquire language skills. A one-year collaboration project has been established between the *Centre for Computing in the Humanities* of the King's College in London (CCH) and InfoUma at the University of Pisa, with the goal to foster new advanced educational activities and to explore research issues in the use of virtual worlds in the field of Humanities Computing. The project consists in creating and running a joint work environment in SL, where to develop shared educational activities. This space is called the *Digital Humanities Island* (DHI).

The project is multi-disciplinary: students learn about history, art, 3D modelling, interaction programming, and communication with new media. The DHI is used as a shared platform for the educational activities of several courses: 3D Graphics, History and Gaming to start with. Other disciplines of the curriculum in InfoUma will hopefully be involved along the way. This virtual space is used by the students of both institutional partners under the supervision of their teachers, following methodological guidelines established and agreed-upon.

In order to assess the utility, potential impact, and future perspectives of the project, a number of meetings, information exchanges, and consultations have been carried out with public organizations (Fondazione Regione Toscana, Università di Pisa, CNR Pisa, Regione Lombardia) and private ones (Opera del Duomo, Big Bang Solutions). As a result, we have gained a strong idea that the job market is going to offer a growing number of opportunities for people skilled in 3D modelling applied in particular to the study and reconstruction of historical-artistic objects. Moreover, we acknowledge that international research in humanities computing recognizes three-dimensional reconstruction of historical objects and buildings as one of the most important and challenging themes (EPOCH).

An important benefit of the collaboration with the CCH has been the introduction to the methodological principles that are currently discussed by the international community interested in the reconstruction of historical buildings and environments (EPOCH). The reference for these guidelines is a document called the London Charter (The London Charter) that establishes internationally recognized standards with respect to the specific qualities of three-dimensional visualisation in historical research and education. The Charter touches upon several properties of such artefacts, namely: intellectual integrity, reliability, transparency, documentation, standards, sustainability, and access.

Since the beginning, the team from Pisa has had a commitment to adopt the principles of the London Charter, particularly those recommending a strong connection between the historical research and the transparency of the applied methodologies. In fact, modelling complex historical monuments immediately raises various issues concerning the external communication of what we are doing: how to pass the methodological validity of what is being made, by which means, and in which circumstances to the visitor? Some solutions have been found in the creation of explicatory panels, audio guides, and interactive objects, such as Iumi, a mascot acting as a mobile guide.

2 The Digital Humanities Island (DHI)

We took possess of the DHI in October 2007 and started building shortly afterwards (http://slurl.com/secondlife/Digital%20Humanities/132/72/32). In a few months the following historical buildings and spaces were created:
1. Galileo's laboratory: a virtual reconstruction of the laboratory of Galileo Galilei;
2. the Leaning Tower;
3. Arketipo: the island orientation centre, built on several stories, hosting meeting and exhibition facilities, teachers offices, and community meeting places;
4. a work area (*sandbox*) where the students have the possibility of experimenting with the construction of objects and buildings.
5. other projects done by the students of CCH, including a reconstruction of the Tower of London.

2.1 Galileo's Laboratory

Galileo's laboratory was modelled after the laboratory set up in the building of *Vecchi Macelli* (the old slaughter house) in Pisa by the Galileo Galilei Foundation (Figure 1).

The students of the 3D Graphics course recreated the laboratory in SL, including some of the objects and experiments contained there. This task was proposed as an intermediate assignment during the course. Students were encouraged to apply techniques and suggestions discussed in class. The lecturer acted as a supervisor, leaving the students free to express themselves according to their artistic taste and technical skills. Students where able to organize in subgroups and distribute the work evenly among them, each student contributing to the group according to his/her capacity.

The students of *Introduction to historical studies* produced historical background information, about Galileo Galilei's life and work, his importance in the History of Science, and his most important experiments. In addition to text, eleven audio files were mixed and edited in a professional manner with music and theme songs. They were made available in the SL Galileo's Lab and from the Galileo Galilei Foundation web site (http://www. illaboratoriodigalileogalilei.it/audio.html) (in Italian).

The interaction between students of the two courses took place in real and virtual meetings: the 3D Graphics students where formally introduced to the London Charter principles (that became a set of shared guidelines in the DHI) and the History students visited Galileo's Lab in SL while it was being built.

Inside the laboratory there is also a library and Galileo's telescope. Clicking on the library, which is divided into three sections (process, life, theories), you get a list of links to books written by Galileo and/or talking about the great scientist. Obviously, they're all accessible online via web. Clicking on the telescope, based on the one located at the Museum of History of Science in Florence, the avatar is teleported "in the centre of the universe", that is a spherical environment where a satellite image of the universe is reproduced on the walls.

The chief architect for Galileo's laboratory was an undergraduate student with previous experience as a SL builder.

2.2   The Tower of Pisa

The construction of the Leaning Tower is part of a more ambitious project which has the approval of the organization who owns the rights of the image of the monument (the 'Opera del Duomo') and aims at visualising the phases of the construction of the Miracles Square in time. The first step has been the construction of the Tower of Pisa.

Given the complexity of the monument, a faithful and detailed reconstruction is really stressing the possibilities of SL as a modelling and rendering platform. It is a fact that the quality of the graphics in SL does not compare favorably with professional productions; on the other hand, we are interested in exploring the opportunities in communication and education provided specifically by SL. A professional 3D model of the Tower was already available from the Opera del Duomo but, due to its complexity, could not be exploited: for this project the Tower had to be built from scratch within SL.

2.3   Arketipo

Arketipo is a reception centre especially designed and built from scratch for the students and teachers of InfoUma and CCH.

The centre makes available a number of services for orientation, information, promotion, and creation of a community, by integrating and merging a number of useful instruments already existing in the InfoUma universe: website, mailing lists, wiki, forum (Figure 2).

Arketipo main goal was to support and enhance the sense of community among students of both institutions and to further support shared educational activities and collaboration. Special care was reserved to the communication and visual interaction strategy, resulting in innovative solutions, such as interactive pillars and Iumi, a mascot acting as mobile guide. Arketipo was inaugurated in September 2008. The opening event, with over 40 avatars participating and more willing to join and blocked by the server, was a great success within the metaverse, and we received enthusiastic comments from SL experts.

3 Opportunities and problems of an interdisciplinary approach

SL offers the opportunity to give classes in laboratory with students learning by experimenting with the virtual environment both for navigating and extending the environment with new objects and capabilities. Moreover, due to the chat capabilities the virtual world is also a natural place for occasional or regular meetings that may take place outside the standard classes that students are required to attend, offering a continuum in the interaction with the teacher, which is otherwise impossible.

The main goal of the course, in which SL was introduced, is to teach 3D modelling. Therefore SL is not only the medium used to communicate, but also the ground where students can put into practice what they learn about 3D models and the tool chain used to convert these models into SL objects. This is not an easy task: it can be difficult for students with background in humanities to face such a rich environment, having to understand usage and limitations of SL, and at the same time encourage them to move to more professional modelling tools.

The availability of an interactive virtual world that can be modified by users through avatars is important because it allows not only a form of e-learning and remote interaction with the teacher, but also a common playground in which students expand their abilities by filling the world with content.

Content is the key player in every SL experience since it is what users look for and students are encouraged to provide. But content can have very different forms in a 3D virtual world, including hypertexts, 3D interactive models, pictures, and videos. To provide content two aspects must be taken into account: gathering of the required information, and having the technical ability to convert this information in the particular media chosen for the presentation.

In the Galileo Laboratory experience in which students have been encouraged in filling with 3D content a building with objects related to the experiments of the famous scientist. In this case the content is made available in terms of interactive 3D models, which the students had realized during the course. Since we were interested in a specific historical period, the first step was collecting the information about the building and the objects to be modelled. In this phase of the project a little historical research was required, especially for the reconstruction of the building, that still exists, but has been subjected to changes over time. Also paintings, carpets and furniture have been selected to be compatible with Galileo's epoch in order to create a suitable context for visitors. In other projects the historical analysis may be more significant, in particular if the goal is to reconstruct a building in its original form starting from the actual one.

The Galileo Laboratory is shaped after a real laboratory that exists in Pisa where famous experiments and instruments have been reproduced in their original form. Students have been asked to use the knowledge from the course to build 3D models of these instruments and place them inside the virtual building. In this way an interactive visit to the laboratory has become possible, including the interaction with the instruments that have taken advantage of the physical simulation engine featured by the SL player to make them work as they would in the real world.

Three-dimensional content is not the only form of content included in the laboratory, students from the History course have produced audio descriptions of experiments and paintings so that the visitor can get a rich amount of information both in audio and text form. Entering the Laboratory of Galileo in the DHI, in fact, you can click on the paintings hung on the walls and you will immediately receive a notecard written by students. Also, the visitor is offered a link, which allows him to listen to streaming podcasts on Galileo or about the History of Science.

The organization of this work – how it is comprehensible – has involved a remarkable amount of work to build an interdisciplinary link between History, 3D Graphic, and Digital Audio. However, the efforts have been rewarded. From the educational point of view, the students have found engaging the perspective to build, to construct, and to elaborate a "product" meant to be viewed, read, and listened outside the University: a most powerful stimulus not only to study, but also to communicate well what has been learned. By choosing to create an audio guide within an historical interactive building we favoured "skills" over "knowledge" – in teaching History. But in the end we also have reached good outcomes in the field of knowledge, because the remarkable engagement in building and discussing has pushed students to study hard and nearly spontaneously, increasing their attitude to criticize; SL makes them feel at ease in discussions and encourages them to clearly state their thoughts (Salvatori 2007).

Therefore in the Galileo Galilei Lab, the formative aspect is central: through this experience students learn how to read and summarize a text, how to create a podcast and they gain 3D modelling skills jointly with an appreciation of the guidelines of the London Charter about the modelling of historical monuments.

So far we have described the laboratory as a static place where the visitor simply looks around and possibly interacts with objects. But by exploiting the capability of the SL virtual world, it is possible to do more since scripts can control avatars. We have created a play using avatars as virtual actors reciting a famous Galileo's dialog. Avatars have been dressed with appropriate cloths and shaped after the aspect of characters inspired from paintings of the epoch.

The play also exploited the ability to control facial expressions and mouth of the avatars so that the visitor can see characters speaking while moving in a room. The only limit of this approach is that actor-avatars must be SL clients connected to SL in order to see them act. Thus, the play is available only if manually started and not upon request at any time.

The worldwide availability of the virtual world also lets students from not only different courses, but also from different universities and countries to interact together. This experience lets students feel like they are part of a whole which is bigger than the class they attend and the persistence and public availability of their work encourages them to put their best efforts in this project. The international collaboration among students (in our experience among University of Pisa and London King's College students) is very interesting because the group-work encourages not only people with different background but also with different cultures to interact with one another. In particular the behavioural rules and other aspects of social interaction tend to vary from country to country, forming an opportunity to learn habits but also offering chances for arguments.

SL is not to be considered just an e-learning media to provide students with content, but as a playground in which content is both consumed and created together, allowing students to collaborate, exchange information, and interact with teachers. Moreover the interdisciplinary aspects that converge allow different courses with different goals to share this playground contributing with their specific knowledge in building something that is not just homework but something that can be used by everyone. If this environment is used consistently over time students in one year may benefit from the work already done in the previous, consolidating existing work as well as creating new.

3.1 Using a Wiki

As understood from previous paragraphs, the construction of the historical buildings in SL and also the realization of the welcome center has involved several subjects taught in our study programme linked by interdisciplinary ties. If at the educational level these ties have been created and managed by teachers, for the operational team, composed of teachers and students, we had to think of a more advanced and effective tool. The choice was made to use a wiki, a collection of web pages designed to enable anyone who accesses it to contribute or modify content and to support collaborative work. This job was done by a student, after an internship in SL, as her thesis project. She started and managed a wiki fully centred on the presence of InfoUma in SL (http://iu.di.unipi.it/wiki/index.php/IU_Second_Life) (in Italian).

Perhaps the most interesting part of the Wiki is the section "SL in education", dedicated to a reflection on SL as an educational environment – where you recreate traditional educational places and objects such as classrooms, chairs, desks –, as a learning content – where you rebuild the objects of study in three dimensions (objects such as molecules, planetary systems, monuments, historical buildings), and finally as a place of exposure, that is as a showcase presentation of teaching.

4 The tension between research, education and implementation

The main challenge, in building the Tower of Pisa and the Galileo Lab, was to obtain the best possible compromise between the principles of the London Charter and the rules and limitations of the 3D modelling and rendering platform of SL.

This Charter aims to define the basic objectives and principles of the use of 3D visualisation methods in relation to intellectual integrity, reliability, transparency, documentation, standards, sustainability, and access. The first two aims, intellectual integrity and reliability, are meant to warrant, by whom accepts the Charter, the intellectual and technical rigour in using 3D visualisation methods: i.e. maintaining proportions, choosing good and well explained texture, making decisions on shapes and colours that match with the discoveries of scientific research (Meulenberg, de Rode 2003; Ogleby 1999).

In the reconstruction of historical buildings the main issues addressed were the exactitude of the proportions and the amount of detail that could be afforded. A choice was made that the correspondence between the virtual monument and the real one had to be carefully respected. This is not an obvious choice to make in SL. In fact, considering that the average inhabitant of SL is two meters high, usability requirements would suggest the creation of buildings with ceilings and doors higher than normal so that avatars can move in them without problems. In this case, the principles of the London charter were given the precedence.

A similar trade-off concerns the amount of detail that can be afforded: a high quality and detailed reconstruction would require complex 3D models and would slow down the rendering thus, again, compromising usability. This issue was especially critical in the Leaning Tower project.

A graduate student was given the important mission of reconstructing the symbol of the town, the Leaning Tower, paradigmatic for its cultural and artistic value, in DHI according to the principles established by the London Charter and taking into account the specific rules and limitations of the SL virtual world.

The challenge was not an easy one. First, she had to study and research the Tower: she consulted the web site (http://torre.duomo.pisa.it/) (in Italian and English) for an appreciation of the aesthetic aspects, and researched in the library of the Department of Civil Engineering for information about the structure and building charts. At first sight it may look like the structure is simple, composed of well defined solid shapes, but looking more carefully the Tower is a building full of surprises and peculiarities. By studying the charts, she was able to appreciate differences that are impossible to notice with your eyes: the heights, the radiuses, the inclinations, and the thickness of the walls, for example, are different from one stage to the next. Every capital is unique: the engraved figures, the writings, the materials used are really diverse.

The work of recreating the Tower proved to be more difficult and interesting than expected. She had to become confident with the modelling environment, not having previous experiences with the SL platform and its rules. The building interface is intuitive enough: ten solid shapes are made available as building blocks (better known as primitives or *prims*), which assembled together, or better *linked*, allow to construct any desired object shape. The first serious problem to be tackled was connected to the requirement that real dimensions had to be respected. SL does not allow users to build cubes larger than 10×10×10 meters, or cylinders with a diameter greater than 5 meters. A big cube is easily built by linking several smaller cubes together up to the desired dimensions, but how to build a cylinder with a 10 meters radius as the one required by the base of the Tower?

By resorting to the community for help, she was able to solve the problem with a specific tool that allows approximating a cylinder by joining together sides with a suitable inclination. Figure 3 shows the creation of a polygon with a 9-meter radius (Figure 3).

The greater the number of sides, the more rounded the surface will appear. The price to pay is that the number of primitives increases and the constraint that every land in SL has an upper limit on the number of prims that can be rendered (15,000 for a regular sim) can become a severe limiting factor. The number of solids tended to increase very quickly since every stage had to be dealt with a composite and independent element; so the builder was subtracting "building material" from her colleagues. The decision to limit the number of sides for each stage and to maintain well defined only the base was a necessary one. For the same reason she decided not to build the 296 internal steps (however useless since avatars are able to fly and can be teleported on top), and refrained from modelling all the different capitals (some of them even lacking suitable photographic documentation).

A further simplification of the Tower was suggested also because of the *lag,* i.e. the delay in rendering introduced by the complexity and potential accessibility problems. The "lag" may be caused by different factors: the presence of too many avatars, buggy scripts, and preference settings concerning the quality of the graphics not adequate for the client hardware. To access SL it is necessary to have a very powerful video board in order to visualize and appreciate all the details of a complex structure. Most users, even if they can navigate with high quality graphic settings, tend to prefer higher mobility to detailed renderings of the scene. High quality is nevertheless priced high by experts in the field (Figure 4).

The result is a careful compromise between the number of *prims* used and the requirement of quality and fidelity to the original. The general impression was achieved by careful planning of the prims and exploiting a number of different textures produced ad-hoc to supply additional detail, even a 'used' effect, in a way that gives justice to the beauty of the monument. The snapshot to the left of Figure 3 gives an idea of the high quality of the result, even at an intermediate stage of the construction; the one to the right suggests the complexity of the model.

From the educational and cultural point of view, the student learned a lot: she had the opportunity to see closer and in more detail a monument that she was used to seeing every day, without fully appreciating its uniqueness. In her words: "It was like rediscovering the Tower by seeing it with new more interested eyes".

5 Applicability of the London Charter

In the previous section we have explained as we tried to resolve some technical problems in buildings historical monuments in SL, in order to create realistic and scientifically correct 3D models. However the London Charter guidelines are not limited to the exactitude of the proportions or the accuracy of appearance. A great part of the Charter principles concern in fact the need for transparency and communication (Cantone 2002; Denard 2005). In short, if the Leaning Tower has several different capitals, and if Galilei has invented the hydro chronometer (water clock) reproduced in the 3D laboratory, how did we obtain this information? How we elaborated these findings and which techniques were used in order to recreate these objects? These questions concern the transparency of information. In fact the London Charter states: "*sufficient information should be provided to allow 3d visualisation methods and outcomes to be understood and evaluated appropriately in relation to the contexts in which they are used and disseminated*".

From this point of view, SL is not by itself a good environment for transparency. Visiting a virtual environment, SL users think to find there almost everything, as SL appears as a "self-contained" world. This is not so: to access SL or to purchase dresses or land or to learn how to move, SL needs information that can be found in the web. If this is true for basic steps, the 3D reconstruction of historical buildings needs – in terms of information – ten or one hundred times more. So obviously SL cannot be seen as separate from the web, it needs the web as a source of information.

So the first choice we made, in order to maintain a certain degree of transparency, was to put the greater part of our information on the Web, in the wiki platform for example, and to link some panels of our SL building with our pages. But this is not enough. In fact, more detailed documents on historical monuments are mostly in libraries and archives. Therefore an authentic "Operation Transparency" would involve the transformation of all the source documents about an historical building in digital form and then, their further transformation in web pages, captured through SL panels. This job has not been made yet, since it involves considerable costs and time, but also because the effective reading of these materials through SL would not be easy. For these reasons we choose to give in SL the link to some useful web pages, but to provide also simplified information, by short texts and audio. We are perfectly aware that this cannot be considered a real transparency, but only a good spreading of knowledge, but we think that now the virtual world can not allow more.

In any case the activation of interactive objects that give back texts and audio, and that can capture websites, video and images, has involved a large effort to communicate correctly experiences and knowledge. This has been possible giving great attention to the problem of the interaction between man and virtual world, topic that is dealt in the next section.

6 Experiments in avatar-computer interaction

HCI (*Human Computer Interaction*) is the discipline concerned with the design, evaluation, and implementation of interactive computer systems for human users. The design of interactive man-machine interfaces is no easy matter, and designing *avatar*-machine interface for *SL* can be even more difficult. In accessing a virtual world, the user must first learn the *client* interface and, then, identify the interface that has been created on purpose for the space where he/she is interacting through the avatar interface, which changes continuously depending on the places *(sim)* being visited.

This can produce a *matrjoska effect* caused by a lack of standardization and often generates confusion.

6.1   Interaction in the Galileo's lab

A main issue in the construction and equipment of the laboratory has been the *affordance* of objects and the environment, i.e., following Norman (Norman 2002), the *property they have to make their action possibilities of use readily perceived to an actor*. In our case, the main problem was how to lead visitors to discover the valuable information provided about Galileo and the experiments, hidden in the laboratory, i.e. in pictures hanging on the walls, books and other objects.

At this stage, SL still does not have strong conventions, as the Web. Apparently, everything that works is fine. Design is guided by common sense and a more or less educated personal taste, but usability guidelines are lacking. So in order to make the interaction of the avatars with the environment as natural as possible we explored several ideas, some of them innovative.

A common solution is issuing notecards when entering a place or touching an object. But how, in a natural manner, to suggest that certain objects carry important information? Or lead visitors to discover which objects hold scripts and behaviour? Among the solutions we have explored to attract the visitor's attention are *rotating signs* and *glowing objects*, borrowing some of the conventions used in other contexts, such a video games. This way these special objects will stand out from the others, by a rule of contrast, and the avatar is encouraged to click on them to obtain information (through notecards, websites or podcasts) or to activate specific behaviour (like the animation of Galileian experiments).

6.2   Interaction in Arketipo

An important issue in DHI was making information easily available to the different types of visitors, ranging from absolute beginners, as first year students, to SL experts or simple lurkers.

The Arketipo reception centre was especially made for teachers and students of InfoUma (but other people are welcome as well), and offers multifaced services integrating and merging equally effective instruments already existing in the InfoUma universe: website, blog, forum, mailing list. Moreover we wanted the centre to become an effective *bonding place* where the reference community could meet and engage in a number of activities introducing them to the InfoUma culture.

Information is available both in *asynchronous* (by way of special panels, interfaces, notecards) and *synchronous* mode (congress hall, interactive virtual guide).

We can introduce some of the solutions adopted by resorting to some fictitious scenarios.
   Sam is a SL expert user. He read on the InfoUma website an article on a SL reception centre for new entry students. By clicking on the *slurl* (*Second Life Universal Resource Locator*) after installing and starting the SL client, he goes automatically to the entrance hall of the centre. A number of monolite-like panels rise in front of him. Each of these interface panels bears a name: *Rules, Teleport Information, IumI*. When approaching the panels, a rotating script effect is activated to attract the user's attention on the buttons, which, when

clicked, will release information or services. If the monolite is clicked by error, the monolite itself will send a message in the local chatroom to suggest the correct way to interact, i.e. clicking on the buttons.

Pam knows little to nothing about SL, but she is interested in the centre. She read on the Arketipo blog (http://arketipo-sl.blogspot.com/) (in Italian) that SL hosts a reception centre of InfoUma and CCH. Following the instructions, Pam came to the reception platform with a newly created *avatar*. She looks around carefully, she is barely able to move around, but, happily enough, the monolites explain everything, and all is at a click's reach.

Tam knows little to nothing about SL, but he has the good idea of taking *Iumi* on his shoulders. He can hardly move around, but *Iumi* talks with him and tells him what to do, explaining that information can be reached by clicking on the various objects. So, Tam gets immediate access to information and services even if he has skipped the introduction.

DHI visitors land exactly in the middle of the arrival platform (as shown in the picture). They are welcomed by the Arketipo interface, a set of four interactive pillars (Figure 5).

Figure 5. Arketipo interface   Figure 6. Rotating text and teleport panel

The best interface is immediately forgotten, thus allowing the user to focus on information. As a design criteria, the builder tries to focus on elegance and essentiality, by combining and arranging the elements in the various panels in an effective and intuitive way. When approaching any of these panels, within a range of 5 meters, a round-rotating script associated to the buttons is enabled and a rotating text appears around the buttons, explaining their function. This is the only *non-static* element and is especially designed to immediately catch the user's attention on the action to be done. This rotating effect only appears within a certain distance from the avatar, thus preventing any visual interference problem.

Contents have different functions and are conveyed in different forms. In some cases, SL standard information *notecards* are offered, in other cases SL's integration features are used to directly access the web.

The *Teleport* deserves a special mention. This panel allows a person to be immediately tele-transported to the required area. In order to differentiate between levels in the building, a legend has been implemented in the *associating perception* style: the user easily associates the two upper buttons to level I and the lower two to level -I by exploiting form and colour as clues. In practice, the black buttons refer to one level, the white buttons to another. This idea was tested on different subjects and proved easily understandable and intuitive.

6.3 Iumi, the virtual guide

When you create a community, it is essential to establish a reference symbol representing a specific group with a specific identity. Happily, this symbol already existed in the logo of InfoUma, a character which is a bizarre combination of a book and computer screen (see the InfoUma web site http://InfoUma.di.unipi.it/) (in Italian).

This logo naturally candidates to the role of a virtual guide in DHI, since it is not an abstract symbol but was designed from the beginning to play the role of *InfoUma mascot* and to be easily animated (in fact it was the subject of a Flash animation in an earlier version of the web site). Moreover it can be further humanized, by creating its own history and psychology to make it nice and funny. By making it speak and interact in the *metaverse*, we were able to adequately utilize the use context without making use of too many explicatory panels, thus making everything easier, more intuitive, and entertaining (Figure 7).

The first step, was the choice of a suitable name. A name is even more important than the virtual representation, for it designates a living person. Beforehand, it was generically called the *Chromozoon* (after the design studio *Cromozoi* that created it). But the name had to be simple, easily memorized and bearing reference to the community it represents. Finally, the choice fell on *Iumi* ("I" for "Informatics", "uma" from "umanistica" with adaptation to "umi" that sounds cuter).

The graphic realization that ensued was rather simple. The idea of representing it in natural size was discarded immediately: the guide should always be to the *avatar*'s side to give precious suggestions and thus a *portable* object appeared more suitable. On the other hand, a rather common fashion among SL residents is taking a *pseudo-animated* pet on their shoulders, usually a *funny animal*. We adopted a similar idea for this solution, reducing Iumi to the size of a "Schtroumpf" to be dressed on the *avatar*, on the right shoulder, with an important difference with respect to the other companion pets of SL inhabitants: Iumi has an important mission to accomplish, Iumi acts as a virtual *adaptive* and *context-aware* mobile guide.

One of the main limitations of SL is that it is not possible to animate *prim* constructions simulating a living being. The SL platform does not support unplaying *avatars*, or *bots,* that is avatars whose behaviour is controlled by scripts rather than human beings. In other words, the usual and complex animations that avatars feature are not available to be used in scripting objects.

However, certain very clever users have implemented programs that can simulate *pseudo-animations*. As a concept, such programs use an *array* of the positions (in the x, y and z axes) of the different primitives and present them cyclically in linear order, with an interval of one second, simulating a movement. Even if the movement is not very smooth to the human eye, this is one of the few stratagems that can be used in SL to give the idea of animation to a set of primitives. One of these programs, *Puppeteer,* was used to simulate a pseudo-animation of 40 seconds to make Iumi appear to be alive.

Once *pseudo-animated, Iumi* had to be scripted to implement the *mobile guide* concept. *Vectors* have been used for this purpose. Such simple panels communicate on a pre-defined channel within a definite spherical space (called *range*) every x seconds.

Iumi has been programmed in such a manner, that it can communicate with the object owner (i.e. the avatar who wears it) over a private channel; communication is triggered upon entering the *range* of this vector and the message is chosen from among a *case* of possible phrases. In practice, the avatar is free to go wherever it wants, and only when it happens to be in a definite context it gets the information relevant to the context. It is also possible to reset and disable help. *Context awareness* is thus a first level of adaptation implemented in Iumi.

Iumi is also able to *adapt* to the avatar profile by offering different contents. Living in a intercultural environment, Iumi is characterized by an identity crisis because it does not know whether it's a book or a screen. Actually one of our missions as educators is to make both cultures coexist in our students, but it is funny to imagine a tension between cultures that are so different, and wise to acknowledge the possibility that our visitors are more technologically inclined or more humanistic inclined. Thus, Iumi implements two profiles: *informatic* and *humanistic*.

By choosing from the special menu one of the two profiles, Iumi will give different information:

- as *informatic,* he will give information more focused on the technological aspects, such as implementation methods and building techniques;

- as *humanistic*, he will give information about the history of the buildings, important related events, and artistic aspects and so on.

Iumi's schizophrenia manifest itself in randomly generated sentences uttered once in a while. The sentences where collected with the help of an InfoUma student forum, where contributors were challenged to invent ways to personalize Iumi's behaviour.

Finally, to introduce first year students to the world of SL and DHI, a number of Iumi's adventures have been created the format of comics and made available from the Iumi web site(http://iu.di.unipi.it/sl/iumi/) (in Italian). These adventures are funny, help better define the character and are instrumental in creating a sense of community (Figure 8).

7 International cooperation

The goals of the collaboration project between CCH and the Humanities Computing programme at the University of Pisa were to develop shared educational activities within SL, and to strengthen and develop cooperation and understanding between teachers and students in higher education institutions of similar standing in two countries.

7.1   SL facilitates international collaboration

The distance learning potential of SL, especially when used in conjunction with voice and Web-based tools, is very considerable.

With these tools, SL allows the creation of virtual classes with people all over the world. This capability makes it possible to establish strong international relations, creating shared teaching activities, where students and teachers from different countries can exchange methods and knowledge. Students are faced with different realities and start to learn simply by beginning to talk amongst themselves, including when they try to negotiate language barriers. The ease of communication permitted by the teaching tools of SL encourages and stimulates international relations, where everyone competes to increase their knowledge and skills. Universities are the biggest beneficiaries from this relational system and researchers can collaborate with their colleagues worldwide, having the opportunity to augment Web tools with a third dimension, and commensurately increasing the potential for further projects. In light of this, it is unsurprising that more than 74 universities already have a virtual presence on Linden Lab's servers (http://secondlifegrid.net/programs/education).

7.2   King's College London – University of Pisa collaboration

DHI provides a place to meet for humanities experiments in teaching, learning and research, as well as offering meeting, exhibition, and collaboration facilities for Digital Humanists, worldwide.

The first teaching and learning pilot project took place during the 2007-08 academic year, built on the similarities between the InfoUma programme at the University of Pisa and similar programmes offered by the CCH at King's College London. Involving the use of 3D graphics in historical studies and cultural heritage, the collaboration aimed to enhance the student experience and to open new frontiers of communication and research in the application of information technology within humanities disciplines.

The Pisa and KCL students undertook a number of visualisations and reconstructions of ancient and modern buildings with some recognisable heritage value. In doing so, they strove to implement the methodological principles set out in *The London Charter for the Computer-based Visualisation of Cultural Heritage* (www.londoncharter.org), which establishes internationally-recognized standards for heritage visualisation with respect to the intellectual integrity, reliability, transparency, documentation, standards, sustainability and access.

7.3   The shared experience of DHI

The InfoUma course at Pisa includes a module on "3D Graphics", while the MA in Digital Culture and Technology at CCH offers a module on "Applied Visualisation in the Arts, Humanities and Cultural Heritage". Although the lessons took place during the same semester, a combination of different timetable requirements and language barriers dissuaded us from attempting to design a shared curriculum in the first year of the collaboration. Instead, the Pisa students worked together on a reconstruction of Galileo Galilei's Laboratory and historic experiments, while each of the KCL students developed a separate visualisation project, ranging from a model of the Tower of London complex to a reconstruction of a "classic" film set. The work on the Leaning Tower, we hope, will be the prelude to further work by the KCL and Pisa partners on the architecture and history of Medieval Pisa.

Given these differences, and the timetable and language obstacles, communication between the two cohorts was minimal. Arketipo was created precisely to facilitate joint meetings, classes, workshops (complete with virtual blackboard, slide projector, movie player and camera), exhibitions, conference presentations, and to assist in building relationships among both staff and students. Iumi was also developed to provide context-sensitive information to visitors to DHI, together with an associated blog and Flickr gallery (http://arketipo-sl.blogspot.com) (in Italian).

The Centre, will be both an agent of community creation, and a focal point for experimentation with new forms of e-learning involving students from both Pisa and KCL. The Centre and Island will also afford space for the presentation of completed projects, together with information on project aims and the methodologies used, as well as introductory materials for the visitor. Student projects, past and in progress, will be able to be materialised ("rezzed") on demand from a menu, as well as packed away when not in use to avoid over-taxing the server.

With the aid of the Arketipo Centre, we will in future be able to support shared lessons, bringing together students from different countries, shared projects, thereby helping them to acquire valuable language and collaborative skills.

With the exception of management meetings and occasional encounters on DHI, so far the students have not taken full advantage of the international community set up in collaboration with CCH.

We faced another major problem along the way, and it was the lack of internal regulations for the Island. The building blocks of modelling in SL are called "primitives", or "prims" for short, and each island has an upper limit of 15,000 prims. However, some early projects used an excessive number of prims, thereby creating confusion and restricting options for others working on the Island; not being able to delete or edit current or past projects, new structures have had to cope with the problem of a lack of prims. When we began to perceive the problem, we began to develop a new framework of prim quotas to strike a reasonable balance between competing priorities. This regulation, subject to ongoing revision as we learn from experience, is still valid and is followed by all users of the island, including teachers and students.

Communication between those with administrative permissions over the DHI has not always been transparent and precise. Meetings took place on the Island, but an accurate record of the discussions was not always made, and without a well-defined hierarchy of responsibilities, there were misunderstandings and mistakes.

In order to avoid these errors for the next academic year, we have agreed upon a document setting to detail the roles and responsibilities of the Management Group, which consists of two coordinators who determine the overall strategy for the Island, two technical directors, responsible for the technical maintenance of the Island, and a number of tutors from both institutions, who oversee teaching and learning activities. Each of these management groups has representatives from both institutions. In addition, we have developed a hierarchy of 7 levels of user privileges, starting from simple visitor up to the owner of the island.

For the second run of the pilot project, which will run during the 2008-09 academic year, we will be strengthening this international collaboration by embarking on a true shared, educational program of teaching.

As scheduling differences remain intractable, the Italian and English students will contribute to different phases of a common study, that of the ancient port of Pisa, which has a rich archaeological record including significant remains of ten boats dating from the third century BC to the fifth century AD (http://www.navipisa.it) (in Italian). In the fall term, the students at Pisa will document and visualise the existing state of a number of vessels as they are still to be seen *in situ* with 3D graphics in SL, while in the spring term, the KCL group will research and model, also in SL, hypothetical reconstructions of the ships in their original, working condition. Teachers from both institutions will be available, virtually, to give tutorial, observe, and advise on the progress of the shared project across both terms, while the interlocking nature of the activity will require the KCL students to consult with their Italian counterparts during the second semester, also within the "Arketipo" Centre.

At the end of the academic year, we hope to have achieved the first shared, three-dimensional reconstruction project carried out by students from different nations following a common set of methodological principles: *The London Charter*.

Acknowledgments

Thanks to our colleagues at the CCH, Richard Beacham and Hugh Denard, for introducing us to the London Charter and to the secrets of SL, and jointly running DHI with us. Thanks to all the students of the 3D Graphics and History courses for their enthusiasm and participation. InfoUma and CISIAU (the centre of computing services for the humanistic area of the University of Pisa) provided financial support for the project.

References

Bardzell, J. (2007), Creativity in Amateur Multimedia: Popular Culture. Critical Theory, and HCI, *Human Technology*, Volume 3 (1), February 2007, pp. 12–33.

Cantone, F. (2002), 3D Standards for Scientific Communication in Archaeological Informatics: Pushing the envelope. CAA2001 Proceedings of the 29th Conference, Gotland, April 2001, Oxford Archaeopress, BAR International Series 1016.

Denard, H. (2005), Visualisation and Performance Documentation Editorial, *Didaskalia* volume 6 (2).

Digital Humanities Island (DHI) (http://slurl.com/secondlife/Digital Humanities/186/167/28/?title=DigitalHumanities%20Island).

EPOCH: The European Research Network of Excellence in Open Cultural Heritage (http://www.epoch-net.org/).

Joseph, B. (2007) Best Practices in Using Virtual Worlds For Education in Proceedings of the Second Life Education Workshop at the SL Community Convention, Chicago, August 2007.

Kamimo Islands (http://slurl.com/secondlife/Kamimo_Island/127/148/25).

The London Charter. For the use of 3D visualisation in the research and communication of cultural heritage (http://www.londoncharter.org/)

Mason, H. (2007) Experiential Education in Second Life, in Proceedings of the Second Life Education Workshop at the SL Community Convention, Chicago, August 2007.

Meulenberg; G. F. & de Rode J. (2003), Truth and credibility as a double ambition: reconstruction of the built past, experiences and dilemmas, *The Journal of Visualization and Computer Animation*, Volume 14, (3), pp.159-167

Norman, D. (2002) The Design of Everyday Things, Basic books, 2002, ISBN 0-465-06710-7.

Ogleby, Cl.(1999), How real is your reality? Verisimilitude issues and metadata standards for the visualisation of Cultural Heritage, in CIPA International Symposium

Prensky, M. (2001) Digital Natives, Digital Immigrants, in *On the Horizon*, NCB University Press, Vol. 9 No. 5, October 2001.

Ryan, N. S. 1996, Computer-based visualization of the past: technical 'realism' and historical credibility, in Higgins, Main and Lang.

Salvatori, E. (2007), Didattica, scienze umanistiche e nuove tecnologie: opportunità, problemi e scenari plausibili nelle Università italiane, *Il giornale dell'e-learning*, volume 1, http://www.wbt.it/index.php?pagina=86

Figure 1. The laboratory of Galileo Galilei

Figure 2. Arketipo as appearing at sunset

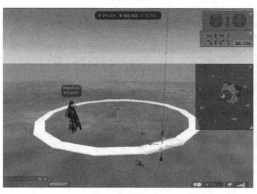

Figure 3. Rea building a large cylinder

Figure 4. The Tower of Pisa complexity of the model

Figure 7. Iumi, the virtual guide

Figure 8. Iumi: the comics

Chapter 10: Performance in Second Life: some possibilities for learning and teaching

Toni Sant, Ph.D.
University of Hull – Scarborough Campus
School of Arts & New Media
Filey Road, Scarborough YO11 3AZ
United Kingdom
t.sant@hull.ac.uk

Chapter Overview: Second Life holds interesting potential for performing drama, music, and live art events. Unlike other virtual worlds, created as games with set rules and stock characters, most of what goes on in SL is created by its users. This makes it an ideal playground for creative people. A growing number of musicians, theatre-makers, and other performers are exploring SL as an alternative stage for their ideas. Furthermore, like other similar massively multiplayer online role-playing worlds, SL is used by a large number of people for creative virtual self-presentation. These activities indicate various possibilities for learning and teaching with performance in SL.

1   Performance: A Broad Spectrum Approach

The study of performance goes beyond the performing arts to consider social roles, performing in everyday life, sports, popular entertainments, and all sorts of rituals. Richard Schechner (1988) calls this point of view "the broad spectrum approach." Furthermore, as Jon McKenzie (2001) has demonstrated, performance studies cannot ignore the way performance permeates activities outside the cultural realm. In assessing functionality and efficiency in technology and organizational settings, performance is an omnipresent term. In this chapter the focus is on the cultural side of performance but a broad spectrum model is explored, particularly to highlight the way things are interrelated and often spill beyond categorical boundaries.

Before embarking on a rollercoaster ride through Second Life to consider some of the more interesting types of performance going on in-world, particularly as they relate to learning and teaching, I'd like to apply what you've just read in the previous paragraph to something that is very specifically about Second Life. Wagner James Au (2008: 217) has identified three principles that keep Second Life going and growing the way it has since 2003, when he was hired by Linden Labs to work as an embedded journalist in this virtual world. It is hard to find any other participant observer who has a more incisive understanding of what goes on in Second Life. According to Au, the three things that keep Second Life thriving are:

- *"mirrored flourishing"* – this is what he calls the idea that what you do in world should make you a better person in First Life.
- *"bebop reality"* - he uses this as a term to signify that Second Life is like a jazz band, improvising and rising to the occasion as needed.
- *"impression society"* – referring to a type of community where how creative you are in adding value to your surroundings matters very much.

Au's observations are particularly interesting because of the way he highlights reality, improvisation, and spectacle, which can be found in some way or other in most performance related activities in Second Life. Each of these three elements will crop up in different guises and combinations throughout most of the examples and ideas presented in this chapter. Although I will not be returning to them directly just to make the point, they should be kept in mind as we move through the labyrinth of performance in Second Life.

2   Technical considerations

There are various technical approaches for presenting live performance in Second Life. Some of these techniques are live media performances while others include pre-recorded elements, which in some cases are not unlike the use of similar inserts in offline performances, such as music, sound effects, and voice-overs.

Following on from the lineage of online role-playing established in text-based massively multi-player online role-playing games (MMORPGs) since the 1980s, avatars in Second Life are involved in all sorts of representational performance. Throughout this chapter we shall be having a closer look at the most prevalent modes of performance in Second Life. All these performances involve avatars in a staged setting designed specifically for the event or appropriated to serve the ends of the show. Parallel to this sort of activity, and most times in conjunction with it, Second Life also embraces streaming media as espoused broadly over the Internet. Live or pre-recorded audio and video streams are integrated into Second Life spaces to compliment or enhance avatar-based performance. In this way, piped-in music provides a soundtrack for dancing and video is used to bring the world outside Second Life into this virtual world instantly, without transcoding the data into a new format. In basic technical terms, any streaming audio or video available on the Internet, which is playable in the QuickTime media player, can be played directly in Second Life.

Besides bringing in audio and video into Second Life, the practice of recording moments in world is quite common too. In most cases, snapshots or brief video clips are captured to preserve a souvenir of a particular experience, which can then be shared with friends over the Internet via email, personal blogs, or websites like Flickr, MySpace and YouTube. Users who are technically more advanced than the average user also capture video from Second Life to create short edited video sequences known as *machinima*. This type of video production will be discussed in more detail later.

As with any other synchronous communication over the Internet, lag or signal delay is a serious problem that can get in the way of planned events and hinder the execution of live online performance. For example, choreography that is dependent of temporal precision can easily be thrown out of sync and become muddled to look at and possibly even unintentionally farcical. Sometimes this can be worked into the piece but when it occurs unexpectedly it merely highlights one of the greater challenges for any performance involving telematics (Dixon 2007: 419-435).

It is essential that anyone exploring performance in Second Life should be at least aware of these technical elements: streaming media, audiovisual capture from Second Life, and lag in synchronous online environments. Different levels of engagement and interest with each of them are needed depending on which aspect of performance in Second Life the user is interested in. A producer needs to be technically proficient with at least one or more of them, while someone who is merely interested in performance as a spectator needs only understand what they are along with the possibilities and limitations inherent in these technical aspects.

3   Expected behaviour during Second Life performances

One of the joys (or headaches, depending on your perspective) of any virtual world is the potential for mischief (Sant 2005). As great as the temptation may be for any resident hidden behind relative anonymity, most performance producers expect their audiences to behave as they would at a similar event offline. Once the initial hurdle of basic technical proficiency is overcome, it is easier to conform to the expected norms of any given event. Any resident who harasses or maliciously disrupts the activities of other residents is commonly known as a *griefer*, and is in violation of the Second Life Terms of Reference. Still, this does not preclude playful spectator improvisation or peaceful social activism.

In 2006, Second Life resident and blogger Salome Strangelove published a set of tips for people attending performances in world. Although there have been some technological advancements since her original posting – particularly the introduction of voice chat in March 2007 – many of her points of etiquette are very useful for anyone attending a live performance in Second Life for the first time. What follows is based on Strangelove's original hints, which were meant mostly for music-related events. This updated and expanded version gives anyone who attends a live performance in Second Life an idea of what to expect in terms of audience behaviour.

- **Enable settings for audio, video, and voice chat:** these are set from the Preferences dialog box in Second Life, which can be found at the bottom of the 'Edit' menu. Make sure that "Play Streaming Music When Available" and "Play Streaming Media When Available" are selected in the 'Audio & Video' tab. In the 'Voice Chat' tab, make sure you select "Enable Voice Chat".

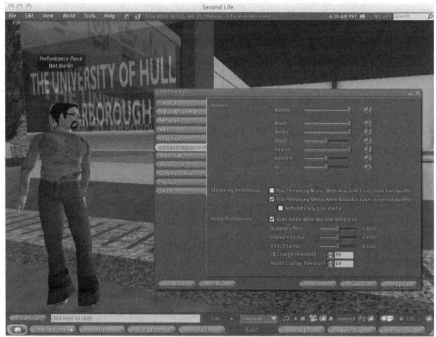

Figure 1. Enabling the settings for audio, video and voice chat through the preferences dialog box.

- **Set the controls for audio, video, and voice chat:** once your settings are enabled, you'll see the controls for music, video and voice appear towards the bottom left of your screen whenever these are available at a location you're visiting. Through these buttons and sliders you can control volume and playback. Music and video are usually known to default to the off setting, so make sure to click on the play button if you're expecting sound and/or video. Audio and video may take a few seconds to start after you press play, depending on the quality of your connection. The voice chat audio is automatically switched to on once it is enabled from the application preferences. Audiences are normally expected not to use their microphone during performances, unless otherwise directly instructed by the event producers. Once enabled, the microphone is turned on using the 'talk' button. Further directions can be found in the 'help' menu or by pressing F1 on your keyboard.

- **Text-chat:** the annoying sound of someone typing loudly at the keyboard, heard whenever someone makes any attempt of public conversation in Second Life, can be easily avoided. You should either speak to other residents using the IM function (which is silent) or you can negate the typing sound (as well as the motion of typing) by simply typing a forward slash "/" at the start of each line of your conversation. Keep private conversations to IM and keep room chatter to commenting on the performance, venue, or public conversation. The etiquette for this really does vary from one type of performance to another, so let the venue environment lead you unless you want to stand out.

- **Gestures:** most performers and other audience members will greatly appreciate restraint when it comes to the use of gestures during performances. You'll probably annoy no one by sticking to modest cheer and clap gestures whenever they seem appropriate. A simple clapping gesture is included in your 'Gesture' library. If you're already familiar with the use of gestures, you can choose the gesture that best expresses your own feelings, of course. However, keep in mind that your gesture sounds override the live audio stream and will be heard over the performer. The best rule of thumb is to keep gestures brief and to use them sparingly at the appropriate time/s. Typing feedback (silently, if done during the show) is also appreciated by most performers, but do bear in mind that they have a lot to deal with during the performance and may ignore your message until a more convenient time or completely.

- **Lag:** be very mindful of lag. Different audience members experience lag differently at the same time. Aside from any creative effort performers put into their shows, it is very common for Second Life residents not to see a performance as it was intended or performed by its producers. This is getting better with faster computers, improved software, and as more bandwidth become available across the Internet.

- **Tipping performers:** many Internet users don't think to pay for anything online but tipping performers in Linden dollars at the end of a show helps pay for basic expenses involved in producing more elaborate performances. Most performers do it just for fun but semi-professional performers have started appearing in Second Life too. Look for a tip jar or donation box. You'll find them at most performances. If you prefer, you can also right-click on the performer themselves and select "pay." The amount is completely up to you, but if there is no admission ticket to pay, about L$250 is an average tip. Just give what feels right for you.

These few pointers should be adequate preparation for attending any staged performance in Second Life. These tips are also useful for performance producers to share with their potential audiences, and some version of them is sometimes offered to in-world audiences.

4 Performance Arts in Second Life: an overview

Second Life holds interesting potential for performing drama, music, and live art events. Unlike other virtual worlds, created as games with set rules and stock characters, most of what goes on in SL is created by its users. This makes it an ideal playground for creative people. A growing number of musicians, theatre-makers, and other performers are exploring SL as an alternative stage for their ideas. The following overview of the different types of performances presented in Second Life is meant to help you find similar works and consider where to start if you would like to produce your own.

4.1 Theatre

Virtual worlds have been used as venues for theatrical activities since the early 1990s. The first use of the Internet for a performance of dramatic literature took place in 1993 after more than a year of preparations and rehearsals on Internet Relay Chat (IRC). This and other examples of text-based online theatre are important antecedents of the related activities in Second Life (Schrum 1999; Sant 2008). The various collaborations at ATHEMoo as well as the work of Desktop Theater and the ABC Experiment in the 2-D online environment The Palace, along with the subsequent work of Avatar Body Collision on UpStage, were further developmental steps before the emergence of theatre in Second Life.

Theatrical activities in Second Life range from play readings and storytelling to experiments in theatre architecture and full-blown productions of classic and new plays. The most elaborate theatrical projects in Second Life include the work of the Second Life Shakespeare Company and Theatron. These two projects were probably not the first to bring theatre-related activities to Second Life, but the magnitude of their scope greatly outweighs other works in this vein.

The Theatron project predates Second Life. The original project was started in 2001 by a European consortium led by participants from the School of Theatre Studies at University of Warwick in England, the Council of Europe's European Foundation for Heritage Skills, the Department of Theatre Studies at University of Amsterdam in the Netherlands, Atelier 4d from Berlin in Germany, and the Department of Engineering at the University of Ferrara in Italy, among others. Their initial interest was in using multi-media to teach European theatre history. Before entering Second Life, they had already produced architectural visualisations, an interactive touch screen kiosk, an archaeological context reconstruction, and an online teaching tool featuring interactive real-time walkthroughs of highly accurate 3D models of present and past theatres across Europe.

In 2007, two branches of the Higher Education Academy – The English Subject Centre and PALATINE the Dance, Drama & Music Subject Centre – initiated collaboration with the original Theatron consortium on the educational component of a new project in Second Life. This involves the importing of a range of pre-existing 3D theatre models into the Second Life environment and supplementing them with existing and new interpretative content through a spectrum of original interactive tools, scenarios and automated tutorials, incorporating manipulability and customisable actors, props, sound effects, lighting and scenic technologies, streaming video and scripts enabling individual and group movement or choreography. In the second half of 2008 visitors to the Theatron region in Second Life saw a breathtaking model of the Theatre of Epidaurus in ancient Greece appear over the course of several weeks on the Theatron sim. The magnificent Teatro Olimpico from Vicenza in Italy soon appeared right next to it, enabling visitors to experience the space in which perspective was brought to the stage in renaissance Europe. Previously, two other theatres were presented on the same space in Second Life. The first was the Hellerau Festspielhaus, considered to be one of the most influential spaces for the development of theatre innovations throughout the twentieth-century, and the other was the theatre of Pompei, restored to its former glory from Roman times.

Several UK-based individuals and institutions are working with the Theatron project in Second Life to produce performances and educational resources (see Table 1 in box below). A quick glance at the titles of these projects shows the exciting possibilities that arise from the creation of a space where students can witness animated performances created in a 3D rendition of the original theatres they read about in their theatre history textbooks.

Table 1: The first batch of Theatron-related projects in Second Life initiated during the 2007/08 academic year, facilitated by The Higher Education Academy in the UK.

Project 1 - Seeing space: Exploring scenographic principles in Second Life
Led by Paul Brownbill at the University of Wolverhampton
Project 2 - Integrating film technologies into Second Life
Led by Joff Chafer at the University of Coventry
Project 3 - 'The fools' zanni': exploring prominent characteristics of the Commedia dell'arte
Led by Gordon Duffy-McGhie at Middlesbrough College
Project 4 - Virtual Poiesis: The New Creative Pedagogy of Second Life
Led by Chris Wigginton, Northumbria University
Project 5 - 'Insubstantial Pageants': learning about Renaissance drama in Second Life
Led by Gweno Williams at York St John University
Further details about each of these projects is available at http://www.english.heacademy.ac.uk/explore/projects/archive/technology/tech2 3.php (accessed 14 September 2008).

The demand for such environments is so high that, there are two models of The Globe Theatre, made famous by William Shakespeare, in Second Life, aside from the one in the Theatron project. The first of these two other Globe theatres in Second Life is on Renaissance Island, where it has rarely been used for live performances but fits in well with the theme of the island and serves as an excellent teaching aid for history lessons about this period in Second Life. Renaissance Island serves as an environment where elements of sixteenth century life in Europe can be experienced within the online environment of Second Life. The other rendition of The Globe was built specifically for the SL Shakespeare Company (SLSC) on SLiterary Island. Set in the confluence of four island sims, this version of The Globe Theatre is designed to accommodate large audiences and stage performances that attempt to control lag as much as possible.

The Second Life Shakespeare Company is by far the most active theatre group in-world. All the sets, costumes, and avatars used by this company are custom-made for each play. They are among the first online performance groups to use live voice in their theatrical productions. Their work on Shakespeare's *Hamlet* and *Twelfth Night*, presented in 2008, employed conventional staging of dramatic literature. This presentation style is not unlike what you would expect to see at any contemporary production of Shakespeare's plays, which does not attempt to appropriate the seventeenth-century drama for anything other than what can be called a straight reading. This does not diminish from the mammoth task that the SL Shakespeare Company has undertaken in building not only a theatre space that is a relative-to-scale replica of the original Globe Theatre in Stratford-upon-Avon, but also what is undoubtedly the most consistently active theatre space in Second Life.

Anyone interested in theatre in Second Life knows (or should know) the work of this company. They are not strictly limited to staging the works of Shakespeare, but they have also produced an original one-act play called *One's a Pawn of Time*, which premiered in September 2008. For this production, audience members who chose to participate, had their avatar camera dynamically directed and moved in real time to follow the action on stage. This technique gives the performance producers the ability to assist their audience in focusing on actors and events as necessary, making for a rather cinematic or televisual montage rather than a live theatre experience.

At about the same time the company also launched the SL Shakespeare Company Academy of Performing Arts. Taught by working actors who are also involved in the world of theatre and performing inside Second Life, this academy aims to teach acting skills and courses on technical aspects of production for Second Life. The curriculum offered during the first season included these eight areas:

1. Beginning voice-over acting for commercial work with an emphasis on Second Life
2. Character development and script analysis
3. Stage craft for Second Life
4. Writing for Second Life performance
5. Producing live events for Second Life
6. Intermediate voice-over acting for theatrical work with an emphasis on Second Life
7. The art of radio hosting
8. Production design

These sessions are taught in a closed environment and the location is made available only to the students who are in the course.

Shakespeare is not exclusively reserved for the SLSC. Various scenes from *Romeo and Juliet*, *Midsummer Night's Dream* and *Much Ado About Nothing* have appeared in-world with varying degrees of complexity. The latter production was related to the creation of the New Globe Theater by Millions of Us, which corresponds with a controversial bid to create a physical space called the New Globe Theater on Governer's Island in New York Harbor. The actual site is a nineteenth-century military fort, which has a blueprint that is very similar to Shakespeare's Globe.

These activities are only an indication of the fairly numerous examples of theatre work in Second Life. Teachers of theatre history and classic literatures would probably be very interested in the work of online theatre veteran Steve Schrum who has also been involved in bringing Greek tragedy into Second Life. The version of Euripides' *Bacchae* he directed in the summer of 2008 showed a mastery of techniques introduced into Second Life by the SLSC, which he undoubtedly superimposed over his experience with text-based performances from the late 1990s.

4.2 Music

In much the same way that Second Life offers a global platform for theatrical activities, it also offers the opportunity for musicians to reach a global audience. This is done by transmitting a live music stream, which is generally somebody performing into a microphone in a small studio or in front of their home computer. As in the rising popularity of social networking websites like MySpace and Facebook, this is an opportunity to reach a potential global audience that might not otherwise be able to hear your music. With the Internet in general, the barriers are lower for people to experience new genres and artists they would otherwise never hear of.

There are hundreds of music events going on in Second Life every week. Simply go to http://secondlife.com/community/music.php to see the full listings, which are updated live with all the music events taking place in-world. On this official webpage you can also find details about opportunities for emerging artists and established musicians to perform in Second Life. It also gives details on how to host a live music event, including ways for DJs to spin records in Second Life.

For educational purposes, particularly with the history and appreciation of western music since medieval times, the Music Academy Online in Second Life is an excellent place to start. This music-centric sim first appeared in-world in January 2007 as an extension of the work done by Music Academy Online outside Second Life to generate interest in classical music. Music Academy Online's CEO Benton Wunderlich believes that his organizations mission of music education, music appreciation, and the promotion of new music and living composers has been greatly augmented through becoming fully involved in Second Life. The organization's ultimate goal is to offer potential students or music lovers the opportunity to chat with living composers, musicians and music educators freely within an appropriate Second Life environment.

The Music Academy Online island in Second Life has developed considerably since it was first created. New exhibits and performances appear regularly, often attracting relatively large crowds. The possibilities for learning and teaching the histories of music are within the same scale as those that can be found in the Theatron project for the history of European theatre. Covering every major period from medieval Europe to the present, music by selected key composers from each era is represented within visually congruous settings for each of the epochs.

The work of Music Academy Online in Second Life promotes music appreciation above everything else. All sorts of genres of music are present in Second Life, but since most people think that classical music is shrouded in convention its presence in Second Life stands out even more. Small recitals by soloists or small ensembles are quite common and usually quite pleasant, if you like that sort of thing. Scale-wise, such musical performances stand in stark contrast with performances given by orchestras.

In February 2007, Sinfonia Leeds, an amateur orchestra from England, was the first large-scale music performance in Second Life. They streamed their music live from Leeds in

England and had avatars represent each of the musicians in-world. Soon after the Leeds Sinfonia concert, the American chamber ensemble Red {an orchestra} presented a live multicamera video stream of their performance from Cleveland, Ohio. Such works came to considerable public attention though a concert given by the Royal Liverpool Philharmonic Orchestra in September 2007. A fairly faithful 3D replica of the Liverpool Philharmonic Hall was created for the occasion, but rather than have avatars on stage, a video stream of the orchestra playing live in Liverpool was broadcast into the sim. A video of the performance remained available in Second Life long after the live event. The video showed only one static long shot throughout the performance, in an attempt to simulate in-world the presence of the orchestra on stage in Liverpool.

Figure 2. The Royal Liverpool Philharmonic Orchestra live concert in Second Life. Photo reproduced by courtesy of Taran Rampersad, under a Creative Commons license 3.0.

Popular mainstream musicians have also explored Second Life as a way to promote their most recent record releases. Regina Spektor was the first major label recording artist to be given this treatment in 2006. In her case, the event was little more than a virtual listening party giving residents the opportunity to preview her new album *Begin to Hope*. Songs from the album were available at six different listening posts in a room made to look like a large New York City loft. Singer-songwriter Suzanne Vega followed suit a few weeks later, but significantly she chose to give a live solo performance using a guitar-playing avatar that looked very much like her established public persona. No other major label performer had done this before, but a few others have explored this format since then.

While popular singers can easily draw attention to their performances in Second Life, there are hundreds of unsigned musicians and singers who perform in world. There are some who perform almost exclusively in Second Life. Most of them perform in clubs and bars across Second Life. Open mic sessions are quite popular. There are also buskers on some of the more popular public regions too.

4.3 Dance

Dance is quite a common activity in Second Life. You can and will find dancing in clubs and dance studios as well as anywhere else where dance is not considered to be out of place. Dancing in Second Life is done for fun, for money, or as part of or a full-blown staged performance. Dancing in Second Life can be performed by all residents through pre-assigned animation scripts that are made available either by the landowner or someone they give permission to.

This sort of dancing in Second Life takes place when a user activates a Dance Animator or poseball, which normally takes the shape of a pink or blue ball. When an avatar activates a poseball the user is actually executing a set of scripts that enable an animation sequence or a menu of multiple poses and animations through a device such as a HUD. The scripts are usually integrated into an object or area in the virtual space. Scripts can enable two or more avatars to dance together. Individual avatars are also able to dance anywhere they can activate a personal dance animation from their inventory.

In places where people gather to socialize, dancing for fun is quite likely to happen. All types of dancing can be seen at various locations in Second Life, from square to lap dancing and salsa to free form. Dance scripts are readily available to copy or buy, but if you have the appropriate programming skills you can write the necessary code to animate selected avatars to move their bodies in any way permitted by the Second Life game physics engine.

One prevalent use of dance is in an activity called camping. The act of camping in Second Life involves placing an avatar in a specific zone where it can earn a small payment (usually between L$1 – L$10) just for being there. Landowners who are keen to populate their islands, particularly in-world retail stores, use this technique to attract avatars to their space with the hope that anyone else who teleports there will not leave because they find themselves in a deserted area.

The act of camping often involves activating a dance script; but sitting or other actions are also popular. Payment is usually made to the dancing avatar after a preset number of minutes have elapsed. There is usually a limit to how much money any individual avatar can earn in one go, but there are often ways around this. An avatar that has reached its payment limit on one dance spot can simply move to another dance spot, provided it is not already occupied by another avatar. This ensures a level of fair treatment to all, and seems designed to discourage any particular avatar from anti-social behaviour and simply visiting that space for the money.

Finish SL resident Maar Auer has created various popular dance animations and acoustic musical instruments. The first musical instrument she built was a double bass but she has also created a concert grand piano and an antique grand piano, which can be seen all over Second Life. These creations are for sale at her main store in Mevatersal Arts. In 2007 she started creating dance animations for a waltz, a slow dance, foxtrot, the Charleston, and a 50's style jive called the SLindy Hop. Her work is just a small example of the activities in this area. Building instruments and programming dance animations is essential for the development of performances that use these types of objects in-world. By the summer of 2008 a total of 651 dancing animations were available for sale in Second Life, according to SLExchange.com, with prices ranging from free to L$8500 for a Female Mega Dance HUD with 35 dance animations.

As in the case of music and theatre, there are also activities organized around staged dance. Doug Fox has covered the intersection of dance and the Internet on his blog since 2005. One of his main aims is to "to help dancers and dance companies use the Internet and their dance videos for marketing, educational, creative and revenue-generation purposes." In the process, he has also chronicled some of the first attempts to bring dance to Second Life. From his initial experience with Second Life in 2006 he immediately noticed that other Second Life users were commenting about the limitations of gestures and dance in this online environment. In spite of this, Fox soon came to argue that dancers should take Second Life and other virtual worlds seriously. He recognizes that the technology is still in its infancy but clearly understands its potential for dance. This has led him and others to continue exploring Second Life in relation to dance and to find ways to make it work better for dancers and choreographers. When he first entered Second Life, he was instantly struck by the possibility to combine a Second Life-based dance performance with video clips of the same performance in a physical space by the same group. This is a technique that's also available to all other types of performance that exist both in Second Life and in everyday life.

Anyone looking for a remarkable collective effort to innovate the potential of dance in Second Life should be aware of the Ballet Pixelle, formerly known as Second Life Ballet. This dance company operates solely in Second Life; the dancers and crewmembers live in various countries across Europe, a handful of states in the USA, as well as Bahrain and Japan. Over a period of about two years, this dance group has produced five productions, starting with the original 3-act ballet, Olmannen in February 2007.

Through their website, Ballet Pixelle address the main question levelled by most people at attempts to present live performance in Second Life: *why do this?* The answers they propose for this pertinent question include the fact that it brings this art form to new audiences without some of the elite trappings that come with ballet in the dance world. Furthermore, they're hopeful that it attracts people to try dancing ballet, even if only in Second Life. It also offers the opportunity to present ideas that are otherwise hard to produce in a physical space where lack of substantial financial backing can thwart the efforts of budding dancers and choreographers.

The work of Ballet Pixelle is noticeably different from most of the casual dancing seen around Second Life because each of the movement pieces shown by avatars in the company is an individual unit, not a loop. Each of the animations has timing within the gesture, personally choreographed by the company's Tokyo-based artistic director Inarra Saarinen. Such work is in direct linage to the work done by the influential choreographer Merce Cunningham, whose interest in contemporary technology led to two decades of work designed with the aid of software called Life Forms, which has developed from prototype choreography software in 1989 to a specialised package incorporating motion capture technology called DanceForms. Both packages are produced by Credo Interactive. Although this software is meant to assist in the choreography of dance in physical spaces, the work done through these software packages is quite similar to that needed to prepare a Second Life avatar to dance in-world. It can be argued that Second Life makes some of the basic components found in Life Forms and DanceForms freely available to all. However, choreographic movement in Second Life is structured through the aid of other applications. Avimator (http://www.avimator.com) and QAvimator (http://www.qavimator.org) are primary among these animation editors and they were created specifically for use in Second Life. They are both free and open sources alternatives to other popular 3D design applications like Poser and Maya.

As this assistive software shares many qualities with CAD packages that have become the workspace of choice for most architects, it comes as no great surprise that a group of architecture students from the Royal Institute of Technology in Sweden, have formed the Second Life Modern Dance Theatre in collaboration with The Stockholm Modern Dance Theatre. Unlike Ballet Pixelle's work, which is exclusive to Second Life, the dance performances produced by Second Life Modern Dance Theatre are presented as hybrid works with offline elements shown to a live theatre audience in Stockholm.

A live dance installation presented in March 2007 took place simultaneously at the School of Architecture and in Second Life. The performance featured eight avatars in Second Life where the set design of the virtual stage changed as other avatars in the in-world audience sat on different seats, which had scripts embedded in them that would change the appearance of the stage whenever someone sat down. The action in Second Life was projected via five different projectors into the physical space at Stockholm's Royal School of Architecture creating a 3D installation replicating the virtual stage in a physical space. As in the Second Life environment, the audience in the physical space could move through the environment and thus the audience in Stockholm became surrounded by the performance in Second Life rather than simply watched it as one would watch a flat projection. The physical environment in Stockholm was then fed back into Second Life as a live video stream, enabling the online audience to see what was going on in the physical space in Stockholm. The Second Life audience could then interact with the event further and change what the audience in Stockholm saw in the physical space.

Other Second Life users who organize what are known as mixed reality parties have adopted this format. These parties are not presented specifically as staged performances but simply as an ordinary party with a Second Life version that is projected on a wall within the physical space where the first-life party is taking place. The popularity of mixed reality events is evident from the fact that such activities have seeped into two diverse television series. The American crime drama CSI: New York (original U.S. air date: October 2007) and Tony Moore's Let's Talk Music (simulcast in Second Life and on national television in Malta: spring 2008). Mixed reality events are not exclusive to dance parties and music. In the world of visual arts it is not uncommon for exhibitions to include both a show in a physical space as well as a presentation of some of the same works in Second Life. In one instance presented by the artist Lynn Hershman Leeson on 24 November 2007, a symposium that coincided with the major retrospective exhibition Autonomous Agents: The Art and Films of Lynn Hershman Leeson, took place at The Whitworth Art Gallery in Manchester and at the same time in Second Life, as part of the The Performing Presence Project, a four-year partnership between the University of Exeter, Stanford University and University College London.

They Live (in Second Life), produced by Paul Sermon for the Futuresonic Festival 2008 in Manchester, is another example of a mixed reality art event (see Figure 3). This particular project falls squarely in the live art category, combining a Second Life exhibition at the SYLGRUT Centre, which had avatars in world meeting festival visitors at Futuresonic, which takes place annually in England. A live video link enabled audiences in the two spaces to listen and dance together.

4.4   Live Art

Live art, or performance art, comes from a tradition of mostly visual artists who use performance to make their art. At the risk of oversimplifying the many different types of live art, for the scope of this chapter it is safe to say that performance art always involves live bodies; in most cases the artist's own body is an integral part of the piece. As in other virtual worlds, in Second Life the artists' body is conspicuous by its physical absence. This enables performance artists to find room to play with discovering new ways to perform.

Re-enactments of historically famous performance art pieces are among the most significant examples of live art in Second Life. Scott Kildall, an American conceptual artist who works with new technologies, produced a series of remediations of several iconic performance art pieces in Second Life between 2006 and 2007, in a series called Paradise Ahead (see Figure 4). This type of work builds up the problematic issue of reproduction in performance art. This theme was originally presented by Fluxus in the 1960s but has recently resurfaced with great prominence through a 2005 event by Marina Abramovic, who reproduced seven historic performance works, two of her own and five by others, under the title Seven Easy Pieces, at the Solomon R. Guggenheim Museum in New York.

Following on from Paradise Ahead, in March 2007, twenty five years after Joseph Beuys' planted the first oak tree at Documenta 7 in Kassel for his work 7000 oaks, Eva and Franco Mattes (also known as 0100101110101101.ORG) re-enacted this in Second Life on Cosmos Island. Beuys' original piece involved the planting of seven thousand trees, each paired with a columnar basalt stone. The artist had intended this to be part of an ongoing scheme of tree planting throughout the world creating one of the first pieces of live art actively involved in significant environmental change. The Mattes' intention is to replicate this in Second Life by inviting residents to plant oaks and place stones from their event on their lands.

Figure 3. They Live (in Second Life) is one example of a mixed reality art event. Photo reproduced by courtesy of Paul Sermon.

Figure 4. *Cut* (2007) by Scott Kildall, Second Life recreation of *Cut Piece* by Yoko Ono. Photo reproduced by courtesy of Scott Kildall.

The Mattes' reproduction of 7000 Oaks launched a series of works by these artists in Second Life entitled Synthetic Performances. After the Beuys piece they went on to re-enact works by Vito Acconci, Marina Abramovic, Chris Burden, Valie Export, and Gilbert & George. The Mattes did not attempt to simulate the original pieces by creating avatars of the original artists but performed all the actions through their own avatars. Performance art re-enactments in

Second Life continue beyond the examples I've mentioned. For example, over a period of 26 days starting on March 12, 2008, performance artist Joseph DeLappe, re-enacted Mahatma Gandhi's famous 240-mile walk in protest of the British tax on salt. This may be an indication that this format may stick around for some more time to come.

Performance art in Second Life is not limited to re-enactments. Second Front, a performance art group based in Second Life was founded in 2006. In the first two years of their existence they have presented a considerable number of original performance works in-world. The group is made up of contemporary artists from different parts of the world, including Scott Kildall. Like the Second Life Shakespeare Company or Ballet Pixelle, the members of Second Front come together formally only in Second Life. The group builds on a tradition of performance introduced in the twentieth century by the Futurists, Dada, Fluxus, and the Situationist International. On their blog they call their works "theatres of the absurd that challenge notions of virtual embodiment," and they are particularly interested in the construction of virtual narrative. Their first works consisted mostly of appropriating the Reuters HQ in Second Life and in the process creating their own event in the virtual space. All their works question the role of the artist in society in one way or another.

More than any other form of performance, these kinds of works bring the relationship between the real and the virtual into question. In the seemingly simple act of creating an avatar, every virtual world user, not just Second Life residents, are performing an identity that may or may not be similar to the way they see or want to see themselves in everyday life. Every avatar is a performance of self. Whenever we make or enhance an avatar we are creating or recreating virtual identities that are marginally or remarkably different from our presentation of self in everyday life.

5   Avatars: Identity Performance

When you first enter Second Life, your avatar (i.e. the way you look in-world) is the most important thing. You get to play with your identity before you even set foot on Orientation Island. Once you log into Second Life you instantly activate the possibility of being someone else; playing the role you've created for and through your avatar. The mechanics of Second Life – its physics and game engine and expected or acceptable behaviour – are the rules that enable you to operate within the online environment. Beyond this, whatever role you chose for your avatar is an identity performance. As Mark Stephen Meadows puts it, "A rule is a function of mechanics. A role is a function of theater" (Meadows 2008: 34). The fact that Meadows, who is not directly involved in any of the performance arts, sees "theater" as an essential part of all avatars, builds on the idea introduced at the beginning of this chapter in relation to the broad spectrum of performance.

It is important to distinguish between the two basic types of identity performance in Second Life: role-play and real-play. Most avatars role-play. Most avatars have a different name than their user but it most often still tells you something about the user, even if it reinforces the way a user wants to be perceived. To some degree or other, the 3D representation looks different from the person operating it, enabling the user to perform a role that is as close or as different from their known self as they make their avatar appear. By contrast, real-play involves avatars whose name is identical to the one the user uses offline. With real-play, the avatar is usually as faithful a representation of the way the user looks in First Life, as much as possible. However, all avatars have the potential to enable real-play for their users. If a truthful exchange occurs between Second Life residents, who known exactly who is behind the avatar they see in-world, then the suspension of disbelief that is essential in successful role-play is disengaged temporarily to enable real-play between the users. The relationship between users and their avatars is similar to that between actors and their roles. For the sake of the user's mental sanity, it is essential to ensure that the role of the avatar in role-play does not take control of the users life as a person. The cautionary tale for this on a large visible scale can be seen with celebrities and typecast actors, who are always seen as their constructed persona before they are seen for the person they are beneath the superimposed layers of identity.

Richard Bartle (2004: 130ff), co-creator of MUD – Multi-User Dungeon, the world's first online massively multiplayer online role-playing game (MMORPG) – identifies four types of users.

- Explorers – uncover the beauty of things and show them to others
- Socializers – like to form groups, build social infrastructure, and throw parties
- Achievers – enhance their avatars by increasing power, wealth, and reputation
- Controllers – dominate, compete, and defeat

Some users fall within two or more of these categories but regardless of the type of user you are, your avatar is a way for you to become an interactive character that is able to choose or change the plot of what goes on around you. Additionally, Second Life offers its users a function that most other 3D MMORPGs do not: the possibility to create completely new or personalized narratives. These two basic ideas have attracted interest in virtual worlds since the days of text-based chat environments like MUDs and MOOs.

Meadows clearly sees this as a function of identity performance when he says, "virtual worlds are interactive narratives, and the avatars are actors in a kind of street theatre where the audience helps improvise the plot" (67). More than this, without referring directly to it, he invokes an established form of interactive performance established by Brazilian theatre-maker Augusto Boal known as Forum Theatre. In this form of theatre, members of the audience are encouraged to become "spect-actors" and invited within the performance space to take over the role of the protagonist with the aim of changing the outcome of the plot. This is one of Boal's techniques in the Theatre of the Oppressed (1979), where theatre is seen as a rehearsal for social change. Equally, "an Avatar can be seen as a rehearsal mechanism we can use to figure out the important stuff in real life" (Meadows 2008: 72). This shows that this virtual world can be used to remodel offline experiences rather than just serve to model experiences from First Life into Second Life.

While there's plenty of room for creativity and scope for innovation in Second Life, the environment can be seen as a tool for simulation. The most effective uses of Second Life fall somewhere between the two extremes: innovation built on the power of simulation. One example of this balance can be found in the technique of machinima production.

6   Machinima

People have been making machinima since the mid-1990s when it became easier to capture live sequences from games straight into a digital video file. Doom (1994) and Quake (1996) were among the first video games that enabled gamers to record sessions and then play them back later. Besides simply playing back captured sequences, creative gamers came to see that they could edit sequences together into short video clips, possibly enhancing the original offering, or even moving away from the original narrative completely. The term *machinema*, later spelt as machinima, did not come into use until some years later. The word is a neologism derived from the words machine and cinema. It is common belief among machinima enthusiasts that the term is spelt the way it is because this way it also invokes animation and even anime, the Japanese form of animation that has an extensive cult following among the more avid makers of machinima.

Unlike bespoke 3D animation, the creation of machinima from environments and avatars already constructed in commercial virtual worlds like Second Life does not require the many hours of designing every single element in the final production. The use of Second Life as an environment for machinima has one important advantage over game environments like World of Warcraft or The Sims, in that everything visible in world is fully customisable, from buildings, landscapes, and furniture, to vehicles, costumes, lighting and so on.

It is common for works of machinima to be described in terms of actors, sets and directors (Carroll and Cameron 2005; Carr 2007). This performance terminology points the way to two approaches towards machinima. One takes into consideration the fact that elements of live performance, within or without a narrative structure, are captured into video clips and then edited into coherent short narratives employing elements of film language, making the final experience for the viewer as different from viewing live performance as cinema is from theatre. The other simply looks at the finished productions of machinima as an example of mediated performance, within the broader spectrum of other screen-based performance like television drama and cinema.

Kelland, Morris and Lloyd (2005) have identified four machinima production techniques: live recording, puppeteering, recamming, and scripting. With the first of these techniques, the machinima simply captures activities as they happened in a documentary or cinema verite style. In the puppetry approach, the manipulation of avatars is performed according to a screenplay, recorded live and edited together in post-production. Recamming goes one step further and involves retaking particular scenes or actions to enable a more aesthetically effective final product. And in the scripting technique the avatars are made to perform in a very specific manner through custom animation scripts such as dancing, which are not among the default ordinary actions within the virtual environment.

Until version 1.20 of Second Life, the software itself offered the option to record sequences of action as they appeared on your screen. Linden Labs removed this feature because they felt that it was unreliable and there are better third-party tools, including free software, which can be used for the same purpose. The most popular of these are listed on the official Second Life wiki. While it may seem that everyone with a computer can produce video these days, the more engaging machinima productions are made by people who are well-versed in the conceptual and post-production aspects of video production. To produce even the simplest machinima production, you need to be fully aware of all the technical aspects involved, including sequence capturing, video editing and post-production. These skills are relatively easy to acquire and there are many online tutorials available to help anyone acquire an entry-level understanding of these techniques.

Aside from generic machinima in Second Life, the technique is employed regularly by SLCN.TV, which produces virtual television programmes directly in-world. This video network is avatar-based, fully employing machinima techniques. It is aimed primarily for in-world audiences, who can view it either at the SLCN sim or on SLCN TV screens that are freely available throughout Second Life. The programmes are also available on the web, reaching an audience that is not necessarily in Second Life. All video clips show live events presented as television shows with and by avatars, as they happen in Second Life.

The network launched in March 2007 with the Texas' Aussie Music Party, broadcasting live coverage of six bands, including live music and interviews. Since then SLCN.TV has also offered live coverage of other major events within Second Life, and the number of regularly scheduled programmes have become full-blown line-ups for Sundays and Mondays. Within just over a year from its appearance, SLCN.TV was producing several sports shows, as well as special interest channels for community and lifestyle, including Music Academy, produced by the Online Music Academy in Second Life mentioned earlier. Other styles of music are catered for in a weekly show called Music on the Isle.

7   The Future of Performance in Second Life

Understanding the basic concepts and having interesting ideas are essential for going beyond obvious simulation and imitation in Second Life. Performance forms that are specific to this virtual world and other 3D environments are slowly emerging. Like other media before it, an initial period of adjustment is necessary to enable creativity to take hold fully. Think of early cinema and how long it took film-makers to start producing movies that approach the sort of thing we've now come to expect from that medium.

Technological advancements will also help in the development of further ideas. Lag issues will be rectified overtime, if not overcome completely. Easier integration of live and pre-recorded audio, as well as video, will occur gradually through user feedback. And while it is relatively easy to use third party solutions for video capture to produce machinima, it would be convenient if Linden Labs were to re-introduce an improved video recording function within the Second Life software itself, possibly as an easy plug-in or an alternative version of the software.

Some of the same ideas presented in this chapter can and will work just as well in other virtual worlds, possibly even ones that are still to be developed. Machinima in particular, is already quite well spread over other virtual worlds, such as World of Warcraft and The Sims. It is very likely that mixed-world machinima, bringing together sequences from different virtual worlds and/or the offline world, may be produced more frequently in the near future. This is not just a futuristic prediction. It follows logically from current trends and general moving image production. In the same way that the less-technically-challenged users move from one application to the other almost seamlessly, it follows that moving from one world or reality to another will eventually become a natural progression. It is also an excellent way to use Second Life productively for learning and teaching.

References

Abramovic, M. Marina Abramovic: Seven Easy Pieces. Retrieved September 17, 2008, from http://www.seveneasypieces.com/.

Au, W. J. (2008). *The Making of Second Life: Notes from the New World*. New York: Collins Business.

Bartle, R. (2003). *Designing Virtual Worlds*. Berkeley, CA: New Riders Games.

Boal, A. (1979). *Theatre of the Oppressed*. London: Pluto.

Carr, D. (2007).Teaching Media and Machinima in Second Life: Interview with Britta Pollmuller. Retrieved September 18, 2008, from http://learningfromsocialworlds.wordpress.com/interview-teaching-machinima-at-schome-park/.

Carroll, J., & Cameron, D. (2005). Machinima: digital performance and emergent authorship. In *Proceeding of DiGRA 2005 Conference: Changing Views - Worlds in Play*. Vancouver. Retrieved September 18, 2008, from http://www.digra.org/dl/db/06276.32151.pdf.

Dixon, S. (2007). *Digital Performance: A History of New Media in Theater, Dance, Performance Art, and Installation*. Cambridge, Mass: MIT.

Fox, D. Dancing into the Future. Retrieved September 17, 2008, from http://greatdance.com/danceblog/.

Kelland, M., Morris, D., & Lloyd, D. (2005). *Machinima: Making Animated Movies in 3D Virtual Environments*. London: Course Technology PTR.

Kildall, S. Paradise Ahead (2006-2007) Digital print and performance series. Retrieved September 17, 2008, from http://www.kildall.com/artwork/2007/paradise_ahead/paradise_ahead.html.

Kildall, S. Second Front. Retrieved September 17, 2008, from http://www.kildall.com/second_front/sf.html.

Kildall, S., Babell, G., Gilks, Y., Hansen, B., Jarvis, D., Lichty, P., et al. Second Front Blog. Retrieved September 17, 2008, from http://www.secondfront.org/blog/.

Mattes, E., & Mattes, F. Synthetic Performances. Retrieved September 16, 2008, from http://0100101110101101.org/home/performances/.

McKenzie, J. (2001). *Perform or Else: From Discipline to Performance*. London: Routledge.

Meadows, M. S. (2008). *I, Avatar: The Culture and Consequences of Having a Second Life*. Berkeley, CA: New Riders Press.

Midgette, A. (2007). Watching a Cyber Audience Watch a Real Orchestra Perform in a Virtual World. *The New York Times*. Retrieved September 16, 2008, from http://www.nytimes.com/2007/09/18/arts/music/18seco.html.

Saarinen, I. Ballet Pixelle. Retrieved September 16, 2008, from http://slballet.org.

Sant, T. (2005). Rape, Murder and Suicide Are Easier When You Use a Keyboard Shortcut: Mouchette, an On-Line Virtual Character. *Leonardo*, 38(3), 202-206.

Sant, T. (2008). A Second Life for online performance: Understanding present developments through an historical context. *International Journal of Performance Arts and Digital Media*, 4(1), 69-79.

Schechner, R. (1988). Performance Studies: The Broad Spectrum Approach. *The Drama Review*, 32(3), 4-6.

Schrum, S. A. (Ed.). (1999). *Theatre in Cyberspace: Issues of Teaching, Acting and Directing*. New York: P. Lang.

Second Life Exchange. Dancing Animations Marketplace. Retrieved September 17, 2008, from https://www.slexchange.com/modules.php?name=Marketplace&CategoryID=44.

Sermon, P. They Live (in Second Life). Retrieved September 17, 2008, from http://creativetechnology.salford.ac.uk/paulsermon/theylive/.

Strangelove, S. Concert Tips and Etiquette. *Linden Lifestyles - The Unofficial Second Life® Fashion Shopping Blog*. Retrieved September 15, 2008, from http://lindenlifestyles.com/?p=146.

From the official Second Life Wiki

Machinima
http://wiki.secondlife.com/wiki/Machinima
Movie Recording
http://wiki.secondlife.com/wiki/Movie_Recording

YouTube videos

Creating & uploading animations for Second Life using Qavimator
http://www.youtube.com/watch?v=h_-3c_aC-O4
Editing & uploading sounds using Audacity
http://www.youtube.com/watch?v=QBVmFafFatE

Dance

The Evolution of Dance in Second Life
http://www.youtube.com/watch?v=HOtI6GHrWUw
How I Dance in Second Life using HUDs (by Phoenicia Sol)
http://www.youtube.com/watch?v=vEdV618BHj4
Second Life Ballet
http://www.youtube.com/watch?v=twrlfOyAtNM
http://www.youtube.com/watch?v=z7MTbAO7dKk
Second Life First Life Dance – Stockholm (March 2007)
http://www.youtube.com/watch?v=InCiE1AXcOo
http://www.youtube.com/watch?v=HsFcxJb1iVc
Second Life ballroom dancing animation by Maar Auer
http://www.youtube.com/user/MaarAuer

Music

Regina Spektor
http://www.youtube.com/watch?v=GP-x_hrSR6c
Suzanne Vega
http://www.youtube.com/watch?v=BFCpsxb6m8s
http://www.youtube.com/watch?v=WpGeRgkOUCE
Liverpool Philharmonic Hall
http://www.youtube.com/watch?v=RVGWeZuxFKA

Live Art

Second Front performances by OntoDistro
http://www.youtube.com/user/OntoDistro

Chapter 11: Spacing Creation:
The HUMlab Second Life Project

James Barrett, Ph.D. student
Stefan Gelfgren, Ph.D.
HUMlab, Umeå University
901 87 Umeå, Sweden
jim.barrett@humlab.umu.se
stefan.gelfgren@humlab.umu.se

> *Text lacks the emotional bandwidth which we crave.*
> Pathfinder Linden, 2007

Chapter Overview: This chapter is both a summary and a glimpse of the future regarding the twelve months of activity in Second Life by the digital humanities lab and studio HUMlab at Umeå University. Art and cooperation have been the emphasis in the early stages of the HUMlab Second Life project. In the few months prior to the authoring of this chapter things began to move quite rapidly for HUMlab in Second Life with numerous projects emerging in relation to the large HUMlab Island. Through a constructivist pedagogical model, and lots of trial and error many lessons have been learnt by all involved. Some of the more interesting learning experiences are related in this chapter.

1   The HUMlab Second Life Project

In June 2007 the digital humanities research lab and studio HUMlab at Umeå University in Sweden purchased a 5120 square meter island in Second Life (SL). Online world platforms had already been used in HUMlab as part of education and research for a number of years. Class work had been conducted by HUMlab in ActiveWorlds (1999-2004), and research and teaching in Online Traveler (2001-present), The Sims (2001- present) and Adobe Atmosphere (2003-2004). The move into Second Life was part of the ongoing research and pedagogical application of virtual worlds in learning and teaching by various HUMlab personnel. From experience already gained in working with online worlds it was understood early in the Second Life project that documenting of the HUMlab Second Life project was essential. A concerted effort was made to document as much as possible from the very beginnings of the project. In this article we go back over almost two years of planning and development within the HUMlab Second Life project to relate and evaluate what has been learnt in that time. We describe a specific case study, the "Holiness in Virtual Spaces" project, where research is being conducted into the manifestations and representations of the Holy in the symbolic and social world of Second Life. While only two years old the work by HUMlab personal in Second Life represents an innovative and extensive approach to investigating the platform. This work is multidisciplinary and experimental, as we shall now explain.

1.1 Background to New Ground

To understand the intentions and actions that were part of HUMlab establishing a presence in Second Life it is necessary to mention briefly the philosophies behind the actual HUMlab organization. How HUMlab functions as a collective entity is summarized on the lab's website:

> HUMlab at Umeå University is a vibrant meeting place for the humanities and information technology. A large and diverse studio environment serves as the most important manifestation of this basic idea which involves bringing people together, looking at information technology as tool, medium, study object, and activist venue, and doing things that have never been done before. (HUMlab Website)

The intention to do what had "never been done before" was a major focus in the overall planning for a HUMlab presence in Second Life. To determine what had been done in regards to pedagogy and the digital humanities with Second Life it was necessary to experience what was happening inworld (i.e. in Second Life). Beginning in September 2006 research was begun into how universities, schools and research bodies were using Second Life in their work. This research lasted approximately three months. It involved attending lectures, teacher 'buzz sessions', art shows, political manifestations, film showings, seminars, lectures, themed islands, museums, gallery and installation openings, visiting virtual campuses, wandering in night clubs, interviewing passers-by and playing in sandboxes in Second Life. Inspired by the Deep Dive brainstorming technique developed by the IDEO group, immersion in Second Life over an extended period of time resulted in a number of assumptions regarding the affordances of the medium.[i] The term affordances (Gibson 1977) can be summarized as the qualities of a tool or object or even environment that permit specific ranges of use and interaction.[ii] What is understood from the work of other groups and individuals using Second Life as indicative of affordances serves as a guide for how the HUMlab Second Life project aims to develop.

From the early research four tendencies of practice were identified in regards to the uses of SL in Education and Learning. The four general uses of Second Life were found alone or in combination/s as

- A three dimensional web portal (links, information and contact details with brand identity important).
- A virtual classroom for distance learning (interactive, synchronized, often multimedia and modelled on the physical classroom).
- An archive (gateway to storage with access to online but offsite files etc.).
- As a means to reproduce in a representative sense an element of the physical learning space (a model or simulation of a campus or physical space).

Each of these tendencies is a perfectly rational and technologically innovative use of the Second Life platform. However, the prior use of online worlds in HUMlab has been driven by a constructivist pedagogical model which "focused on student creativity rather than teacher or supervisor creativity." (Svensson 3 2002) It was and still is the intention for the HUMlab SL project to allow students degrees of self expression and determination that are quite often difficult to actualise in traditional classroom situations. The details of these efforts to realise student creativity shall be described later in this article.

1.2 Planning the HUMlab Island

The purchase of what was to become the first HUMlab Island in SL was preceded by a long process of looking for a suitable piece of virtual real estate, seeking advice, developing contacts and learning the market inworld (i.e. in Second Life). All inquiries into land purchases were documented with chat records saved (cut and pasted into Word Documents, this was prior to voice chat in SL which creates archiving issues), screen shots or inworld snapshots taken. The invite friends' function in SL becoming a valuable tool as contacts could be maintained with avatars who worked in SL real estate and related areas. Email and the blogs of HUMlab were the in-house means of keeping HUMlab personal informed of developments in SL regarding land negotiations and the events related to the developing presence.

In planning the HUMlab presence in SL a document was produced to frame the expectations and thoughts which accompanied the project in its early stages. *A HUMlab Presence in Second Life?* was submitted to the director of HUMlab on 1 May 2007. The questions that were asked in this paper were:

1. What are the affordances of Second Life in relation to HUMlab?
2. Who would occupy and used the space of HUMlab SL?
3. What would be the goals of a space for HUMlab in Second Life?
4. How big/small, multimedial, archival, pedagogical, and integrated with the actual
5. HUMlab will the HUMlab SL site be?
6. How much $L are we willing to spend?

The *A HUMlab Presence in Second Life?* paper raised the issue of coding restrictions in SL, a development from the business model, whereby (in May 2007) "Second Life does not allow the user to directly import the objects (prims) that make up structures in the world." (Barrett 2) The situation has not changed much in the sixteen months since those words were written. Second Life is a closed (although vast) platform which does not allow for ease of movement in and out of. Artists, students, researchers, and teachers who create work in SL are dependent on the platform for the continued existence of the products of that work.[iii] The products of working in SL cannot at this time be moved out of SL or exist independently of the platform. The proprietary control over all work created on the SL platform is an important consideration for educators. The remainder of the paper A *HUMlab Presence in Second Life?* discussed the four dominant tendencies of practice for teaching and learning in Second Life, the affordances of the medium and discussion around a sketched design of a possible HUMlab facility inworld. A month after the paper was presented to the director of HUMlab an island had been purchased in SL and work could begin.

1.3 HUMlab Island One

The island which the HUMlab project in SL settled on was purchased from a private landlord for $L55989 ($US210) with a monthly surcharge of $US37. We purchased an island of 5129 sq meters and began working with a landlord who became over the following six months a valued teacher. There were restrictions on the island which would affect our work there and ultimately lead to HUMlab leaving the island. A height restriction with no high-rise and "No Flying Structures over 300m altitude" was imposed on the sim as well as no lag scripts, although this last criterion was enforced by the contractual land covenant and not by having the scripts disabled on the parcel purchased. The first HUMlab Island was in a French area of SL and our neighbours included an Israeli version of MySpace, a Swiss genetics research group and an Italian aircraft company. The small islands hosting these businesses within the sim were generally empty. Initial interest in Second Life was not great from the university population where the actual HUMlab is situated. One of the first acts following the purchase of the island was the organizing of a short course in HUMlab on "Your Second Life: Living and Building in Second Life" on 31 May 2007.

Understanding the benefits of virtual online worlds such as Second Life in an active, critical and pedagogical sense in tertiary contexts can be a bigger hurdle than many people expect. Huge areas of SL are ghost towns, with buildings and scripts running but no avatars present. An empty classroom is just a room, as an empty site is Second Life may as well be a conventional webpage. In running short courses in HUMlab, such as 'Your Second Life', we have attempted to both connect with individuals around campus who are already involved in the related areas and to introduce new ideas and practices to the wider university and broader community. Second Life has proved particularly popular with certain demographics, but it is also a difficult concept for many people to come to terms with. Building a community of practitioners regarding digital humanities takes time. It is for this reason that a supportive environment is necessary for a high standard of practice to develop in relation to teaching and learning in Second Life.

HUMlab projects are often conducted by a number of researchers or academics who work with technical support personal to form a team. A team model for research or teaching is not common in the humanities disciplines but it is a valuable mode for working on projects such as Second Life. The affordances of Second Life permitted us to call in team members in a virtual sense, who could set up a presence on the new HUMlab Island and work over distance (including time zones) on projects. The first major project was an interactive art installation commissioned as part of a large exhibition for the National Art Museum of Denmark. The artist who created the work was living a thousand kilometres away from HUMlab but was very connected to it through working on the Second Life island.

1.4   Arrival of the N00sphere

The Japanese/Swedish artist Sachiko Hayashi began working on the N00sphere Playground installation on the HUMlab Island in August 2007 (see Figure 1). Prior activity on the HUMlab Island had been restricted to small building experiments and occasional visitors. By deciding that the HUMlab Second Life project was going to be a constructivist user driven exercise there were risks involved. The emphasis on results shifted from the facilitators to the users in the project and as there were few people who either had the time, ability or willingness to engage and create with HUMlab in Second Life, there was little happening on the island. For this reason the arrival of Hayashi and an international networked art project was welcomed. At this time the role of the island manager emerged for the first time.

The role of manager was never intended to be attached to the island, but with space and collaboration come borders and goals. How the manager of such a space fits in with constructivist pedagogical principles has been an interesting and rewarding development in the HUMlab SL project. The role of the manager on the island became the point of first contact in support for island residents from the larger HUMlab apparatus. The contexts for this support included the fact that Second Life has its own time frame; it is pan-global and open twenty four hours a day seven days a week. Clock time in SL runs on Pacific Daylight Time (PDT), but in practice time is much more flexible inworld. People are online and working outside any single normal working schedule. The potentials of the flexible time frame of SL are resources rather than restrictions that need to be approached in a creative way if they are to be utilized to their full pedagogical potential. The use of inworld Instant Messaging (IM) connected to an email inbox allowed an almost round-the-clock communication channel to be open between those working on the island and the support networks that were available from HUMlab. Contacts over time zones has the potential to result in a kind of global shift-working culture whereby an academic, technician or student in one time zone works with a project while others are sleeping through their nighttimes, only to resume when the 'night shift' finishes. While such a system is only beginning to be established on the HUMlab Island it complies with the 24 hour 7 days a week access policy the actual lab has on campus.

Mediation between agents inworld on the HUMlab Island has been an important function of the manager role. In the traditional classroom setting the teacher may be a source of structure and instruction, but in a SL context such a figure struggles with the contingencies of the medium. The alternative to a central figure which directs and attempts to control activities in the (virtual) learning space is a facilitator, perhaps more akin to a stage manager than a teacher. During the first year of the HUMlab SL project several conflicts have arisen which required arbitration and were resolved without major personal or professional long term consequences. The intensity of conflicts in the collaborative working space of the HUMlab Island can be compared to the issues which can arise in an actual shared living environment. Space, and subsequently place, have a deep and defining connection to personal identity. Even virtual space exerts a powerful influence over identity through self expression and as a gestalt to feelings of control.

In the HUMlab conflicts it was intrusion and exclusion and a respect for the (virtual) property of others that lay at the centre of exchanges on the island. These are interesting issues in themselves and could be developed much further, however in the context of this discussion it is necessary to say that an open ended structure with defined rules is important at the start of the project. Trying to accommodate all opinions and actions can be difficult after the event and it is better to lay down clear structures early than attempt to patch things up after. The structures for collaboration in SL are determined by the materials of the platform, and learning them will allow structures to be established in a project. On the HUMlab Island it was separating and defining areas which helped with conflict situations. Parceling land and granting it to individuals is often a better course of action than more communal arrangements. Sandboxes are great for learning, but the conflicts of the sandbox can damage relations within a project for the long term. Compatibility between site, goals and actors is a difficult equation to master but it is absolutely essential if a project in SL is to develop. In many ways HUMlab Island One can be described as the sandbox stage of the project, where basic lessons were learnt and simple experiments run. The move from HUMlab Island One to the current

HUMlab Island Two was the result of an incompatibility between project goals and site affordances. The move occurred in January 2008.

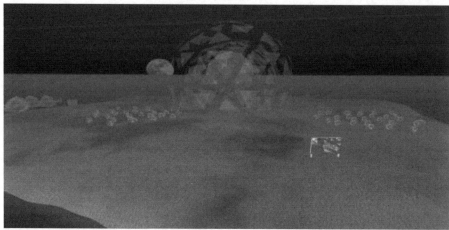

Figure 1. The N00sphere Playground, complete on HUMlab Island two

Figure 2. Live Lecture Stream on HUMlab Island

1.5 The HUMlab Region

The purchase of an educational sim of 65,536 m² by HUMlab became a necessity as the complexity and size of projects we were interested in made working in a domestic land parcel impossible. Due to the Linden Inc. business model the amount of scripted actions that can be run is tied to the amount of land in space assigned to the parcel or project. The 5129 m² HUMlab Island allowed for 1175 prims or virtual objects to be in place. The new island allows for 15 000 prims to be in place as well as parceling of land, landscape manipulation (terraforming) and multiple projects to be run simultaneously. The move to the new island was conducted within the N00sphere Playground project, which tested the HUMlab support network outside of Second Life. When it became clear that the scale and demands of the first large project to be conducted on the island, the N00sphere, was not compatible with the rules of the estate, a decision had to be made quickly regarding a solution. The N00sphere artist, Sachiko Hayashi, contacted the island manager via email IM late in the evening. The situation was that the artworks created so far within the project had to be moved very soon. The same evening the manager of the island emailed the director of HUMlab outlining the situation. Within two hours the decision had been made to purchase a private island and the order had been placed with Linden Inc.

That form finds expression rather than expression finding form is a grounding principle of HUMlab's work in Second Life. This means that once a medium or tool is introduced, it is people which develop its uses, in a sense they create its meanings. These uses can conform or diverge from what could be termed intended use. With the expansion in SL represented by the new HUMlab Island came new agents. Through the HUMlab Island agents were enabled to deepen and develop their involvement with the SL platform. The N00sphere opened as part of the 'Virtual Moves Exhibition 4 Exhibitions by Tagging Art' at the Statens Museum for Kunst (The State Museum of Art) in Copenhagen, Denmark and in Second Life in January 2008.[iv] At the opening of the Tagging Art exhibition part of the new HUMlab Island had been taken up by Oz Gate, a long term virtual world's project conducted by a veteran of numerous online worlds. Between the N00sphere and the Oz Gate there existed a number of use issues which were interesting in regards to the affordances of a collaborative space in SL. The N00sphere project involves the affordances of gallery spaces and the perimeters of the work as intended by the artist. The Oz gate project is based on pushing the virtual world medium (in this case Second Life) to its limits by testing its affordances. The testing of the possibilities of SL by Oz Gate included flying vehicles, video streams, bandwidth heavy kinetic scripts, light shows, and audio. The potential for conflict between these two approaches is obvious and it required negotiating skills and an awareness of the platform materials to navigate through the issues as they arose. By prioritizing projects and delegating areas it became clear over time that agents can be coordinated within a tapestry of projects. A skybox several hundred meters over the island and a restriction of running scripts on the ground became the solution to integrate two radically different projects on the HUMlab Island for the duration of the exhibition.

Following the Tagging Art exhibition more groups were established on the HUMlab Island. By the beginning of March 2008 the Avatar Orchestra Metaverse (AOM) had been granted 5168 m².[v] Land on the HUMlab Island is sold to agents for nothing which allows them to Deed to Group, making it a collective project or to keep the land in a single name. The AOM is an innovative group of international artists and performers which use Second Life to collaborate over distance on audio visual installation and performance projects in real time.[vi] Their work is extremely bandwidth heavy and relies on Heads Up Display (HUD) devices for the running of pre-recorded samples in orchestrated live sequences inworld that can also feature video and scripts. Performances by the AOM can also involve physical performances that often are coordinated with what is happening in the SL performance. Because the AOM only use the HUMlab Island as a practice and studio space there has been no need to alter anything from their presence. The AOM works from skyboxes, platforms hundreds of meters above the HUMlab Island. Thus far there has been little contact between the AOM crew (up to 40 avatars) and the other residents of the island. However, with the more recent start of undergraduate student projects on the island it is hoped there will be some informal contact between the AOM members and the students. Many of the AOM are professional artists and any contact between them and students has the potential to be interesting. The concept of mentorship is not unrealizable in Second Life and by having a semi-professional organization like the AOM on site it is hoped there may be some developments in that direction.

With the expansion of the population on the HUMlab Island the use of metamedia (media extra to the SL platform) was recognized as being useful in building a community of practice around the activities involving SL. These media included the formation of a Google Groups list were people who were interested in the activities of the island but did not spend much time in Second Life could get updates on activities and events. Blogging continued as is a valuable portal for the broader public to gain an insight into what is happening on the HUMlab Island. Several parallel projects have begun as a result of blogged content and a connection with on campus with someone who is interested in working with Second Life (see the second part of this article on the Holiness in Second Life project as an example of this). Email is a media thread which runs through most of what is done in relation to the HUMlab SL project. Other forms of communicative metamedia that seem appropriate for the SL project but have yet to find a role are SMS messaging and an expansion of online video from inworld activities. There are a variety of screen capture video programs available and their use in relation to SL is already well established (see the AOM website for some good examples of practice). The use of media to support activities mediated by SL should be a constant consideration for anyone using the platform. One of the primary weaknesses (or perhaps it is an open field waiting for structure) is the difficulties that can be experienced with archiving materials from SL. At the present stage of development everything that is created with Second Life stays in Second Life on the Linden Inc. servers. The best that can be done to archive what is produced and what occurs via the platform is to document everything. The use of metamedia assists in the process of documentation greatly.

The general principles described so far in this chapter are beginning to be applied to practical pedagogical situations. Teaching and research is now conducted daily on the HUMlab Island in Second Life. Students are meeting researchers and creating their own works on the island. We would now like to describe further some of the practical issues and situations that have emerged in relation to HUMlab work in SL so far.

1.6 Teaching and the HUMlab Island

In September 2008 a class of sixteen third term museum studies students from the Department of Culture and Media at Umeå University began their term work on the HUMlab Island. The use of the HUMlab Island centered on the idea of the students building exhibitions and installations based on what was discussed in lectures, and what emerged from their research, both inworld and out. Gender, Nation, Religion, Ethnicity and Class are foci in the course lectures and these concepts are expected to drive the work conducted by the students in Second Life. The students work began in Second Life in a communal sandbox, which ran for a week. The use of a group space at the start of the curse was designed to let them to get to know each other and the platform as well as give them the opportunity to help each other while working in close proximity. No building was done prior to the beginning of the course. It was rather left to the students to

Figure 3. Meeting with church members in Second Life.

Figure 4. Students from the Museology Course on the HUMlab Island for the first time.

construct the environment in which they would be working. From experience with earlier HUMlab virtual world's projects it has been found that academic work in virtual world platforms lends itself to networks. If the students help each other, all benefit from it. Students who work alone and insulate themselves from group dynamics will generally not do as well at tasks in Second Life as students who adapt to network structures.

The early stages of the Museology course look promising. The Museology students broke into four groups and each one was granted 8700 m². In informal workshops the students have been guided through the basics of getting started in SL (only one of the sixteen has any experience with the platform). Touring relevant sites in Second Life the students have been taking screenshots and chatting to avatars who work on the projects of interest. Issues related to the foci of the course, in particular representations of gender in SL have already provoked discussion and orientation in lines of inquiry over the longer time frame of the course. Communication between students and facilitators and documenting of development is done via blogging. Four group blogs for the students and a single central blog for the HUMlab personal.

The museology class has also given us input to further pedagogical experiments, for example a live video stream of a lecture was broadcast on the HUMlab Island in the first week of the course. While the lecture was being given to the students in the actual HUMlab the scene on the HUMlab Island of the screen broadcasting the lecture was being shown on a large screen in HUMlab. The lecture stream on the island was attended by several avatars, some of which were the students attending the lecture in the actual lab space (see Figure 2). It is this augmented reality configuration with mixed spaces being used in teaching that is looking like the next area for investigation for HUMlab in relation to the uses of Second Life.

2 A Case Study: SL as a Platform for Research

The interest for research in Second life is still developing at HUMlab. Many ideas are around about interesting and challenging projects, and so far some research projects have taken shape, and others are discussed and planned. One project is called "Holiness in virtual spaces" and involves four scholars, two from religious studies, one from English literature, and one historian of ideas. The aim is to study the presence of holiness in different virtual spaces – how a sense of holiness is created, and how creators of "holy" environments relate to their creation of sacred places in different virtual worlds such as Second life and World of Warcraft. Created sacred places give prerequisite and a structure for religious faith and practices, and the project wants to analyze how the use of digital media affects faith and practices.

It is a well known fact, that Internet has changed and still changes the setting for contemporary religion. Internet and digital media is often considered anti-hierarchical, democratic and interactive in a way often contrary to traditional religious structures (Barker, Schultze). The question is how this influence religiosity. Previous studies have mainly studied how consumers live their religious lives on the net. This research project instead focuses on the providers of holiness – such as Churches, designers and other representatives for and from the religious sphere. Early case studies shows that the creation of holiness differs widely – from making digital representations of, for example, Cathedrals with symbols, music and everything else related to a sacral place in the physical world , to quite anonymous rooms with only some symbols or signs showing the sacred character of the room. Many sacred places emphasis its openness and tolerance but the meaning differs widely. Some places are open to anyone to come there, while others are in their practice more explicitly tolerant toward different worldviews and stress the importance of interaction and all inclusiveness.

Maybe it is not obvious but there are many parallels between what is happening within the field of religion and within pedagogy. Analogous with the development on the Internet which is labeled as a shift from Web 1.0 to Web 2.0, it is possible to claim that this shift is taken place both within religious and educational practices. Web 2.0 is characterized by creativity, interactivity, sharing information, and collaboration, to a higher degree than its predecessor. This description is valid also for what is happening in sacred and educational spaces as well. Experiences learned from the project "Holiness in virtual spaces", have given us a deeper understanding of what can be done in Second Life regarding education.

HUMlab is also, together with Umeå live (umealive.se) and the Swedish Church, involved in a project aiming at conducting a church service simultaneously in Second Life and in First Life, linking these two worlds together through audio-visual technology. The idea is to hold a service at a physical Church in Umeå, with clergies and a congregation. And at the same time a service will be held in NoWay Church in Second life. The clergy will be represented in SL through an avatar, and the two congregations will appear on displays on each location. The liturgy will involve moments of interaction between the two worlds, for example through sharing experiences, or through the possibility of sending prayers through SMS or IM. Audio-visual technologies will also be used as a part of the service to highlight or emphasis certain parts of the liturgy.

Research issues raised are for example how the distribution of people will affect the view of the congregation. How does a traditional world like the Church relate to an anti-traditional world such as SL when it comes to the role of the clergies, the congregation and the liturgy? In what way does Internet and virtual worlds influence religious faith and practices in the physical world?

This project has certainly also given input when thinking about Second Life and pedagogy, and especially to concepts such as blended learning (Osguthorpe) and the so called extended classroom (Schneider). Within these concepts lies a mixing of traditional classroom learning and different e-learning tools. On possibility is to bridge time and distance between teachers and students on campus and student groups off campus. A teacher could for example give an introduction in a traditional classroom and then let the students use various forms of information technologies in their work, i.e. use technology as a tool to enhance learning. Or video conference technologies can be used to connect different geographical locations to each other.

In this context Second Life could be used both as a virtual classroom and as a tool for searching and presenting information – both possibilities reflect traditional pedagogy. Here has been interesting to see how SL can further develop the idea of blended learning, and, as mentioned before, to expand the limits of the traditional use of digital media in education. The question is: What and how can a virtual 3D world, such as Second life, contribute to the pedagogical work at a university?

3 Second Life as a Pedagogical Sandbox

HUMlab has experimented and used Second Life in different ways but here we would like to emphasis two ways which differ from traditional education. According to the well known expression from Marshall McLuhan "the media is the message", and hence has its own affordances. So what is the message contained in SL, with bearing on education? How can a 3D environment as SL be taken advantage of, and used in a way not possible through other media technologies?

These are at least three ways which explore SL's potential as a means for education, each one with a potential beyond what is possible to do in a traditional educational setting, and with all ready established media. We identify the following three ways:

1) Extension of the classroom – in bridging the virtual and the physical classroom.

2) Engineering humanities – as using the possibility to build and create environments in SL as a way to support the learning process in using practical elements combined with ordinary intellectual processes.

3) Experience based pedagogy – since SL gives the possibility to simulate real world conditions in a spatial environment at a low cost and at hand from anywhere (if you have a computer).

HUMlab has been involved in thinking, brainstorming and developing courses on undergraduate level together with several different disciplines at the Faculty of Humanities at Umeå University. Different approaches apply to different disciplines, but one general experience is that the use of Second life effects what kind of pedagogy to use at a certain occasion.

3.1   The Extension of the Classroom

It is a well known method to use Second life as a virtual classroom in which you can give lectures, have seminars and other meeting for group discussion and supervision – pretty much according to patterns established in a traditional university.

However, during this last semester HUMlab has started experimenting with an augmented mixing of Second Life with the physical world through live streaming seminars and lectures to a learning environment at the HUMlab Island in SL, a technique similar to what will be used in the planned church service project. The idea is to use SL as a means to merge the two worlds together into an extended classroom (in its literary meaning). The Second Life environment, with present avatars, is simultaneously displayed in the physical world as well. The avatars can watch the lecture and also interact through chat.

Student from both groups can have joint meetings and also socialize in Second Life, activities which both bridge the geographical distance and enhance the feeling of belonging to the same group. The student can also give presentations in both worlds through using for example voice chat and a power point presentation or other audio visual techniques.

We want to simulate and give a feeling of belonging to a shared community within the auditorium, no matter if you belong to the on campus student group or not. Through giving the SL-avatars presence in the First Life, the on campus students will be aware of the extension of the classroom as well. This is of course also possible through conventional video conference technologies. One advantage with SL is that it adds a social dimension, outside the actual lecture and classroom. It is quite difficult to imagine a couple of students to use for example video conferences such as Marratech or Skype, or learning platforms as Sakai or Moodle, for socializing. And the importance of the social aspect should not be underestimated in distance education.

Blending a virtual world with the physical world opens up new possibilities of which we have only seen the beginning. We have used Second life but it is possible to imagine mixing different worlds and platforms with each other in a near future.

3.2 Engineering Humanities

Another important feature in Second life, with potential for humanities, is the possibility to build/create objects – from the smallest item to whole environments. Then it is possible to take the role of an engineer. Traditionally an engineer is person who builds and uses machines and other technical devices. An engineer combines both practical and theoretical skills, and the concept of technology has its roots in both crafts and science. When the engineer, as a modern profession, was established during the 19th century both aspects were emphasized, with patterns from the Parisian school of higher education École Polytechnique (founded in 1794). One important aspect of the education of engineers is to teach them to feel and get a sense of technology – to train their so called tacit knowledge. This was done (and still is) through practice in for example sketching, drawing and constructing (Ferguson). Within humanities tacit knowledge is often neglected, but we firmly believe that involving different senses and a variety of learning techniques enhances and adds new aspects to the learning process.

This semester HUMlab is, as aforementioned, involved in a program for students in museum studies. It all started when representatives from the discipline wanted a dialogue about if and how HUMlab could enrich their traditional courses. The semester intends to give the students a deeper understanding of Gender and Sexuality, Class and Social stratification, Religion and Ethnicity, and Nation and Locality. Second Life is of obvious reasons a good ground for empirical research, but the question is if Second life could give the students even more then only research material. After discussions it was decided that the students in the end also shall build an exhibition in SL, and at the same time learn and relate to different forms of presentation techniques.

The whole exhibition project is founded on the idea of problem based learning. We, as teachers, facilitate the island and give the students guidelines about how to use SL and a theoretical understanding of virtual worlds related to each theme during the semester. The HUMlab teachers also show them different kinds of existing museums and exhibitions – ranging from digital representations of First life museums, to constructed historical sites and exhibitions of more imaginative character. The aim is to inspire the students to think outside preconceived concepts and to use the multi modal, 3D environment in which the physical laws can be bent in many creative ways.

Simultaneously, the world and life in SL question and reemphasize categories such as gender, ethnicity, religion and locality, so in this specific course SL contributes with a context to the different theoretical themes. Making an avatar, teleporting around the world, meeting people from different places, and learning the social codes, all generate discussions about what the students are learning and reading about. The students also have to work with and practice Second life in order to think three dimensional and understand the possibilities to combine different media and layers of information, which is not easy if you have your educational background in a text-based environment. This process is parallel to how engineers traditionally are thought to think. You have to work up the feeling for what you are doing. And activating different senses and different parts of the brain enhances creativity, which must be considered as an important thing to do at a university.

For students in museum studies this means they have to relate to and think in spatial terms. They will also be able to evaluate different ways of presenting information and how they relate to each other. It is too early, but it is interesting to think how the experiences the students get in SL can influence their thinking about curating in the physical world.

The use of the building feature in SL can also be used for other student groups, for example students in different historical disciplines. Having to build a three dimensional historical building, a representation of a whole historical setting or a thematic environment (such as a city, a market place or a 18th century park) demands a high degree of historical understanding and interpretation, a level of knowledge which can be difficult to achieve through only reading and discussing text in a more traditional way. For example, to build a city you have to understand how a city, during a specific age, was built, and why it grows the way it does, how different functions interact with each other and what kind of materials are available for constructing.

4 Experience Based Pedagogy

Since Second Life is a digital simulation of the physical world, it gives the prospect of experiencing (almost) any aspect of life – often much easier then in real life, only a mouse click away. And the possibility to build and interacting in-world gives the user an opportunity to simulate real world scenarios. This can of course be used with pedagogical purposes, which HUMlab has developed and will do even further in collaboration with different disciplines at the Humanities faculty at Umeå University.

HUMlab's collaboration with museum studies has already been mentioned. But apart from building, and skills combined with that, other experiences can be drawn. Through building their own exhibition students can practice, for example, how to work as curator for a museum. This can be done in the physical world, but it is much more difficult to manage, due to practicalities such as space and expenses. A Second Life exhibition can never replace the experience in making a physical exhibition, but the similarities are good enough for making a trial-and-error mock up version of a "real" one. If you are a student and new to the profession Second Life can be a useful sandbox for making mistakes and to learn from them.

HUMlab is currently discussing with faculty of fine arts about possibilities for future collaboration. Both the opportunity to curate (as discussed above) and to display art is relevant, in this discussion. Once again Second Life makes it possible to show a piece of art in a context, in for example a whole environment (some art is made in Second life and should of course be shown inworld). The possibilities a virtual 3D world give is valuable especially if you want to show architecture on site. The reconstruction of destroyed ancient environments, such as Stonehenge, Alhambra or Rome, can both give the students a feeling for architecture and give input to a discussion about how history or a historical narrative is presented.

For students within disciplines which study culture and human behaviour, such as Ethnology and Religious Studies, it is easy to point out the benefits of using SL as a platform for participatory studies. The aforementioned students in museum studies are studying such topics as gender, ethnicity, social stratification and religion, and they are at the same time analyzing these subjects. When making their avatar, finding clothes, choosing body shapes, having to define sex, and so on they have to reflect upon for example gender issues. Then having to search SL for inspiration for their own exhibition, they have to meet and interact with other people inworld. First some students were afraid of leaving the safe haven of the HUMlab Island, and even more intimidated by interacting with others but soon they flew out into the larger world. This process causes a lot of pondering upon their own cultural background, which deepens the students' understanding of various forms of identity related issues.

For students of religious studies Second life gives an opportunity to work with a variety of sacral places and to participate in various religious rites. This is possible in the First Life as well, but both financial and cultural restrains can inhibit a student. It is easier to go to an obscure cult disguised as an avatar then showing up in "real life". Once again the mere construction of the sacral triggers a discussion of how holiness is constructed and perceived in both worlds. In such an activity it is possible to understand the pedagogical role of Second Life as a simulation. By creating a near enough model to what could be described as the actual event, the conditions allow for a reflective evaluation of the event and ongoing analysis.

5 Summary

In HUMlab we have a fairly long experience of education in relation to virtual worlds, stretching back to ActiveWorlds in 1999, and via Online Traveler, The Sims and Adobe Atmosphere, HUMlab is now experimenting with Second Life today. One founding idea for HUMlab's involvement in virtual worlds has always been to explore the potential of what can be done. This is not so much a technical issue, but more a mental. One advantage with the environment in HUMlab is the fact that many different disciplines meet and interact in often creative ways, which we hope stimulate the desire to explore.

Over the last year HUMlab have been contacted by representatives from different disciplines at the Faculty of Humanities at Umeå University regarding education in different ways. Drawing from experiences in history and different current projects related to Second Life, we have started to explore Second Life as a platform for enhanced pedagogy. In doing so we would say that the greatest potential, as we see it today, lies within the possibility for extending the classroom through mixing Second Life and the physical world, and through the possibility to build and simulate familar scenarios. The option of building in a three dimensional world, and using a more practical oriented part of the mind, we believe makes it possible to learn and think in more imaginative ways than is often the case within the Humanities. Finally SL gives a unique chance to participate in, and study numerous aspects of ordinary human life and culture.

Notes

[i] The similarities with the IDEO Deep Dive include onsite contact with problems/issues, a familiarity with the forms and processes of the site, attention to the cultures which contextualize the site, and a learning of hierarchies and power within the structures of the site.

According to IDEO founder David Kelley "The trick is to find these real experts. The people who are really getting the info are out in the field meeting with people." (IDEO) For documentation on the Deep Dive, See Boynton and Fischer, (2005) .

ii Gibson's ecological concept of affordances are "action possibilities" latent in the environment. "Different layouts afford different behaviors for different animals, and different mechanical encounters" (Gibson 1979, 128).

iii Interoperability is a major issue in SL and other virtual world platforms. In July 2008 Linden Inc and IBM "claim to have successfully transported avatars from IBM's OpenSim virtual world server to a Second Life preview server." Nichols, 2008.

iv For more on the Tagging Art exhibition see the website http://www.taggingart.org/ Accessed 13 September 2008.

vThe Sustainable Communities Project was granted 9920 m² of land in May 2008 for research into simulations for sustainable agricultural and social models. Perhaps the most natural science orientated of the projects on the HUMlab Island, Sustainable Communities has had some success with academic presentations and conference papers.

vi For more on the AOM see http://www.avatarorchestra.org/ Accessed 12 September 2008.

References

Baker. E. (2005). "Crossing the Boundary: New Challenges to Religious Authority and Control as a Consequence of Access to the Internet", in *Religion and Cyberspace*. Højsgaard M. T. & Warburg M. (eds.). London: Routhledge.

Barrett J. *A HUMlab Presence in Second Life? (Unpublished paper)May 2007.*

Ferguson, E. S. "The Mind's Eye: Nonverbal Thoughts in Technology", *Science* 197(4306), 827-836.

Gibson, J.J. (1979). The Ecological Approach to Visual Perception. Boston: Houghton Mifflin. (1986)

Hayashi, Sachiko. *The N00sphere Playground*, HUMlab Island. Second Life. Virtual Moves Exhibition 4 Exhibitions by Tagging Art 2008.

HUMlab Websitehttp://www.humlab.umu.se/humlabinenglish Accessed 16 September 2008.

Kirkpatrik, David. *Second Life to Go Open Source*, Fortune Magazine January 8 2007http://money.cnn.com/2007/01/07/technology/secondlife.fortune/index.htm Accessed 10 September 2008.

Olsen, Eric. *DAC IDEO shopping Carthttp://skellogg.sdsmt.edu/IE345/Supplement/ideo.pdf* Accessed 10 September 2008.

Osguthorpe, R. T. & Graham, G. R. (2003). "Blended Learning Environments: Definitions and Directions", *The Quarterly Review of Distance Education* 4(3) 227-233.

Nichols, Shaun. Second Life "Avatars Teleport to IBM", *World Information Reviewhttp://www.iwr.co.uk/information-world-review/news/2221122/second-life-avatars-teleport Accessed 10 September 2008.*

Schultze, Q. J. (2008) "Following Pilgrims into Cyberspace", in *Understanding Evangelical Media: The Changing Face of Christian Communication*. Schultze. Q. J. & Woods, R. H. (eds.). Downers Gorve: InterVarsity Press.

Scneider, A. (1998). "Sociology: The Internet as an Extended Classroom", *Social Science Computer Review* 16(1), 53-57.

Svensson, Patrik. "Building a Virtual World for Learning, Collaboration and Experience. Project Report for Project 138-98" *Virtual Weddings and a real wedding of linguistics, Literature and cultural studies* Accessed 9 September 2008, http://www.myndigheten.netuniversity.se/download/3263/x/svensson_patrik_98.pdf.

Chapter 12: Future Directions for Learning in Virtual Worlds

Mats Deutschmann Ph.D.
Department of Humanities, Mid Sweden University
871 88 Härnösand
Sweden
mats.deutschmann@miun.se

Judith Molka-Danielsen, Ph.D.
Molde University College
Britvn. 2, 6402 Molde, Norway
j.molka-danielsen@himolde.no

Chapter Overview: This book has partly dealt with specific case studies, with different focuses. However, the common goal that runs through each of these cases is the focus on learning and the roles of learners and educators in learning activities. Do virtual worlds assist learning and do they create new opportunities? The answer from these analyses is "Yes" and this book illustrates "how" to make use of the affordances of the virtual word of Second Life as it exists today. Yet, many questions remain both for practitioners and researchers. To give some examples: On what principles should learners' tasks be designed? What other projects are being conducted in SL? What is the future of virtual worlds in a learning context? In this chapter we attempt to address some of these issues.

1   The Learner's Task

Throughout this book we have advocated that innovative ways of learning and teaching should be applied in a new learning environment, such as 3D virtual worlds. The chapters of Action Learning and Active Learning show that new opportunities do exist in Second Life. This leads to the question of how to design learning spaces that build on these opportunities. The pedagogic goals are clear. Learners need to actively engage with the content of the learning tasks and get a sense of shared accountability in the learning process. A design methodology for learning tasks has been developed by Jane Vella (2001) with these goals in mind. She advocates that the learners' tasks be designed with open questions that invite inductive and creative reasoning, and that collaboration and experienced based reflection and review are needed in any effective learning program. She emphasises the role of the "open question" as most important in the learning process:

> "We set a learning task to engage learners in the active learning of substantive, new material. We respect their life experience and their unique context and offer the task as

an open question, inviting their reflective response. Some learning takes place in the mind (cognitive), some in the heart (affective) and some in the muscles (psychomotor) (Vella 2001: 8).

Vella (2001:33) defines four types of learning tasks: (1) inductive tasks that connect learners and what they already know with their context; (2) input tasks that invite learners to consider new content and the concepts, skills and attitudes associated to these; (3) implementation tasks that get learners to do something directly themselves with the new content; and (4) integration tasks that incorporate what they have learned into their lives. While not directly stated, such tasks involve learners in Action Learning and these definitions give direction on how to design tasks in virtual worlds.

While it is believed that all of these types of learning tasks can be implemented effectively within SL, only some work has begun to design and actually test their implementation in SL. One example is "Access to Virtual and Action Learning live Online" (AVALON), funded for 2 years (2009-10) within the EU program on lifelong learning. The project, in which the authors of this chapter are involved, has as one of its aims to design learning tasks and artefacts together with learners and educators for learning in SL. The outcome will result in shared resource repositories and teaching programs for educators who would like to extend their e-learning skills to include virtual teaching worlds. The project has a number of set goals which include: the creation of case studies which will include field-tested communicative scenarios and the guidance on how to utilise them; the provision of the necessary skills for language teaching professionals to work in these new online environments through a targeted training course; the facilitation of easier access in cases where there are limited computer resources; and the promotion of general awareness in mainstream educational contexts of the potential of these environments.

2   Recognising Other Projects

Various research and education activities are taking place through numerous projects in Second Life. The limited scope of this book can in no way give recognition to all such activities. However, we wish to highlight some examples in particular.

The SLENZ project is currently investigating the potential of Second Life education in New Zealand (SLENZ, available at http://slenz.wordpress.com). This project has been built on the former experiences of the Nelson Marlborough Institute of Technology with Koru Island as was outlined in Chapter 5 by Atkins and Caukill. As part of SLENZ, a process for the methodical construction of SL 'builds' is being developed and will provide the framework within which two major pilot education projects will be created. The SLENZ team have identified that all work undertaken in this area is of an experimental nature and they state that there are no clear guidelines or best practices as yet.

Jarmon, Traphagan & Mayrath (2008) report on an interdisciplinary project to create a virtual presence for two green, sustainable, urban housing designs called the Alley Flats. Using *team approach*, the pedagogy focussed on enhancing communication between researchers and students. The project has also tried to involve existing communities in SL and other groups of interest. The participants took so-called "field trips" in order to engage other SL communities, as well as architects, educators and other interested parties. This all culminated with a formal ribbon-cutting ceremony in SL in which guests from all over the world participated in a virtual presentation and walk-through of the two Alley Flat virtual homes.

The projects presented in this book have mainly addressed the learning needs of adults in higher education, but there are examples of ongoing projects where the target audience are primary and secondary school children. One such project aimed a school children is "Skoolaborate" (http://www.skoolaborate.com/), which uses Teen Life grid to bring together learners from various parts of Australasia to practice their listening and communication skills. Skoolaborate is organised around various projects which encourage cross-cultural collaboration. These do not stop with mere communication and contact, but include the joint constructions of buildings, such as a mall, where students will set up various shops and commerce. The project makes full use of many of the affordances of SL such as voice and text communication as well as the building tools available in the environment.

The Second Life in Education wiki (http://sleducation.wikispaces.com/educationaluses) is a good resource for locating former and new educational projects in distance education, training and skills developments, and self-work tutorials. They make reference to one of the early teaching experiences in SL that was lead by Harvard™ Berkman Center for Internet and Society that featured the course "Cyber One: Law in the Court of Public Opinion". Another rich resource for educators is The New Media Consortium (NMC: http://slurl.com/secondlife/NMC%20Campus/138/225/43) Campus in SL, which hosts educational events including classes, demonstrations, art exhibits and other learning materials. Teachers Buzz (http://sl.nmc.org/wiki/Teachers_Buzz_Session) is the NMC wiki that reports on the various experience stories and activities of the NMC Campus.

One striking feature of almost all the above projects is their innovative nature. Another common feature is the general tendency to accommodate 'freedom' of direction. It is very often the participants, be they school children, university students, educators or researchers that decide on the direction and content of the projects. Finally, it is also encouraging to see how many of such projects are interdisciplinary, breaking up the traditional boundaries and creating new focuses of learning.

3   The Near Future of Virtual Worlds

In recent years, various consulting groups have started to recognize the impact of virtual worlds and are now trying to predict their future significance. The Gartner Group, for example, predicted in April 2007 that "80 percent of active Internet users will have a "Second Life" in a Virtual World by the End of 2111." While we do not intend to project in percentages, we will, however, breifly summarize the present landscape and point to some of the indications of where things might be heading in the near future.

By the beginning of 2009 Second Life® will be one of the most prominent virtual worlds in education. Other 3D worlds have existed longer, such as Traveler® (since 1994) and Active Worlds® (since 1995), but relatively speaking, membership and activity indicate a stronger and growing interest in SL. Recent statistics from Linden Lab show 16 million resident accounts with approximately 500 000 member logins within a 7 day period. The SL economy is also booming with 400 000 residents having made a total of 22 million transactions (SL 2008). In the area of education, Linden Lab has reported 200 educational institutions to be members of SL in 2008, and the Chronicle of Higher Education (Young 2008) indicates an even larger figure. According to this source, 25 percent of the US campuses have reported a presence in SL in 2008 compared to 16 percent in 2007. This does not account for the fact that over 60% of the residents of SL are from outside of the US.

What lends SL to growing acceptance? We think the primary factor is that it represents an innovative way for both learners and educators to participate in the world in general, and to control the learning activities in particular. It is possible for both students and teachers to create 3D objects and information content, to build learning artefacts including custom interfaces for learning management systems (such as SLoodle with Moodle), or to establish and administer in-world groups. It is an environment that allows for self-governed activities of the learner (Molka-Danielsen 2008). In brief, a key factor to Second Life's adoption is that it is conducive to all members (residents) being able to create content, and not just those responsible for courses within educational institutions.

Several see the dominant interface of the Internet within the next 5-10 years to be a 3D-Web or "Metaverse" that will seamlessly integrate the applications of the 2D-Web. Progress will be made in the factors of virtual worlds supporting various areas of interest such as Physics (full Newtonian, chemical processes, hydro, aerodynamics, electromagnetic spectrum, etc); document and applications management; real "eye" 3D rendering; lifelike avatar appearances; sense based avatar interactions (based on sight, voice, and touch); virtual agents (virtual touring, negotiations), and broader variety of user interfaces (including tactile, augmented reality, neuro-controlled and neuro-feedback interfaces) (Daden 2007). Since January 2007, Second Life has allowed for open source on the client side, encouraging development of interesting viewers such as "Windlight" and better in-world atmospheric rendering, thus enabling the creation of ever more immersive learning spaces. The developers of Second Life, Linden Lab, do not see other virtual worlds to be a threat to the ongoing adoption of SL (Wagner 2008). Rather they see worlds such as Google's Lively (www.lively.com) or OpenSim (http://opensimulator.org/wiki/), an open source platform based on SL and in part on reverse-engineering SL published APIs and portions of open source code, as increasing the interest in and applications of virtual worlds. Indeed, developers of SL are working with the open source community and with OpenSim with IBM work to find ways of integrating virtual worlds, to allow for the movement of avatars between worlds and for the sharing of objects between worlds (Gonsalves 2008). When this is achieved we will be taking great steps towards a 3D-Web.

4 No Simple Roadmap or Grid

In his article on SL in education Stevens (2006) asks what SL has to do with education and points out that no matter where we believe SL is heading, the answer to the question has to be "a lot". He, and many other with him, point to the fact that SL is revolutionising the way we view education, opening "doors to creativity and imagination". SL *is* in other words making an impact on education. Whether SL will survive or should be seen as a "prototype for some future form of learning" as Graham Stanley puts it, remains to be seen, but it is clear that SL is making an impact here and now, having caught the imagination of thousands who "see in the depths of their computer screens how their work can be made more enjoyable, productive, and interactive in the course of encountering others attracted to 3D virtual spaces" (Stevens 2006).

"Why?" one asks. What makes it so special? Patrik Svensson (2003) perhaps puts his finger on a key issue when he claims that "paradoxically, virtual simulations often turn out more 'real' than ones that are carried out in the classroom". The key element here is, according to Svensson, not the technology, the simulations or the effects *per se*, but the fact that SL and worlds like it allow for meetings with "real people ('playing' themselves or having alternate personas), for working collaboratively with remote participants" and, for the creation of a "place and a unified spatial interface" for such meetings. While specific software may come and go there are two aspects fundamental to human nature remain that make us predict that we have only seen the beginning of the development of 3D virtual environments in e-learning contexts: we are *social* creatures that have evolved in a *three dimensional* world.

References

Daden, , (2007). "Virtual Worlds – a Roadmap to the Future?", Daden Limited. Accessed: http://www.daden.co.uk/downoads/Virtual%20Worlds%20-%20A%20Road%20Map.pdf

Gonsalves, A. (2008). "IBM, Second Life Demo Virtual World Interoperability", Information Week, July 8, 2008. Accessed:
http://www.informationweek.com/news/personal_tech/virtualworlds/showArticle.jhtml?articleID=208803274

Jarmona, L., Traphaganb, T. & Mayrathb M. (2008). Understanding project-based learning in Second Life with a pedagogy, training, and assessment trio. *Educational Media International* Vol. 45, No. 3, 157-176.

Molka-Danielsen, J. (2008). "Learner Support in Multi User Virtual Environments", Moe, C.E. ed., in NOKOBIT 2008, Tapir Akademisk Forlag, Trondheim, pp.157-169, ISBN 9788251 923873.

SL (2008). Economic Statistics, Second Life, November 20, 2008, Accessed: http://secondlife.com/whatis/economy_stats.php

Stanley, Graham. http://www.pod-efl.com/video/Web%202.0%20&%20Language%20Learning.mov

Stevens, Vance. (2006). Second Life in Education and Language Learning. TESL-EJ, Volume 10, Number 3

Svensson P. (2003) "Virtual worlds as arenas for language learning". In Felix U. (ed.) Language learning online: towards best practice, 123-142. Lisse: Swets & Zeitlinger.

Wagner, M. (2008). "Second Life Faces Otherworldly Competition", InformationWeek, October 10, 2008. Accessed:
http://www.informationweek.com/news/personal_tech/virtualworlds/showArticle.jhtml?articleID=210602205

Vella, J. (2001). Taking Learning to Task: Creative Strategies for Teaching Adults, Jossey—Bass Publishing, San Francisco. ISBN 978-0-7879-5227-3.

Young, J. (2008). "Technology Survey Reveals Budget Cuts and Concerns About Staffing", The Chronicle of Higher Education, Today's News published October 29th, 2008, Accessed: http://chronicle.com/free/208/10/6130n.htm

Index

Chapter 1: page 16: A student "blue dragon" shows the teacher the group's 3D-design of a ship

Chapter 2: page 30: Getting to know each other around the camp fire

Chapter 2: page 30: Giving formal presentations in the Peer Gynt Rotunda

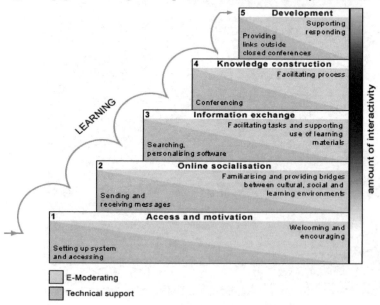

Chapter 2: Page 32: The Five Stage Model (Salmon 2004)

Chapter 3: page 51: Shows a Business Talking Course Launch

Chapter 4: page 66: There is a secret cave behind the waterfall on Kamimo Island.

Chapter 4: page 66: A class meeting held around a campfire.

Chapter 4: page 68: Demonstration of a video clip on a display in a Kamimo Island classroom.

Chapter 4: page 71: The "About Land" control panel can be found by clicking on a virtual land's name in the top centre of the client window. Here is "Guru Meditation"

Chapter 4: page 71: Selecting parcels in necessary before subdividing or joining land.

Chapter 4: page 72: Public sandbox is a popular free building parcel on Kamimo Island.

Chapter 4: page 74: After selecting a group a control panel reveals rights and roles.

Internet Protocol Addressing (IPv4)

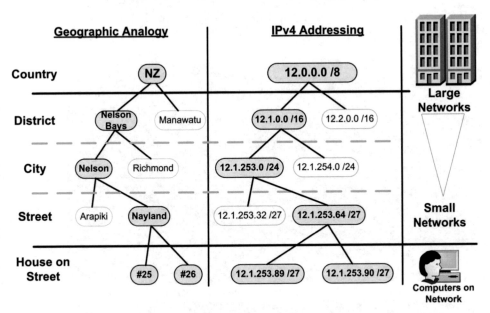

Geographic Analogy		IPv4 Addressing	

Country — NZ — 12.0.0.0 /8 — Large Networks

District — Nelson Bays, Manawatu — 12.1.0.0 /16, 12.2.0.0 /16

City — Nelson, Richmond — 12.1.253.0 /24, 12.1.254.0 /24

Street — Arapiki, Nayland — 12.1.253.32 /27, 12.1.253.64 /27 — Small Networks

House on Street — #25, #26 — 12.1.253.89 /27, 12.1.253.90 /27 — Computers on Network

Chapter 5: page 82: graphical representation of subnetting using a geographical analogy

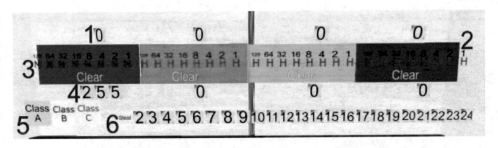

Chapter 5: page 84: A close-up view of the student's IP subnetting tutorial interface

Chapter 6: page 95: Learning Set Meeting on Terra Incognita Island, Second Life

Chapter 6: page 98: Decka's Decks - The classroom in large group mode

Chapter 6: page 98: Hand show chair with animation (Created by Angrybeth Shortbread)

Chapter 7: page 106: Virtual Harlem in Second Life

Chapter 7: page 106: Virtual Harlem in Second Life.

Chapter 7: page 106: Virtual Montmartre in Second Life.

Chapter 7: page 106: Dancing at the Cotton Club on Virtual Harlem

Chapter 8: page 120: Example of a typical multi-party video conference screen showing the participants as a set of talking heads. Used with permission of Mats Deutschmann.

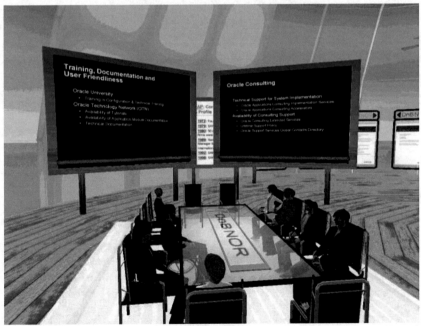

Chapter 8: page 121: Meeting held in Second Life. The image is from our pilot role play in the purchase management class at the DnB NOR site in Second Life.

Figure 1. The laboratory of Galileo Galilei

Figure 2. Arketipo as appearing at sunset

Figure 3. Rea building a large cylinder

Figure 4. The Tower of Pisa complexity of the model

Figure 7. Iumi, the virtual guide

Figure 8. Iumi: the comics

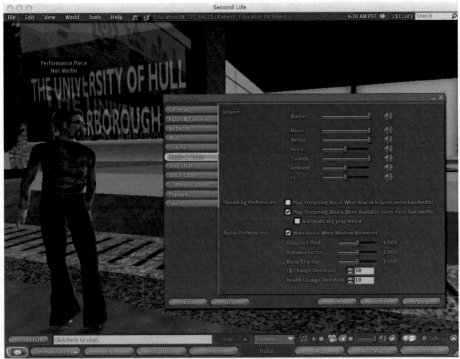

Chapter 10: page 148: Enabling the settings for audio, video and voice chat through the preferences dialog box.

Chapter 10: page 154: The Royal Liverpool Philharmonic Orchestra live concert in Second Life. Photo reproduced by courtesy of Taran Rampersad, under a Creative Commons license 3.0.

Chapter 10: page 159: They Live (in Second Life) is one example of a mixed reality art event. Photo reproduced by courtesy of Paul Sermon.

Chapter 10: page 159: *Cut* (2007) by Scott Kildall, Second Life recreation of *Cut Piece* by Yoko Ono. Photo reproduced by courtesy of Scott Kildall.

Chapter 11: page 172: The N00sphere Playground, complete on HUMlab Island two

Chapter 11: page 172: Live Lecture Stream on HUMlab Island

Chapter 11: page 175: Meeting with church members in Second Life.

Chapter 11: page 175: Students from the Museology Course on the HUMlab Island for the first time.